The Psychology of Spirituality

The Psychology of Spirituality

An Introduction

Larry Culliford

Jessica Kingsley *Publishers*
London and Philadelphia

Quote from Campbell 1995 is reproduced by permission of Souvenir Press.
Quote from Cousineau is reproduced with permission
from Red Wheel/Weiser/Conan Press LLC.

First published in 2011
by Jessica Kingsley Publishers
116 Pentonville Road
London N1 9JB, UK
and
400 Market Street, Suite 400
Philadelphia, PA 19106, USA

www.jkp.com

Copyright © Larry Culliford 2011
Cover artwork: *The Golden Tree* by Hilary Hope Guise,
from the series *Not Silenced by the Darkness*
Printed digitally since 2012

Library of Congress Cataloging in Publication Data
Culliford, Larry.
  The psychology of spirituality : an introduction / Larry Culliford.
    p. cm.
  Includes bibliographical references and index.
  ISBN 978-1-84905-004-3 (alk. paper)
  1. Spirituality--Psychological aspects. 2. Psychology and
religion. 3. Psychology--Religious aspects. I. Title.
  BF51.C85 2010
  204.01'9--dc22
                                          2010017902
British Library Cataloguing in Publication Data
A CIP catalogue record for this book is available from the British Library

ISBN 978 1 84905 004 3
eISBN 978 0 85700 491 8

*For helpmate Sarah
and newly born Thomas,
with love.*

Uncover what you long for, and you will discover who you are.

Phil Cousineau
The Art of Pilgrimage[1]

CONTENTS

PREFACE

Many people are discovering the relevance of spirituality. It helps us make sense of the important things because of its irrepressible, if at times paradoxical, logic – logic with poetic as well as conventional, rational properties.

The relevance of the spiritual dimension shows itself particularly where there is human pain and suffering; a point demonstrated, for example, when medical and psychiatric patients are helped and some healed, 'made whole', by a sense, an experience, an intuition of something spiritual. An attempt at clarification of the psychology of spirituality, by introducing a new 'psycho-spiritual paradigm', seems timely.

At school, in order to go on to study medicine, I first studied biology, chemistry and physics, and have been a lover of science ever since. My teachers made it clear, though, that science has limitations. While it may provide useful information, it does not address and cannot fully answer important questions about meaning and values. In fact, answers to the big scientific questions tend to open up deeper mysteries.

I left school for university in 1967. Later, in the 1980s, physicists discovered two important sets of ideas that have profoundly changed the way human beings understand themselves and the universe. The first came from quantum physics. The second was 'chaos theory'. The science of psychology is still catching up and accommodating to these momentous ideas.

The implications are considerable. A new, unified theory is required, a new model or paradigm involving 'heart' (representing the emotions) and 'head' (representing awareness, the physical senses and thinking) in harmony with each other and attuned to a higher plane, the spiritual dimension. This is the poetic vision, backed up by science, of heart and head interacting seamlessly together as 'soul'.

In 1982, Paris-based physicist Alain Aspect and his team conducted an experiment demonstrating that a measurement made on one photon (a particle of light energy) has an instantaneous effect on another photon, its twin, emitted at the same moment from the same light source. The two were linked inextricably, at whatever distance, despite the fact that they were flying apart from one another at the speed of light. Information, in the form of a message, could not be passing between the two, because nothing can travel faster than the speed of light, which is 186,000 miles per second.[1] The results were confirmed and extended in 1983 at the University of Sussex by Terry Clark and his team.[2]

'Super-luminary' communication between the photons could not be explained by conventional physics. The implications were and remain very significant for all of us. Whatever happens in one place, author Gary Zukav has explained:

> Is intimately and immediately connected to what happens everywhere in the universe, which, in turn, is intimately and immediately connected to what happens elsewhere in the universe, and so on, simply because the 'separate parts' of the universe are not separate parts.[3]

'Non-separateness' turns out to be a key element in the new psycho-spiritual paradigm.

The seamless interconnection between two photons at a distance is known as 'non-locality'. A comparison for the psychologist is provided by the mother who jumped up in alarm at the exact moment her son, far away, met his death in a car wreck, or the father who knows across the world that his daughter has just gone into labour. There are many similar cases on record. Many people 'know' who is calling at the instant the telephone rings, and 'know' too when they are being looked at from behind.

Something genuinely happens. It is not enough to dismiss these telepathic effects as weird, decide that they probably don't matter, package them simply together as 'paranormal' and dismiss them. The true social scientist cannot afford to ignore what are, to many people, profoundly meaningful experiences. They are part of our present, just as they have always been part of our human past, our history, our myths and religions, our spirituality.

There are those who try explaining such phenomena by saying that the brain makes use of quantum effects.[4] Others describe the universe itself as being in some way conscious, that it has a mind.[5] These ideas can be helpful, but they are not sufficient. To cope, to make sense of 'non-locality' and other phenomena, psychologists are obliged to develop a new map or

---

1   See, for example, Zukav, G. (1984) *The Dancing Wu Li Masters: An Overview of the New Physics.* London: Flamingo, pp.302–17; also Gribben, J. (1984) *In Search of Schrödinger's Cat: Quantum Physics and Reality.* London: Corgi Books, pp.3–4 and 226–9.

2   See Gribben, *ibid.*, pp.231–4.

3   See Zukav, *ibid.*, p.315.

4   Hameroff, S. (1994) 'Quantum coherence in microtubules: A neural basis for emergent consciousness?' *Journal of Consciousness Studies 1*, 1, 91–118.

5   See, for example, Dean Radin's book (1997) *The Conscious Universe: The Scientific Truth of Psychic Phenomena.* San Francisco, CA: HarperEdge.

guide, starting from and building on what we already know. This is the new paradigm that forms the substance of this book.

The discovery of non-locality is potentially linked in some way to the spiritual principle of 'reciprocity', according to which the intention to do good and the actual completion of helpful actions bring rewards to the person concerned. Similarly, the intention to harm and the carrying out of hurtful or destructive actions brings misfortune to the perpetrator. This misfortune could then have a positive aspect, providing the person with the opportunity to learn from the situation, amending their thoughts and behaviour in future.

In Buddhism, this is referred to as 'the law of cause and effect', also known as 'karma'. In theistic religions, it is frequently considered a vital aspect of 'God's will', on which is based the 'golden rule': 'To do unto others only as you would wish them to do unto you'.

Chaos theory, like non-locality, also emerged in the 1980s. The meteorologist, Edward Lorenz, discovered the Butterfly Effect, according to which, famously, 'Butterfly wing-beats in Brazil can cause a tornado in Texas'.[6] The principle of reciprocity is similarly complicated. Human beings affect each other in close proximity and at a distance, and in ways that are both coarse and subtle, both immediate and delayed. It is seldom possible to predict fully the results of our actions, or to establish precisely afterwards what these consequences might have been. So many factors are involved, and the nature of human experience is inexorably dynamic, ever-changing. There are no fixed points. And we cannot go back in time.

Psychology, which has for some years attempted to remain 'objective' and 'value-free', immediately takes on an ethical or moral dimension for this reason. Intention becomes paramount: the intention to behave either well or harmfully. Attempted neutrality, if it leads to indifference, is suspect, resulting so easily in care/less/ness. Carelessness is destructive.

Unpredictability concerning the results of our intentions and actions causes many to doubt the worth of what they think, plan and do. The missing ingredient is faith: faith in the principle of reciprocity; faith, in other words, in the nature and eventual reality of the blessing or boon, the rewards of behaving well. Such faith both accompanies and promotes spiritual maturity: the main aim – according to the new paradigm, as we shall soon see in these pages – of everyone's journey through life.

Working in the health and social care professions, whether deliberately to further one's personal and spiritual development or otherwise, offers frequent opportunities to help others, and to grow in both compassion and wisdom. In the ideal situation, one's training will take account of this.

---

6   See, for example, Gleick, J. (1988) *Chaos: Making a New Science.* London: Sphere Books.

The relationship between brain structure and mental functioning is complex. Much has to be assumed, even today. No comprehensive and therefore fully satisfactory account of the psychology of the healthy mind is currently offered, for example, either at the beginning of psychiatry training or later. Medical students usually study the structure (anatomy) and functions (physiology) of the healthy body before being taught about its pathology, about what can go wrong. For those studying psychiatry, it is different. My experience in the 1970s, after qualifying as a doctor, was that we psychiatry trainees immediately started learning about psychological problems and diagnoses. To fill in the gap, I began thinking for myself about what mental health really means.

To ensure completeness, it seemed to me, the many components of mental health are best considered as five seamlessly and circularly interrelated systems or dimensions: molecular, biological, psychological, social and spiritual.

Back then, spirituality was considered inextricable from religion. In a healthcare environment dominated by secularism and the 'objective', pre-quantum, pre-chaos science of the time, spirituality was out of favour, ignored and almost completely forgotten. I was pleased to discover later that, like me, others also thought this a mistake. The realization was beginning to dawn elsewhere too that everyone is deeply affected by the spiritual dimension, whether aware of it or not. The effects may be difficult to describe and harder to quantify, but they are present, whether a person is actively engaged with religious organizations, practices and beliefs or not.

Today, books are being written with titles like George Vaillant's *Spiritual Evolution: A Scientific Defense of Faith*,[7] Frank Parkinson's *Science and Religion at the Cross Roads*[8] and Amy Corzine's *Secret Life of the Universe: The Quest for the Soul of Science*.[9] Forty years ago, however, medicine, and particularly psychiatry, lacked any attempt to reconcile science and spirituality. Eventually, however, people did start making and refining a distinction between religion and spirituality, developing a language of spirituality that was not derived from any particular faith tradition, and that would not be offensive to those who were religious. This is the language, for example, of 'spiritual awareness', 'spiritual values', 'spiritual skills' and 'spiritual practices'.

With the formation within the Royal College of Psychiatrists of a 'Spirituality and Psychiatry' special interest group in 1999,[10] and the 2001 publication of John Swinton's book *Spirituality and Mental Health Care:*

7   Vaillant, G. (2008) *Spiritual Evolution: A Scientific Defense of Faith*. New York, NY: Broadway Books.

8   Parkinson, F. (2009) *Science and Religion at the Cross Roads*. Exeter: Imprint Academic.

9   Corzine, A. (2008) *Secret Life of the Universe: The Quest for the Soul of Science*. London: Watkins.

10 See www.rcpsych.ac.uk/spirit, accessed 18 May 2010.

Rediscovering a Forgotten Dimension,[11] interest in the revived subject gained official sanction. Today, according to the Department of Health, it is UK government policy. Some National Health Service (NHS) trusts have prepared and published strategy documents, calling for the training of healthcare staff on the subject of spirituality. At least one NHS trust has begun appointing 'spirituality advocates' to assist their professional colleagues in relating to this aspect of patients' welfare.

Training material is required. Although much has been said and written, a satisfactory and accessible overview of healthy human psychology incorporating the spiritual dimension has not yet appeared. This book, intended to fill that gap, is designed to be read principally by health and social care professionals and students, and people from related disciplines, including healthcare chaplains. Spirituality, however, knows no boundaries. It is relevant to all spheres of human contact and endeavour, as well as medicine and psychiatry. Chapter 7 on childhood spirituality indicates, for example, that it may be particularly important in the field of education. Meditation, where it has been introduced, has been shown to help children remain calm and better focused on their schoolwork.[12] Teachers are already beginning to take notice of this.

The psychology of spirituality affects social groups as well as individuals. Some in the fields of corporate enterprise, finance and politics may want educating about it too. One of the case examples in this book is Barack Obama, the current US President; another is Etty Hillesum, the victim of Nazism, the extreme 20th century political and military movement. As will become clear, personal and social psychology are intricately interwoven. The more people discover and learn about the spiritual dimension, the better things will be for humanity at large.

There remains hesitation, even opposition, to addressing spirituality in the healthcare system and elsewhere. It is understandable. A dearth of suitable training results in a widespread and embarrassing lack of knowledge. This, in turn, breeds uncertainty and lack of confidence. The separate chapters here have been written to provide opportunities, both for personal exploration of an intriguing and rewarding subject, and as a basis for student and staff training in groups.

A more subtle cause of hesitation could be that it is hard to study spirituality without addressing one's own spiritual development. People are, in an important sense, their own best experimental material. 'I know where I

---

11 Swinton, J. (2001) *Spirituality and Mental Health Care: Rediscovering a Forgotten Dimension.* London: Jessica Kingsley Publishers.

12 Campion, J. and Rocco, S. (2009) 'Minding the mind: Evaluating the effects and potential of a school-based meditation programme for mental health promotion.' *Advances in School Mental Health Promotion 2*, 1, 47–55.

am spiritually. I know what I believe and disbelieve. I do not want to change.'
These are perfectly reasonable thoughts. But someone *completely* secure in
their ideas will not feel challenged, and need not therefore fear to engage in
further thought and discussion. When there is a sense of challenge, even of
threat, this often indicates a need to expand one's world view or philosophy.
Facing up to different perspectives with which we disagree offers an ideal
opportunity to reconsider our position and either affirm and strengthen it, or
to change and develop.

Achieving a mature perspective on life requires regular review of one's
priorities and assumptions. It involves discovering and giving new precedence
to spiritual values; and it involves developing what are referred to in this
book as 'spiritual skills'. To encourage co-operation alongside competition
in this way makes for more contented workers in the fields of health and
social care. It motivates them towards helping to heal people – making them
whole again – in addition to the more limited objective of simply curing
their symptoms. Spiritual development therefore makes for more amenable
colleagues, and greater numbers of more satisfied patients.

An account of the psychology of spirituality, to be useful, must carry
conviction. Statements throughout this book are therefore expressed with
assertion. Where there is evidence, sources will be cited; but it must be
acknowledged that the evidence base for this extensive topic is incomplete.
We are still exploring new territory. This is an introduction to a large and
complex subject. Much will be dealt with only briefly. Some aspects will
necessarily be left out altogether. The emphasis will be on healthy psychology;
so there is little here, for example, about specific mental illnesses, spirit
possession or poltergeists.

Spirituality has deeply personal aspects involving subjective experiences
rather than objective observations. This presents a problem, which the Taoist
author, Chuang Tsu,[13] put like this:

> Perfect is the man who knows what comes from heaven and what
> comes from man. Knowing what comes from heaven, he is in tune
> with heaven… However, there is one difficulty… How do I know
> that what I call heaven is not actually man, and that what I call
> man is not actually heaven?

His response:

> First, there must be a true man; then there can be true knowledge.[14]

---

13   Chuang Tsu lived in China in 4th century BC. The quotation is from Chuang Tsu (1974) *Inner
     Chapters*. Trans. G.-F. Feng and J. English. London: Wildwood House, p.113.

14   Compare this with the following words from 13th-century theologian, St Thomas Aquinas:
     'The First Philosophy is the knowledge of truth, not any truth but truth which is the source of
     all truth.' Aquinas, T. *Contra Gentiles: On the Truth of the Catholic Faith*. Book One: *Of God as He
     is in Himself*, Part One: 'The Function of the Wise Man' (trans. A. C. Pegis). Available online at
     http://maritain.nd.edu/jmc/etext/gc1_1.htm, accessed 8 June 2010.

Much of what follows in these pages will seem familiar to some readers for two reasons. First, many people are gifted with reliable intuitions about spiritual matters. This book will confirm and expand on what, deep down, you already know. Second, what will be presented in mainly secular terms is consistent with spiritual wisdom passed down through the ages via the world's major religions. Specific Buddhist teachings and practices, for example, resonate particularly well with some contemporary notions from science and psychology.[15] Nevertheless, these pages do contain much original thought, together with original interpretation, expansion and adaptation of the ideas and theories of others.

I cannot claim to be a true man in tune with heaven, but do feel sure I have encountered many such men and women during six decades of life. I am fully trained in science, medicine, psychology and psychiatry. I have read widely and studied with a number of spiritual teachers from a range of world religions. I have given many lectures and workshops on the topic of spirituality. I have heard and tried to respond honestly to arguments from many perspectives over the years, frequently by having to admit to not knowing the answer.

These are my author's credentials. In addition, like everyone, I have had plenty of experience of life's ups and downs. I find it helpful to engage daily in spiritual practices, including meditation, prayer and scripture reading, and I regularly attend Anglican services of worship. I refer to myself as an ecumenical or 'universalist' Christian, to indicate openness to the teachings and practices of other world religions, respect for the spiritual truths at their hearts, feelings of great kinship with true devotees of different faiths, and satisfaction from visits to their places of pilgrimage and worship. My personal attitude to religion can be summarized simply: 'God is love, and those who abide in love abide in God, and God abides in them.'[16]

I have muted it deliberately, but this background and the bias it introduces cannot be removed completely from the account of the psychology of spirituality presented here. It will therefore be wise for readers to take into account our differences and overlook what seems false or incomplete. I am happy for people to disagree with me. It means, I hope, that they are engaging with the material and thinking deeply about it. This is excellent. However, readers are encouraged to be generous and open-minded, rather than merely critical.

---

15 Buddhist ideas and practices have already been adapted very successfully for healthcare and mental healthcare purposes, beginning with the programme at the Stress Reduction Clinic at the University of Massachusetts Medical Center: see Kabat-Zinn, J. (1990) *Full Catastrophe Living.* New York, NY: Delta Books. See also Zindel, V., Segal, J., Williams, M.G. and Teasdale, J.D. (2002) *Mindfulness-Based Cognitive Therapy for Depression.* New York, NY: Guilford Press.

16 First Epistle of John 4:16.

My aim is to awaken interest, to shed light on mystery and promote harmony, rather than cause or aggravate conflict. I hope to help people understand themselves and each other better, to expand their vision, to see and grasp the bigger picture, and to do so not just as an intellectual exercise, but by which to live more satisfying lives.

Our hearts and minds interact in harmony as a 'soul', which holds to and expresses an innate reverence and wonder at the combined order and mystery of the natural world and the cosmos. Just like photons from the same light source, we are all seamlessly interconnected and intercommunicate. Mature spiritual awareness fosters in us a kind of 'wisdom mind' or soul-consciousness that, when accessed, provides each of us with a reassuring sense of belonging, and is our link to the ultimate source of meaning and purpose in human life: the spiritual dimension. 'Soul', underpinning all notions of freedom, truth, wisdom, compassion and love, finds its expression in turn through 'hands', through action, including *social* action: through the 'hands of friendship'.

Freedom, truth, wisdom, compassion, love…and joy: these are among the precious rewards of spiritual enquiry… And they are to be shared.

Larry Culliford

PART I

THEMES AND VARIATIONS

'What Goes Round Comes Around'

Chapter 1

INTRODUCTION

This introduction provides an overview, covering in brief much of what follows throughout the book. Each set of ideas will be developed in later chapters. It is not necessary for readers to grasp everything right away.

Wholeness

Spirituality is about wholeness. This point cannot be overemphasized. It is important to recognize the principle of an entirely seamless and interconnected reality that this entails.

To illustrate, from a spiritual perspective everything runs something like a Möbius strip that extends in every direction with no beginning and no end. It is easy to make such a strip and examine it. Take a 30 cm length of paper about 20 mm wide, blank on one side and dark or lined on the other. Half-twist the strip and connect the opposing ends, blank side to lined. This is your Möbius strip. Draw a pencil line along the centre, or simply run it between thumb and index finger. Where does it end?

We human beings, however, do not very often experience indivisible wholeness like this. Our lives much more commonly feel fragmented. We are used to disjunction, to beginnings and endings, birth and death, to ageing, the passing of seasons, of day and night, waking and sleeping, the discontinuity of turning our minds from this to this to this…to desires and aversions…to thoughts, feelings, perceptions of the senses and impulses to action…back and forth between experiences within the mind, within the body and 'out there', in the world…close by and at a distance…in the present, the past or the future…in plain consciousness, in twilight states, in dreams, in memory and imagination. We seldom experience our lives as seamless, or spiritual, at all. Nevertheless, when we do, 'something happens'. It has meaning at a deeply personal level.

Spirituality links the deeply personal with the universal.

In everyday life, changes of focus occur either with gradual subtlety or suddenly, even with violence, as this or that intrudes abruptly into consciousness, demanding our attention. The seamlessness, the sense of linked order, is easily lost and forgotten. The psychology of spirituality in its purest essence involves recapturing an appreciation of wholeness, of indivisibility, and concerns reconciling this with the apparent disjunctions of material reality, of time and space. It is as much about attitude and about acquiring attentive skills as it is about gaining knowledge.

Discovery

The German chemist, August Kekulé, first described the six-member ring of carbon atoms, the benzene ring structure, in 1865. His immensely significant discovery was central to the understanding of organic chemistry, the chemistry of biological systems. He later said that the ring shape came to him after a daydream about a serpent that was curling into a circle to take its tail in its mouth.

After a period of meditation one day in 1980, it was similarly that the discovery concerning the circular interactions of human emotions came to me. Meditation, allowing the mind to settle down and focus upon itself, plays an important part in understanding the psychology of spirituality, and on this occasion seems to have produced a genuine moment of creativity.

As with the benzene ring structure, circularity emerged again as central to ideas concerning human reactions to threat and loss, but circularity with a difference, circularity plus. In this case circularity leads onwards to progression, to emotional healing and, at the same time, to personal growth. The circle develops into a kind of forward spiral. This was the essence of the discovery.

I had been working with a number of deeply distressed psychiatric patients. I felt certain that there would be some kind of logic to their painful feelings, if only I could fathom it out. That day I had been listening to a radio broadcast about the composer Schoenberg and his development of 12-tone musical composition. The principle, as I remember it, was that all 12 notes – including sharps and flats, the black as well as the white keys on the piano – must be used in each composition, but that introduction of the twelfth note should be delayed, bringing duration and perhaps tension to the piece, before its entry signalled completion of each section. The pattern (or a variation of it), concluding eventually with the same note from the musical palette of 12, could then be repeated to make up a kind of musical Möbius strip.

To appreciate 12-tone musical compositions therefore involves developing, more than usual, the ability to listen to a sequence as a whole, and to listen also for what is missing – until it finally appears. This can be difficult, and not everybody finds this type of music pleasing. Nevertheless, the idea sank into my mind and became constructively connected, during that brief meditation, with my thoughts about the emotions. I understood in a flash that emotional healing cannot take place unless the whole scale or spectrum is present or at least somehow represented in the experience of the sufferer. When the sequence is completed, (all the emotions in the scale having broken through a persons's defences and been experienced in some way) it will be as if a dam has been breached. The painful energy is released and flows away, leaving peace. This is how circularity leads to progress. When a loss is fully accepted, and only then, something is completed and the process can move on.

One meaning of the word 'perfection' is linked to completion, to making something whole rather than flawless. This aspect of finding or reaching wholeness is what makes emotional healing a spiritual process. The resulting 'psychological' development equally implies growth of a 'spiritual' nature.

As the turning point is reached, the painful emotions do not disappear but are transformed by the 'catharsis', the release of energy, into their pain-free counterparts. That is why crying and laughter are important. They result directly from the release of energy that was previously invested in some form of emotional attachment.

As a result of the process, anxiety, for example, is transmuted into calm, and sadness into joy. The emotions can therefore be thought of as 'bi-modal', paired in such a way that when one aspect is present, the other is absent. (See Box 1.1, below.) The appropriate diagram is therefore not a single circle but a double one, as in the infinity symbol.[1] For example, you can feel guilty and blameless in sequence, but not both at the same time.

This process, and the basic set or spectrum of eight pairs of emotions, will be described in more detail later. For now, it is enough to say that, when the emotional healing process is complete, people are left with greater and lasting degrees of equanimity and emotional resilience, have more natural courage in the face of possible losses thereafter, are more engaged in the present moment, and are therefore able to live more spontaneously.

Less fearful for themselves, people in such a condition are also able to notice and share constructively in the suffering of others, bringing a measure of calm and hope to painful situations. Burdensome attachments are released as people grow increasingly mature. Progressively more content with the way

---

1   When first presenting this theory, I used the more poetic symbol of two butterfly wings attached centrally to each other. I called it the Butterfly Theory of Emotion and Personal Growth.

things are, their horizons thus lifted and broadened, they start awakening to new truths about themselves and to new 'spiritual' values, discovering a new kinship with others, and intimacy with the natural world and the cosmos.

Box 1.1: Painful and pain-free emotions – the bi-modal set

Wanting – Contentment
(both desire and aversion)

Bewilderment – Clarity

Anxiety – Calm

Doubt – Confidence

Anger – Acceptance

Shame – Worth (self-esteem)

Guilt – Innocence (purity)

Sadness – Happiness (joy)

Purpose in suffering

Purpose can therefore be discovered in suffering. For personal and spiritual growth to occur, adversity – and therefore at least some measure of emotional pain – is essential. In consequence, although it may seem sensible, time and energy spent trying to avoid distress and discomfort may only prolong or intensify painful experiences.

Many people need to revise their assumptions and re-educate themselves about this. The blessing though is that, as cuts, abrasions and bone fractures can mend, nature has also provided a mechanism for the healing of emotional wounds. Just as pain draws our attention to injury, and bleeding begins a healing process, so emotional pain signals something we need to attend to and sets off the process of repair.

We have learned to bring broken bones and cut flesh together with plaster casts and sutures, also to keep wounds clean and free of infection. Through knowledge of natural processes and the time required to heal, we have learned to plan ahead, to endure the necessary span of discomfort and disability with confidence and greater patience.

We have, in addition, discovered convalescent methods that help restore function and strength to wounded parts. Knowledge has thus allowed us to support nature in healing wounds. In the face of loss, by analogy, better knowledge about the process of emotional healing will permit improved wisdom to be brought to bear in helping people undergoing many forms of psychological trauma.

The discovery back in 1980, about a system of emotional interplay linked to healing and growth, significantly advanced my understanding in a way that has been of direct benefit in my work, and through that also, I hope, to my patients and colleagues. It seems natural to want to share what has been rewarding and helpful with others, but to do so has required much further investigation and thought, and has involved building on the ideas and research findings of many others.

Spiritual development

One of those pioneers was James Fowler who, in 1981, described six stages of faith development through the life cycle.[2] In order to build on Fowler's ideas, it will be necessary to outline them and describe how he came to develop and validate them. To make them more accessible and easier to remember, they have been given simpler names.

Box 1.2: Renaming Fowler's Stages of Faith

(Stage 0. Infancy and Undifferentiated Faith – *Infancy*)

Stage 1. Intuitive-Projective Faith – *Egocentric Stage*

Stage 2. Mythic-Literal Faith – *Conditioning Stage*

Stage 3. Synthetic-Conventional Faith – *Conformist Stage*

Stage 4. Individuative-Reflective Faith – *Individual Stage*

Stage 5. Conjunctive Faith – *Integration Stage*

Stage 6. Universalizing Faith – *Teaching and Healing Stage*

---

2   See Fowler, J. (1981) *Stages of Faith*. San Francisco, CA: Harper.

Fowler wrote about infancy for completeness, but only to dismiss it as a period before a child has become conscious of its own existence, of being a separate self.[3] His list properly begins with Faith Stage 1 (Egocentric Stage) involving a self-aware child being egocentric, oblivious to the perspective of others. In Faith Stage 2 (Conditioning Stage), older children, better capable of deductive reasoning, develop mental representations of a more orderly and dependable world. Resonating with others, they are now particularly susceptible to social forces and conditioning.

This prepares children for Faith Stage 3 (Conformist Stage), and a period of adolescence with strong pressures to strengthen allegiances and attachments, and so to conform within their community and culture. The interests of the group now take precedence over individual inclinations, as they do in tribal societies.

With time, though, the wish to be independent, to go it alone and think for oneself, emerges in opposition to the desire for safety and security, and the desire to belong to a large group. This is a critical stage in personal and spiritual development. A person enters Faith Stage 4 (Individual Stage) when the balance swings towards independence.

According to Fowler, it is only a minority of people who manage this, and fewer still who enter Faith Stage 5 (Integration Stage) whereby, one by one, they start to recognize a kind of universalism, and begin taking their true and equal place among the vast diversity of humanity.

The final stage, Faith Stage 6 (Teaching and Healing Stage), is entered by people with no personal agendas remaining, whose virtue is not forced or fickle but arises from a deep-seated, spiritual awareness of the interconnectedness of all things and all people. Such people may not be as rare as Fowler originally suggested. Nevertheless, humble, they tend to keep out of the limelight, so it is hard to be sure.

Beyond Fowler

In order to go beyond Fowler (as we will in Part 2), it is necessary to look more closely than he did at the transition points between stages, asking, 'How do people grow psychologically and spiritually?' This involves examining in particular how people develop through confronting adversity and as a result of the emotional healing process.

This will lead to further discussion (especially in Part 3) about meditation and other spiritual practices that are useful for developing additional spiritual skills. These are skills that can prepare people for, and ease their passage through, experiences of threat and loss that involve the giving up

---

3   Fowler's infancy may be referred to as 'stage zero'.

attachments and aversions (discussed later in this chapter) and the acquisition or affirmation of universal, altruistic, holistic, 'spiritual' values.

The sharing of values is common within social groups, communities and cultures. Pressure to conform in terms of values is powerful, and some of the adversity people face arises when personal values and those of their social group clash. To go beyond Fowler, then, it is also necessary to consider the interplay between personal and social psychology.

Spiritual insights can again be helpful with this. Spiritual values include honesty, trust, kindness, generosity, tolerance, patience, perseverance, discernment, humility, courage, compassion, wisdom, beauty and hope. Temporal or worldly values appear at odds with these. They are more materialistic and commercial, and often frankly self-seeking. It is instructive to examine how people at different stages of faith development approach these two apparently opposing sets of values.

To seek a suitable balance between them seems wise. This is achieved by using the 'both/and' rather than the 'either/or' approach. When both sets of values are adopted, but with the spiritual set taking ultimate precedence over the temporal set, a very different state of affairs results than when their positions are reversed. What would work better in a community, spiritual values dominated by temporal values or vice versa?

People in the Conformist Stage of spiritual development (Faith Stage 3) and earlier have little choice but to agree to and abide by the value set adopted within their group culture, whereas people from Stage 4 onwards do have – and tend to insist upon – a measure of personal choice.

The spiritual growth of communities will therefore depend on multiple individuals making progress towards independence of mind, rather than on some kind of mass conversion. A tipping point of some kind will have to be reached. What, then, is the goal of personal spiritual development? Rather than trying to change the world, or anything over which one has no significant influence, it involves the discovery and release of one's true self.

The everyday ego and the true self

After accepting each major loss, people grow closer to fulfilling their potential and to discovering their true selves. The true self is a spiritual concept.

According to Fowler's scheme, we begin life spiritually immature and develop maturity in stages. According to other authors, however, we have a priceless advantage. We start life with an important viable seed of spiritual maturity, which we carry with us throughout.

According to Donald Winnicot, for example, (quoted by Victor Schermer[4]) people start life with what he refers to as a 'pristine ego', the pure forerunner of a spiritual core or 'true self' that stays with us and influences us all our days. This is confirmed, according to researchers David Hay and Rebecca Nye,[5] by children of primary school age who are found still to demonstrate a natural spiritual awareness. Hay and Nye also report, however, that in contemporary UK culture children are encouraged to suppress and abandon any tendency towards spirituality or religiousness and adopt a predominantly secular world view. By the teen years, spiritual awareness has withered and in many cases vanished from sight.

As external influences grow, the true self is increasingly obscured by the 'everyday ego', referred to by some as the 'false self'. In adolescence and adulthood, except during mystical states when a person briefly experiences spiritual harmony with the temporal world, or until full spiritual maturity (Faith Stage 6) is achieved when it is regained on a more permanent basis, there is therefore dissonance between the two. From a spiritual perspective, this discordant gap between the 'everyday ego' and the 'spiritual self' is the origin of suffering; one that cannot be entirely avoided.

The everyday ego is the 'me' we experience most of the time, the personal self that interacts from birth with mother, father, siblings, the wider family and the social group at community, cultural, national and global levels throughout life. Through this ego, we form attachments and allegiances. We develop likes and dislikes concerning people, places, objects, activities, sensations, ideas, ideologies, and all manner of things, including myriad things created solely by our imagination.

We are engaged both with our surroundings, and with the world of inner experience. By thinking of them in terms of positive and negative, as pleasurable and painful, it is clear that we also entertain preferences about our emotions. Paradoxically, then, a person can feel positive about painful emotions (like anger) and negative about pleasurable ones (like joy).

Creatures of habit who find comfort in consistency, it depends largely on what we get used to. Enduring patterns of emotional response configure a person's 'temperament'. Usually thought of as being less fixed throughout life than 'personality' (which has biological and genetic determinants), one's temperament can change with experience (see Vignette – Mark and Vignette – Vicky).

---

4   See Schermer, V. (2003) *Spirit and Psyche: A New Paradigm for Psychology, Psychoanalysis and Psychotherapy*. London and New York, NY: Jessica Kingsley Publishers, p.67.

5   See Hay, D. and Nye, R. (2006) *The Spirit of the Child* (rev. edn). London and New York, NY: Jessica Kingsley Publishers.

Vignette – Mark[6]

Mark ran a financially successful manufacturing business, employing about 20 people. Although not fully aware of it, his main way of motivating employees involved intimidation. His anger and general irritability kept staff on their toes, vying with each other for his approval. He liked the situation, and would have said that, when angry, he felt good. It gave him both a sense of power and of being in the right. Later in life, after experiencing setbacks and situations he was unable to dominate and control, particularly when his only son developed a severe form of leukaemia, his attitude mellowed. He became more comfortable with people and they with him. He was surprised to discover that as the workplace atmosphere grew more relaxed, discipline was maintained nevertheless. Problems were resolved quickly, and productivity actually increased.

Vignette – Vicky

After her mother died when she was three years old, Vicky was raised by an emotionally distant father and an unfeeling, often punitive stepmother. She grew up with low self-esteem and a highly anxious disposition. She always expected things to go wrong for her, so when as a teenager she met David who treated her with kindness and respect, the brief and intermittent periods of joy she felt soon gave way to anxiety and foreboding again. She was sure she did not deserve to be happy. Later, as she learned to trust David's loyalty, she grew less fearful, smiled more often and developed a cheerful sense of humour.

A central characteristic of the spiritual, 'true' or 'higher' self involves being a stranger to desire. It does not form attachments or aversions. Dwelling in the moment, it wishes for nothing. Accepting the way things are, it has no sense of lacking anything; and in this acceptance lies the antidote to painful emotions like doubt, anxiety, anger and sorrow. Their absence leaves assuredness, calm, inner peace, contentment and joy: the emotions of spiritual maturity.

Spiritual development tends to form an arc or parabola. The everyday ego, seeking to survive and prosper, to meet and mate and procreate, to work, to join and participate in society, regularly meets with success, frustration and failure. Success brings the threat of loss, of losing what has been acquired: loved ones, friends, partners, wealth, position, security and so on. Frustration and failure bring both threat and actual loss too.

People normally react to these challenges with bewilderment, doubt and anxiety in the face of threat; with anger in the face of impending, but still seemingly recoverable, loss; with self-recrimination (shame and guilt) when loss appears inevitable, and sorrow when it is happening and no longer

---

6 The names of individuals in the vignettes have been changed to protect their identities.

deniable. Sadness and tears indicate acknowledgement of the finality of the loss, and so herald the onset of healing. Together with desire and aversion (two sides of the same coin) that set the attachment process in motion, these are the principal painful emotions. The full spectrum of complementary pairs is listed in Box 1.1 earlier.

Desire, attachment, threat and loss are central to human psychology, but the story is incomplete without chapters on healing and growth.

Discovering the true self

The dynamic relationship between the everyday ego and the true self can be clarified using the metaphor of a metal guitar string. Imagine this length of wire under tension between two points. It forms a straight line. Pluck it once in the middle and it begins to oscillate. The air around it is moved back and forth and a sound results. The greater the force applied, the bigger the amplitude of the resulting arc and the louder the sound. Eventually, unless additional force is applied, the string returns gradually to a straight line once again and falls silent.

According to this metaphor, each person is a string that life sets in motion. The true self – silent and motionless – is immediately lost to sight, its silence obscured by the blurred activity of the everyday ego, the string vibrating in its symmetrical arc or parabola.

At first, the string of life remains pristine and in tune, responding to its own internal rhythms of heartbeat and the flow of breath; but many forces are operating to distort its symmetry. The self in this analogy is not in a vacuum. Playing upon it are the background vibrations of nature: of the earth, of sun and moon, of the planets, stars and galaxies, and of the universe. Some are rhythmic and gentle, like the tides; some are at times cataclysmic.

On a daily basis too, the single string of the apparently separate ego is surrounded and influenced by other strings, other egos, other selves, all in vibrant motion. Their characteristics differ, and the sounds they bring forth vary. Some appeal, others repel. To further the metaphor, the individual string, pulled in different directions, is at risk of becoming distorted in a way that makes it hard to revert back to the silence and stillness, and revert to the original pristine condition; but hearkening back, actively listening to the silence in meditation, is a good way to make progress.

The split between everyday ego and true, spiritual self normally grows quickly in the early years of life, especially during Faith Stage 3, when the personal ego is largely subordinated to the priorities and values of the social group (see Figure 1.1). A peak is reached in Stage 4, during which a sense of genuine individuality and self-control asserts itself, allowing the processes of reconnection and reconciliation between the everyday ego and the spiritual

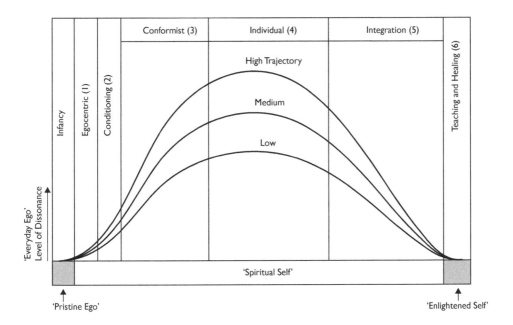

Figure 1.1: Fowler's six Stages of Faith showing high, medium and low trajectories of dissonance between the 'everyday ego' and the 'spiritual self'

self to advance. Progress towards this re-harmonization grows more quickly during Stage 5 and is completed by Stage 6.

In later chapters, the different 'trajectories' of faith – high, medium and low – are discussed. Put simply, people on a high trajectory are worldlier, more secular in outlook and less spiritual throughout life than those on a low trajectory. They are more likely to remain at earlier stages of faith development unless 'something happens', unless they undergo some kind of persuasive experience like an epiphany. Healthcare professionals may especially witness episodes of serious physical or mental ill- health in others which, if handled sympathetically, can contribute to this valuable change of direction. Illness can, of course, challenge a person's faith too.

Practical and poetic vision

To grasp the psychology of spirituality fully, both practical and poetic types of understanding are required. The use of metaphor demonstrates this. The practical approach involves analysis, the scientific method of enquiry and examination that makes use of dissection, of cutting big things methodically into smaller things so as to observe and understand them better. It makes use of the rational approach and the logic of 'either/or' thinking.

It is difficult, however, both to cut things up and easily retain a sense of their wholeness, or a sense of the greater wholeness of which they are part. This is a different skill that also requires training and involves developing poetic vision, employing widely the use of metaphor, as already demonstrated in the case of the guitar string, and the 'both/and' style of thinking. Practical and poetic methods of enquiry are complementary. They support one another.[7]

Think of the word 'universe'. 'Uni' obviously denotes oneness, something single. 'Verse' originally in English referred to the turn and furrow of the plough (as in 'reverse'). Then – through metaphor – it came to mean a line of writing; and thence lines of poetry, psalms, scripture and song.

The universe, indicating all existing matter, space and other phenomena regarded collectively, can therefore be thought of as a harmoniously ordered whole that is dynamic, beautiful, poetic, polyphonous, all parts contributing somehow to the great song: now lament, now lullaby, now anthem, now jig, now theme, now variation, now chorus, now solo, now crescendo, now pianissimo, now plainsong, now boat song, now procession, now dance, now silence.

This is poetics, and these are metaphors for the richness and harmony of the whole; yet the word 'universe' also points in a more practical direction. It can mean not only one verse, but also one 'version', a consensus, one shared interpretation – essentially an astronomical interpretation – of what humans have discovered about the planets, stars, galaxies, nebulae, dark matter and whatever else may be observed or deduced from telescopic observation and mathematical calculations.

Astrophysicists report that our world may be part of a single universe that is multi-dimensional, beyond space and time. They say too that it may somehow be related to many alternatives, our universe as part of a 'multiverse'. Nevertheless, only a very few people can be expected to understand the physics and mathematics involved, and to what degree these ideas are still speculative. The rest of us can only use imagination; and this leads back to the necessity for us of poetic vision and experience, alongside a more practical and analytic overview.

Imagination necessarily leads in turn back to an emotional, as well as a cognitive, response. It causes people to react with awe, wonder, excitement, bewilderment, fear and trembling, disquiet, gratitude, inner peace; with a full dictionary of complex emotions, that may not always be easily given in words.

---

7   See, for example, Finnegan, J. (2008) *The Audacity of Spirit: The Meaning and Shaping of Spirituality Today.* Dublin: Veritas, especially Chapter 3 Towards a Poetics of Spirituality.

Two halves make a whole

Human brains have two distinctively functional but well connected halves – the 'right brain' and the 'left brain' – that are well adapted to interpret experience in both ways, poetic and practical, and to maintain communication with each other about it.

The right side is more poetic, looking wordlessly at the whole picture as with a floodlight. The left brain is more practical, focusing sharply down on the detail, as with a searchlight. It is capable of language, of words to describe what it encounters. Spiritual awareness involves the fusion of poetic with practical. It involves the whole brain working as one. Meditation studies, referred to in Chapter 11, support this observation.

Whatever else, the dynamic universe human beings inhabit demands and elicits personal responsivity. Everyone is involved, not only psychologically – through our thoughts, feelings, sensory perceptions and actions – but spiritually. That, too, is what spirituality is about: non-separateness, the deeply personal linked seamlessly to the universal, the one engaged with the whole.

And, by inference, if each is connected to the whole, then through this we are all seamlessly linked to one another. Thus is repeated the idea that the psychological and social dimensions of spirituality have an intimate bearing on each other. Understanding this, we are beginning to grasp that spirituality fulfils a different kind of logic. It begins to make a poetic kind of sense.

Given the poetics of the situation, the most *practical* deduction to make is that as many people as possible should learn how to enquire into their spiritual nature and discover their true selves. Spiritual development should therefore be restored as the bedrock of education, healthcare, social care, and therefore also of commerce, of local, national and international politics. Then all will be better off. It follows too that spiritual development should be given more emphasis than has generally come to be the case at the heart of every religion. More people than at present will then find religious teachings and practices relevant, even useful, in the search for personal spiritual maturity.

Learning about the psychology of spirituality, about the interplay between both personal and social dimensions, necessarily combines both practical objectivity and poetic subjectivity. Readers are invited to consider this book on the subject, chapter by chapter, as a guide to a journey, a journey through an educational adventure park, a spiritual journey of both learning and fun, a homecoming journey back towards the true self. Everyone alive is on this journey already. The pilgrimage has already begun.

Summary points

1. *Wholeness*

Spirituality is about wholeness. Life commonly feels fragmented. Nevertheless, the psychology of spirituality involves rediscovering an appreciation of the essential qualities of indivisibility and non-separateness.

2. *Purpose in suffering*

The full spectrum of eight paired emotions is involved in emotional healing, a process leading naturally to personal growth. Adversity is unavoidable and necessary for spiritual development. Time and energy spent trying to avoid distress may only add to it.

3. *Spiritual development*

Ways of developing Fowler's six stages of faith involve examining the transition points, and paying more attention to the interplay between personal and social psychology. Conforming to group influences can result in unwelcome restrictions and loss of independence. Spiritual and temporal values may clash.

4. *The everyday ego and the true self*

At birth, the 'pristine ego' precedes a spiritual core or 'true self' that becomes obscured by an 'everyday ego' that develops attachments. Attachments and aversions make people vulnerable to threat and loss, and thus to painful emotions. A split in the dynamic relationship between the everyday ego and the true self normally reaches a peak in adulthood. Reconciliation begins during the 'individual' Stage 4 of faith development. With progress, the journey comes to feel like a homecoming.

5. *Two halves make a whole*

Both practical and poetic types of understanding of spirituality are required. The first involves analysis. Poetic appreciation, in contrast, involves preserving a sense of the greater wholeness of which everything is a part. The two distinctively functional but well connected halves of human brains are well adapted to interpret experience in both poetic and practical ways, and to maintain communication with each other about it. Spiritual awareness involves the whole brain working as one. Meditation studies support this observation.

Exercises and questions for personal reflection and as a basis for group discussion:

1. If you have not yet done so, make (or imagine) a Möbius strip and examine it.

2. Which of these statements fits when you are faced with alternatives?

   (a) 'I like to know where I stand with a degree of certainty, and feel secure using practical logic ('either/or' thinking).'

   (b) 'I am happy with the use of metaphor, and feel comfortable with the poetic ('both/and') approach.'

3. In considering Question 2, did you automatically think of choosing only one answer? If so, reflect on the possibility that both answers may reflect (or come to reflect) the truth about you.

4. What do you know about the way cuts and bone fractures heal? What kind of things prevent, distort or delay healing?

5. How good are you at recognizing emotions in other people? What are the telltale signals of bewilderment, anger, guilt and sadness, for example? How about calm, contentment and joy?

6. How good are you at recognizing your own emotions?

7. Read the vignettes again. Think about them. Discuss them with someone, perhaps a friend or partner.

Chapter 2

THEMES AND VARIATIONS

The spirituality adventure park

'The spirituality revolution is a spontaneous movement in society, a new interest in the reality of spirit and its healing effects on life, health, community and well-being.' These are the words of Australian author, David Tacey.[1] His message, that everyone should become better informed in order to get more involved, means spirituality is not a mere object for analysis or specimen for dissection and scrutiny. It is better considered as a kind of adventure playground to be explored; a vast domain offering inexhaustible opportunities for play and education.

This park is to be imagined containing many different themes. Some parts are apparently dominated by a particular religion, faith or wisdom tradition. Some appear anti-religious, and others non-religious or secular. Many of the themes seem opposed to each other, but all reside and find harmony within the great compass of spirituality.

Just as there are roads and pathways, pipelines, conduits and cables, necessarily criss-crossing real theme parks, so there are a number of connecting ideas in this book, helping unite people wherever they find themselves within the park, with whatever areas they at first feel most comfortable. One theme already mentioned, for example, involves attachment and loss. Everyone experiences attachment: the threat of loss is ever-present, and losses occur repeatedly. Another involves adversity: challenging situations which concern losses and threats offer good opportunities for personal development.

---

1 Tacey, D. (2004) *The Spirituality Revolution: The Emergence of Contemporary Spirituality*. Hove and New York, NY: Brunner-Routledge (p. 1). Tacey is a professor of psychoanalytic studies and reader in arts and critical enquiry at Melbourne's La Trobe University.

To continue the analogy between spirituality and an adventure park, readers might imagine taking an intimidating ride for the first time. Naturally, many people are terrified at the prospect.[2] Others feel challenged and excited. Those who have seen people survive the ride and enjoy it will feel encouraged to follow their example. Those who have actually made the trip will have a sense of achievement and may want to do it again, experiencing the thrill of anticipation beforehand, and joyful excitement during the ride. This may be followed by relaxation and contentment when back on solid ground, and perhaps the desire to go round once more, or try something similar elsewhere. Devotees of such rides often want to share their enthusiasm, and encourage others to participate. Others will not have enjoyed the experience, and may be left with a sense of aversion and an unwillingness to repeat it.

So it is with spiritual experiences, which tend ultimately to be safe but may offer extreme degrees of challenge. They are also generally highly rewarding, full of experiences to share; and whenever associated with a negative initial response, the opportunity for personal growth is present as well.

Dislike of something, however intense or persistent, does not have to be permanent. An intermediate attitude between likes and dislikes, a middle way between attachment and aversion, is 'detachment'. This refers to informed and mature involvement in something with a clear mind and emotional balance, equanimity. A caution is necessary, however. Detachment is quite unlike, and should not be mistaken for, 'indifference', which retains an element of aversion leading to only superficial engagement with its target, or even frank neglect and avoidance.

Exploring spirituality

Fruitful exploration of spirituality is both recreational and educational. Recreation speaks of excitement and enjoyment. '*Re-creation*' refers literally to transformation and renewal; and this is what happens to those purposefully engaged with spirituality. Recreation can also involve relaxation, becoming refreshed. As with real theme parks, there are important restful and beautiful aspects to this spirituality park too.

The use of adventure or the theme park analogy is not intended to trivialize a serious topic, but to suggest that, whereas solemnity is appropriate at times, so too are attitudes of joyful play and innocence. Adult guidance is sometimes necessary (for example, on obedience to the rules of safety, keeping the harness fastened during a ride, and avoidance of anti-social behaviour). A sense of proportion, between codes of appropriate conduct on

---

2   Note how these often have challenging names like 'Oblivion' or 'Nemesis'.

the one hand, and freedom and fun on the other, is ideal for everyone to draw the best out of any theme park experience.

Additional themes in the park

A number of general connecting themes concerning psychology and spirituality have been touched on in Chapter 1. Some will be repeated and developed in the following paragraphs; others have been added (see Box 2.1).

Box 2.1: Spiritual themes

- Joy and wonder
- Reciprocity
- Meaning and purpose
- Life as a journey
- Death
- Religions
- God and the names of God
- Belief as a form of attachment
- Faith
- Love
- Non-dualism
- Two ways of experiencing time

- An inner source of knowledge
- Mysticism
- Wisdom
- Unity of body, mind and soul
- The avoidance of conflict
- The language of spirituality
- Five dimensions of human experience
- Emotions – healing and growth
- Sacred universality
- Human stories

JOY AND WONDER

Suppose there is a merry-go-round at the heart of the spirituality theme park, and on it a small child whose parents are standing by. Imagine the experience of parents disappearing and reappearing repeatedly, of waving goodbye one instant, and then almost immediately waving hello again, over and over. Children of a certain age seem to adore this, experiencing both joy and wonder in response. Wonder is one of the five capacities through which children's spirituality seems to flow, according to researcher Tobin Hart.[3] Joyfulness and wonder are often reflected in the experience and expression of adult spirituality as well.

---

3   Hart, T. (2003) *The Secret Spiritual World of Children.* Makawao, HI: Inner Ocean.

RECIPROCITY

The merry-go-round image demonstrates other features of spirituality. Standing beside it, watching the back of a child recede into the distance, we soon enough see another aspect, the front of the same child, reappearing from a slightly different horizon.

A woman once described herself in casual conversation as 'spiritual but not religious'. Asked what she meant by this, she replied that it was hard to define, but that she believed firmly in the idea that 'What goes round comes around.'[4] This is no mere modern cliché but shorthand for a genuine profundity implying that, as with the funfair ride, life presents people with the same situation, often including a challenge to be met, both repeatedly and from a slightly different angle each time. The same phrase implies too that a person's every thought, word and action (or moment of inaction) has a consequence for them. In other words, 'You reap what you sow.' Wish for, intend and do good to others and you benefit. Wish for, intend and do harm and you suffer.

According to anthropologist Douglas Davies,[5] this principle of reciprocity is the only principle shared by all main religions, whether described in terms of Buddhist karma ('the law of cause and effect'), for example, or aspects of Christian theology concerning love and forgiveness. It reflects the notion of a holistic universe in which everyone and everything is seamlessly connected to everyone and everything else. The Buddhist monk and spiritual master, Thich Nhat Hanh, has referred to this principle as 'Interbeing'.[6] Zen Buddhist teachers speak of awakening similarly to 'non-separateness' as one of the major fruits of meditation. It is a principle to which we shall return throughout these pages.

MEANING AND PURPOSE

According to a leaflet published by the Royal College of Psychiatrists,[7] 'Spirituality is identified with experiencing a deep-seated sense of meaning and purpose in life, together with a sense of belonging. It is about acceptance, integration and wholeness.'

The definition continues, 'The spiritual dimension tries to be in harmony with the universe, strives for answers about the infinite, and comes especially

---

4   I am grateful to Prof Patricia Casey of University College, Dublin for relating this conversation she had with the woman on a plane journey.

5   In a lecture, 'Salvation with Spirituality in Mind' given at the Royal College of Psychiatrists on 20 November 2009.

6   Thich Nhat Hanh (1991) *Peace is Every Step.* London: Rider, pp.95–6.

7   *Spirituality and Mental Health* from the 'Help is at Hand' series, published by the Royal College of Psychiatrists, London. Also available as a free download at www.rcpsych.ac.uk/mentalhealthinformation/therapies/spiritualityandmentalhealth.aspx, accessed 19 May 2010.

into focus in times of emotional stress, physical and mental illness, loss, bereavement and death.'

These situations are all examples of loss and the threat of loss. Medical students instructed to ask patients with a wide range of medical, surgical and psychiatric conditions about what gives their lives meaning and what helps them face serious difficulties (such as ill-health), have discovered that many speak in terms of either a recognized religion or some kind of intuitive faith.[8]

To maintain psychological and spiritual health, it is important for people to make sense of their lives, not just once but continually. The great sages and teachers of history have all said much the same.[9] Refreshment, renewal and recreation are vital. Many people find it difficult to find and express what gives their lives meaning and a deep-seated sense of purpose without using spiritual concepts and spiritual language.

LIFE AS A JOURNEY

The idea of journeying through life with the constant possibility of growth towards personal maturity – through both challenge and tranquillity – is one of spirituality's main themes. The journey outwards from birth, later seems more like returning homeward. The journey is *within* rather than *to* the spiritual theme park. It is not a place to go and visit. It is where everyone already exists. Located everywhere and nowhere, it is an ever-present theme park of the mind.

DEATH

Life's journey on earth ends in physical death. This is a difficult, and not always popular, subject. Yet, the concept of extinction, associated with the anticipation of physical death, is unavoidable when discussing the psychology of spirituality. It is an ever-present possibility; for death can come unexpectedly, at any moment.

The prospect of death, its certainty, provides the maximum possible psychological challenge for a human being. It seems to entail absolute loss, the loss of everything. At the same time, it may equally represent the best opportunity for personal development. People respond differently to the idea of their own extinction at different stages of personal and spiritual maturity. As we explore the subject in later chapters, it will become clear that, for some, it holds no fears at all.

---

8   See Culliford, L. (2009) 'Teaching spirituality and health care to third-year medical students.' *The Clinical Teacher 6*, 1, 22–7.

9   See, for example, Butler-Bowden, T. (2005) *50 Spiritual Classics*. London: Nicholas Brealey Publishing.

RELIGIONS

Spirituality could be described as the 'active ingredient' of religion. Religion and spirituality are linked, but can be distinguished from each other and considered separately.

To use another image, like that of Hilary Guise's painting on the book's cover,[10] spirituality can be thought of as the essential and nourishing roots of a great tree, the main branches of which represent the different world religions. The smaller branches and leaves represent smaller scale denominations of the major religions and faith traditions. Even atheistic belief systems can have spiritual roots.

GOD AND THE NAMES OF GOD

The word 'God', and the various names given to God,[11] are highly charged, full of meaning and significance. However, they have different meanings and significance for different people, and are therefore contentious. Worshippers are apparently at one extreme of a continuum, for example, with atheists at the other.

This makes use of the words and the names for God problematic in a book written for readers from different traditions. Nevertheless, in discussing spirituality, words to indicate a supreme deity are required, as are words for related evocative concepts like: 'sacred', 'divine', 'enlightenment', 'godhead', 'heaven', 'holy', 'paradise', 'providence' and so on; similarly: 'demon', 'devil' and 'hell'.

Readers are advised to approach these and similar words with care, and with minimal preconceptions about their meanings and significance. As a guide, any reference to God or divinity is intended to imply an overarching, sacred and indivisible unity at all times (see Box 2.2).

This means a concept of God as all-inclusive: a principle of both creation and destruction, for example, according to which matter and energy are continuously being recycled. This is most obvious in terms of biology; biomass and bio-energy flowing constantly through different life forms as plants are harvested, prey taken, as age, illness and injury take their toll according to the natural order.

The principle is made explicit in the Hindu faith, where the triple godhead includes a God of Creation, Brahma, and one of destruction, Shiva. The third God, Vishnu, is the Sustainer, maintaining creation in a balance of opposites. In Hinduism, Vishnu is said to have taken many human incarnations at

---

10 From her series of 40 paintings 'Not Silenced by the Darkness', inspired by passages from the Old Testament.
11 For example, the Absolute, Alaha, Allah, Almighty, Brahma, Christ, Creator, Elohim, Father, the Godhead, Great Spirit, Messiah, Yahweh.

different times, for example as Lord Rama and as Lord Krishna. Some Hindus incorporate teachings from other religions by including, for example, the historical Buddha and Jesus Christ in the list of Vishnu's incarnations, acknowledging the divine nature and inspiration of these holy persons.

Box 2.2: Aristotle's Law of Contradiction contradicted

According to Aristotle's 'Law of Contradiction',[12] the same attribute cannot at the same time belong and not belong to the same subject and in the same respect. The philosopher explains, 'It is impossible for the same man at the same time to believe the same thing to be and not to be; for if a man were mistaken on this point he would have contrary opinions at the same time.'

Whereas this makes obvious sense when applied to a universe made up of opposites, it contrasts with the philosophies of Eastern spiritual traditions (especially Taoism and Zen Buddhism) and with mystical experiences during which someone has some kind of direct experience or communication with the divine. Such experiences, likely to involve the whole brain, with right and left halves in unison[13], seem to offer incontrovertible evidence that God (the Creator, and therefore the creator of opposites) is indivisibly whole, incorporating and fulfilling all opposites; including beginning *and* ending, life *and* death, existing *and* non-existing.

These terms have no meaning when applied to the supreme deity, who can therefore be accepted as eternal, indeed as being both existent and non-existent. According to the mystics, the arguments about whether or not there is a God are therefore rendered meaningless. The point is beyond doubt and certainty, because God created doubt and certainty both. Rational, 'either/or' discussion is redundant. God, the supreme deity or Godhead may be referred to as 'Absolute' (or 'the Absolute'), and concerning whatever is absolute, only poetic, 'both/and' ways of thinking are adequate.

Imagine a new, high definition, digital television set, capable of showing an infinite number of channels. According to this metaphor, the comprehensive cover provided by the set represents the wholeness and interdependence of spiritual reality. Viewers choose channels to watch. Strong feelings in favour

---

12   Aristotle *Metaphysics* IV, 3. Available at http://classics.mit.edu/Aristotle/metaphysics.4.iv.html, accessed 9 June 2010.
13   See, for example, Austin, J. (1998) *Zen and the Brain*. Cambridge, MA: MIT Press.

or against some of the programmes arise; but no one programme or channel can offer anything other than a partial view of the seamless reality of the divine realm or of God.

Watching many programmes on many different channels may help, but it might only add to a person's confusion, especially when apparent contradictions are encountered. The only solution is to become attuned oneself to the spiritual dimension – by developing spiritual skills, particularly meditation skills – and so do away with the need for the intermediary of an external receiver like a television set.

BELIEF AS A FORM OF ATTACHMENT

A belief is a form of attachment: attachment to a thought, idea or set of related ideas. Holding to a system of related beliefs therefore represents attachment to an ideology. Attachment to one ideology often implies aversion to opposing ideologies. Attachment and aversion always go together, like day and night.

Any attachment brings automatically the possibility of threat. Beliefs can similarly be threatened. Ideas may be challenged both by new and apparently contradictory experiences, as well as by arguments from other people. These challenges are often met with denial and justification, but they also often awaken emotions like anxiety, doubt and anger. Such an emotional response indicates the presence of an attachment, and the strength of emotion corresponds to the strength of attachment, rather than the correctness of the idea or belief.

FAITH

Faith goes deeper than belief. It is rock solid. It faces challenges with fearless equanimity, rather than anger, doubt or anxiety, because it does not depend on attachment to an idea or to anything else.

Faith is based on spiritual wisdom and awareness. It is not faith 'in' anything partial or incomplete. Faith – if 'in' anything – is faith in the divine nature of a seamlessly whole, universal reality. To have faith in God, a God of wholeness, amounts to the same thing for many people. The experience of doubt is an inevitable aspect of the journey towards fully established personal faith. Mature faith of this type is one of the principal goals of the spiritual journey.

Vignette – Nathan
Nathan was baptized in infancy and raised by devout Christian parents. When he left home to go to university, he believed fully in the gospel message of Christ. Nevertheless, he found himself growing angry when

others, non-Christians, challenged his beliefs. He also met devout followers of other religions, and could not help but be impressed by the calm inner strength they seemed to derive from beliefs and spiritual practices different from his own. He became a little bewildered, and began to experience doubt concerning the adequacy of his beliefs. This marked the start of his search for some greater kind of spiritual truth than the rather rigid and exclusive system of beliefs he had grown up with.

LOVE

Love is also a vital aspect of spirituality. People love whatever and whomever they feel inseparably, intimately and eternally bound to. When we love a person, place, object or idea, it means we feel wholeness in combination with whoever, wherever or whatever. It seems to complete us. We enjoy a deeply satisfying sense of closure; and so we identify ourselves according to our loves. 'This is me,' we feel; and this 'me' expands to include that which we love.

There is a paradox to loving. It has a timeless quality. We experience our loves as if they will and must last forever. In this, they have spiritual significance. Nevertheless, in terms of everyday, worldly reality, they are temporary; only at best, 'Until death do us part.'

The core 'spiritual' or 'true' self identifies with, is totally immersed in and loves only the sacred whole of creation. It is not discriminatory in any way. It can love each component (including each person) equally because each part is seamlessly linked to the whole and reflects the whole. This is perfect love, the holistic and absolute love of total completion.

The everyday ego loves imperfectly, retaining a distinction between self and not-self, between self and other, until spiritual maturity is attained when the everyday ego merges with the true, spiritual self.

Immature love is strong on desire, attachment, possessiveness and dependency. When attachments are intense during interpersonal relationships, for example, we naturally want to be with the one we love. We are averse to even brief separations, and suffer intense feelings of distress in the face of threat – through infidelity or life-threatening illness perhaps – and during the actual loss involved in a break-up. With experience, however, the pain need not be so great.

The journey towards maturity involves learning to love with diminishing degrees of dependent attachment. Love often begins as passionate: exciting but anxious, inexperienced, often forceful, impulsive, self-absorbed, possessive and personal. Later it becomes more compassionate: frequently joyful, mostly wise, gentle, patient, considerate of others, outward-looking and universal. Attachments to ideas and ideologies can follow a similar path.

NON-DUALISM

It is worth repeating often that, being especially about wholeness, spirituality is about seeking completion. It involves a 'holistic' appreciation of a universe in which everything is seamlessly connected with everything else. However, most people learn to have a 'dualistic' understanding of themselves and the world they inhabit, as if standing outside it. In this 'self/non-self' universe, opposing features are emphasized: for example, a person may be considered *either* young *or* old, but not both at the same time.

In contrast, holistic appreciation envisions a person as part of the universal continuum. It acknowledges people in the present as having *both* young *and* old characteristics and capabilities, recognizing life as stretching throughout time. The 'both/and' thinking of holism does not negate the 'either/or' thinking of dualism. It complements it.

The Taoist 'yin-yang' symbol demonstrates the principle of wholeness in all scales, from infinitesimal to cosmic. It can be considered a poetic 'both/and' symbol that invites holistic thinking as follows: the dark ground (yin) has a small central white spot, and the light ground (yang) has a small central dark spot. The entire symbol is to be imagined as dynamic, constantly changing. The primal powers never reach a standstill. Just as day and night forever precede and become one another, what is light gradually becomes dark, and what is dark becomes light repeatedly over time. The opposites counteract, balance and turn into each other, comparable similarly to the changing seasons of the year.

According to the Taoist tradition, yin (the dark) and yang (the light) have become extended to include several polarized forces in the universe, including night and day, earth and heaven, receptive and creative, yielding and firm, feminine and masculine.

There are many opposites that similarly define each other, among them negative and positive, hot and cold, dry and wet, north and south, east and west, up and down, inside and outside, ancient and modern, infinite and finite, bad and good. Without one, there cannot be the other. Wisdom involves knowing that such pairs are inseparable. Bi-modal emotions, such as sorrow and joy, are similarly linked. When one is present, the other is absent and vice versa. The complementary form may not be present, but its potential is there, as behind a veil, and may not be far away.

TWO WAYS OF EXPERIENCING TIME

Many wisdom traditions suggest that there are two ways of experiencing time, which also interpenetrate one another like the white and dark parts of the yin-yang symbol. The two Greek names for time are 'chronos' and 'kairos'.

Chronos is the familiar clock time, advancing steadily in linear fashion, day by day. Kairos was the name of the Ancient Greek god who symbolized chance, fortune and synchronicity, the one who knocked and came calling at the right time, the perfect moment when all was ripe and ready. Kairos is therefore sometimes described as spiritual time (or 'God's time'), and has a different quality altogether from chronos. Subjectively, when gripped by kairos, it may feel as if clock time has frozen, slowed right down or stopped completely. Paradoxically, it may also feel as if time has speeded up, so that minutes, hours, days, even weeks and months can go by as if in a flash.[14] Some athletes experience it, for example, when they get 'in the zone' during a burst of peak performance.

Kairos is in play when things happen unpredictably, but at just the right moment. Eternity and clock time seem to intersect for human benefit and instruction. Such an experience, when something eternal appears to break through into everyday life, is called an 'epiphany'. Heaven and earth may seem briefly to coincide and…'something happens'! Something new and profound, something inspiring and potentially life-changing, may be revealed in an instant.

New wisdom feels right because it tends to resonate powerfully with something already present, deep inside. It feels like a reminder and confirmation of something already known but forgotten. Such revelations may herald a kind of spiritual awakening, a key moment of transition on life's journey towards spiritual maturity. As the fallen leaf never rises to rejoin the tree, so is this a point of no return. And the significance of these experiences is reinforced by 'synchronicities', unexpected but meaningful coincidences, such as may occur when two people meet for the first time who are later to become life partners. It was a coincidence, for example, that I was thinking deeply about the nature of and relationships between painful and pleasurable

---

14 See, for example, Needleman, J. (2003) *Time and the Soul.* San Francisco, CA: Berrett-Koehler Publishers.

emotions when I heard the radio programme about Schoenberg (see Chapter 1).

Synchronicities and serendipities – unexpected discoveries – often go together. There is a kind of mystery about kairos. Kairos is spiritual time.

AN INNER SOURCE OF KNOWLEDGE

People learn and grow through experience, a process of 'education' whereby (according to the word's Latin roots) knowledge is drawn or led out, exposed to the pupil's everyday conscious awareness from somewhere within. Study, external guidance and teaching are helpful, but it follows from people's epiphany experiences that a source of essential knowledge already lies somehow within each person. It is accessible through intuition.

Education and intuition go together; and education of this type is assisted by a number of spiritual skills and practices, particularly meditation and silent forms of prayer, that heighten a person's natural intuitive ability (see Chapters 11 and 12). Conscious awareness of the spiritual dimension may be spontaneous, but it can also be improved deliberately by meditation and prayer.

Exploring how this works gets to the heart of the psychology of spirituality, because it involves deliberately allowing the everyday ego to quieten, in order to pay greater attention to one's spiritual nature in direct communication at all times with the great, pervading spirit or life-force of the universe. To use religious language, it is the soul in direct communication with God.

MYSTICISM

'Mystic' is a term that need not now be considered particularly mysterious. It simply refers to people who have become adept in terms of spiritual awareness. Having a spiritual self and an inner source of knowledge, accessible through intuition, everyone is a mystic, containing at least the spark of mystical ability.

This can be compared metaphorically to having a two-way radio transmitter-receiver, a personal connection to the universal, spiritual realm, which mystics tend to keep turned on and tuned in while going about their otherwise ordinary, everyday lives. Some people tune in regularly; but for many the link remains unconscious and in the background – until and unless 'something happens', in the form of a spiritual breakthrough.

Revered mystics of former times, the powerful spiritual masters and saints of all religious traditions, were people with naturally potent radio receivers, so to speak, who recognized their value and invested time and effort in developing their abilities to pay attention and give priority to the signals they received. This involves contemplation – thinking in a deep and sustained way about a meaningful topic – as well as meditation and other spiritual practices.

Contemplation, at its simplest, means taking time to think about and make sense of one's life. It involves appraising and reappraising one's values and priorities. Many people have developed their own methods, building them into rhythmical and relaxing activities like knitting, jogging, sailing or taking long walks; and feel better for including periods of contemplation regularly as a kind of discipline in their daily lives.

WISDOM

Contemplation soon reveals that there are different kinds of knowledge. What can be observed, measured and tested gives rise to scientific knowledge; but there is also the knowledge of how to be and behave, of how to grow and mature throughout life. This is wisdom or spiritual knowledge.

Science uses the linear time, cause and effect, rational, 'either/or' thinking approach of dualism. It seeks reproducible facts and objectivity. Wisdom incorporates this and goes further. It also sees people and situations from many different perspectives at once.

Wisdom seeks what is best for all, thus acknowledging a different logic: the logic of the bigger picture and advantageous ('wholesome') outcomes. It involves intuition and experience applied to situation-specific, one-off circumstances. Wisdom, the child of kairos rather than chronos, although often referred to as 'timeless', is therefore reborn and reinvented moment by moment. What may be a wise and beneficial action today could have destructive effects tomorrow when the circumstances have changed.

Wisdom also enables the penetration and resolution of paradoxes, many of which arise in the context of spiritual life and growth. For example, there is a paradox in the preceding paragraph. Can anything be both timeless and reborn continually?

The answer requires the application of holistic, rather than dualistic, thinking, and poetic rather than practical logic. Wisdom is not one thing. It is not a simple object. It can therefore be *both* timeless (in one sense) *and* continually reborn (in another). To put it differently, great timeless wisdom, the child of kairos, is born into chronos, and must be interpreted appropriately in each moment for each situation in everyday linear time.

UNITY OF BODY, MIND AND SOUL

People are bio-psycho-spiritual in nature. The body, mind and spiritual essence are one, indivisible. Suffering therefore affects a person's body, mind and soul. It has physical, psychological (especially emotional) and spiritual components.

Despite this, people have learned to pay attention to each aspect differently. Healthcare professionals have come to recognize that some people find it easier to attract attention, help and sympathy by concentrating on physical pain and symptoms, rather than admit to psychological problems. This has also been more socially acceptable. Although a degree of stigma remains attached to mental illness, the situation is improving. Many people now acknowledge suffering from anxiety and depression, for example. Even fewer people, though, think in terms of having a spiritual component to their problems. As a result, many effective ways of preventing and treating health problems are undervalued, even completely ignored.

THE AVOIDANCE OF CONFLICT

Wisdom is about promoting harmony, and minimizing and learning from suffering that cannot be avoided. There are lessons to be learned from Eastern traditions. For example, Jains[15] teach as a major life principle the concept of 'non-onesidedness'. They say that whenever an argument is put forward, the proponent should seek to understand the counter-argument, to genuinely and energetically try to see the matter from the perspective of an opponent. Similarly, the Taoist teacher from the 4th century BC, Chuang Tsu, wrote, 'When there is questioning, there is something beyond the question… Those who dispute do not see'.[16]

Conflict between people usually has oppositional, dualistic, 'either/or' thinking behind it, along the lines of, 'If what I say is true, what you say cannot be true.' Conflict is reduced and harmony promoted by the more unifying, holistic, approach. For example, 'What I say seems to conflict with what you say, but under some circumstances, or from one viewpoint, what I say seems true. Equally, under different circumstances, or from a different viewpoint, what you say seems true. Perhaps you can agree that we may both be partly right, and may both have therefore something still to learn.'

This is the application, if nothing else, of good manners, a form of civility devised to avoid unnecessary conflict and bring harmony to social interactions. The Buddhist principle of 'sympathetic joy' also assists in conflict avoidance. Buddhists teach the wisdom of a selfless attitude that prompts a person to enjoy and celebrate the success and good fortune also of others.

---

15 Jainism is one of the world's oldest religions, already well established by the 6th century BC. Over 10 million Jains are said to practise their faith currently in India, its country of origin, with significant Jain communities also in USA, Western Europe and Australasia.

16 Chuang Tsu (1974) *Inner Chapters*. Trans. G.-F. Feng and J. English. London: Wildwood House, p.37. Taoism emerged in China about 2500 years ago, remaining a powerful cultural influence there and elsewhere. See also Lao Tsu (1973) *Tao Te Ching*. Trans. G.-F. Feng and J. English. London: Wildwood House.

THE LANGUAGE OF SPIRITUALITY

Conflict can also be reduced by careful use of language. It is a question of compatibility, so it is worth developing a language of spirituality that does not depend upon, or appear to be biased in favour of, one or another religion, faith or other type of wisdom tradition (including shamanism, paganism, humanism and atheism).

Spiritual knowledge is synonymous with wisdom. This and other terms like 'spiritual awareness', 'spiritual skills', 'spiritual practices' and 'spiritual values' have also been mentioned and are useful. Each of these terms will be developed later in a way that allows interpretation by each reader according to personal preference and understanding. The hope is the discovery of common ground with other people, including those from different traditions and with different experiences.

An interest in language and its use to convey ideas is often helpful in promoting spiritual knowledge. For example, 'enthusiasm' is from ancient Greek (from 'en-theos') and refers to the idea of being infused and energized by God ('theos': as in 'theology').

Similarly, the word 'inspiration' means two things: first, the in drawing of breath and second, divine prompting or guidance towards original ideas or creative activity. The word for 'spirit' is the same as for 'breath' (and sometimes also 'wind') in many languages. Seamlessness between body, mind and spirit is thereby emphasized once again.

To take another example, the words 'whole', 'holism', 'holy' and 'healing' have common (Germanic) linguistic roots. To be healed as a person can therefore be understood as being made whole again. Healing (people) can therefore be considered qualitatively distinct from 'cure', when this word is applied only to symptoms.

In other words, it is possible for a person's symptoms to go away without the full restoration of inner peace and tranquillity. For example, when a person is cured of the symptoms of a sexually transmitted disease, but continues to feel stigma, shame and a degree of social exclusion, possibly too an element of spiritual transgression, they may no longer feel whole. This emphasizes the psychological, social and spiritual components that may accompany the more obvious bodily aspects to ill-health and healing.

FIVE DIMENSIONS OF HUMAN EXPERIENCE

It is worth repeating that health has many components, best considered according to five seamlessly interrelated systems or dimensions: physical (molecular), biological, psychological, social and spiritual. In that the spiritual dimension creates, informs and inhabits the others, what at first appears as a kind of hierarchy of increasing complexity is also revealed to be circular.

Another, equally acceptable interpretation is that spirituality lies central to the other dimensions. These different views of the same phenomena can be displayed diagrammatically (see Box 2.3).

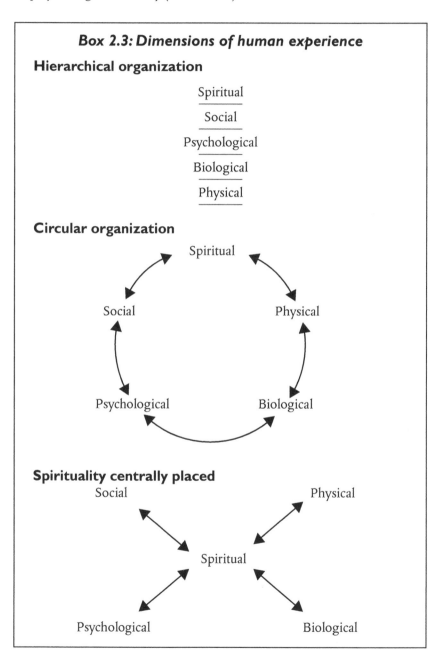

Box 2.3: Dimensions of human experience

Hierarchical organization

Spiritual

Social

Psychological

Biological

Physical

Circular organization

Spiritual

Social   Physical

Psychological   Biological

Spirituality centrally placed

Social   Physical

Spiritual

Psychological   Biological

Since Albert Einstein's revolutionary theories were verified experimentally, and demonstrated publicly later by the detonation of nuclear weapons, the scientific view has acknowledged matter and energy to be interchangeable. They turn out to be linked by an equation involving the speed of light: energy equals mass times the velocity of light squared ($e=mc^2$). This aspect, speed, therefore links time (chronos) to energy-matter occupying space. Our solar system, our planet and we humans exist in time and occupy space, being created of matter and energy. Most of the millions of molecules in our bodies were made during the final destructive events of stars now long vanished from the universe.

The scientific view is therefore, in itself, more or less poetic. The ultimate source of matter and energy remains under debate. It is a debate which may, in scientific terms, ultimately be futile for several reasons.

First, there is no point of objectivity. We are part of the universe we want to examine and cannot get outside it. It cannot be ruled out that our observations are affected by the act of observation, and the interpretations we give them are biased according to psychological and social factors that are equally hard to pin down.

Second, time and space – our universe – seem to have begun, according to Big Bang theory, in a single instant at a single, infinitesimal point called a 'singularity'. Things have been in motion since, according to linear time and to the continuous expansion of space. The idea of a big bang may make us think of an explosion, like a nuclear explosion, which we can observe and think about. But it would not have been like watching it from a safe distance or on a television screen because the seeds of what and who we are were within it, were created within it. Time was created with space, so there was no 'before' the big bang, and there was nothing 'outside' the big bang; nothing that our sense organs, our minds or our scientific instruments could reach, examine or identify. We are left only with poetry and with our intuition; and mankind has applied those faculties to describe the origins of our planet and its people in many allegorical ways. Science has simply been giving us a new allegory.

For many people, either named or unnamed, an original and creative source lies at the heart of what they understand to be spiritual. The new allegory of the Big Bang does not invalidate those that already existed. It complements and expands upon them, for example by introducing the concept of 'non-locality'. Both/and thinking applies.

Looking further into the allegory of science, the chemistry and physics of inanimate atoms and molecules form the basis of biology, of reproduction, of plant and animal life. For many, the creation and maintenance of life remains as much a mystery and source of spiritual wonder as does the origin of the universe.

Biology, in turn, gives rise to organs within organisms, and in humans to a nervous system capable of advanced consciousness, the essential ingredient of psychology, and another great mystery. The psychology of the individual (intra-personal psychology) contributes in turn to the next dimension, the psychology of families, groups, communities and cultures (social psychology).

These four dimensions, together with the spiritual, hold an essential key to human understanding of humanity and the universe. It is important that they are distinguishable from each other; but it is also important to note that they are fully interdependent and seamlessly interconnected. Much conflict and confusion arises when explanations, both for human experiences and for so-called 'external' or 'objective' phenomena, are offered in one, two, three or even four dimensions, rather than all five.

The seamless nature of the universe is what allows for the spiritual whole. Spirituality can be thought of as a connecting principle at the heart of what holds the cosmos together. For many, this 'interbeing' is at the centre of all awe-inspiring mysteries, great and small, both cosmic and deeply personal.

EMOTIONS – HEALING AND GROWTH

Returning to this theme, the emotions are vital to a sense of being alive, to one's life having any sense of meaning or purpose. They are often therefore mediators of spiritual awareness, forming a bridge to the other core components of personal and social psychology: thinking (cognition), sense perception, and the impulses to action and speech (at times similarly to refrain from action and speech).

In terms of spirituality, the value of emotions lies in their immediacy and power. When people congregate to witness and share the experience of a solar eclipse or a beautiful sunset, for example, they stand in silence. There is no thinking to be done, and no words that are adequate. The experience is visual and emotional. Feelings like amazement, delight and wonder arise, associated perhaps with reverence, peace and contentment.

The everyday ego responds to beauty and mystery differently from the spiritual self, the human soul, which seeks silently to bathe in it, moment by moment, without seeking to grasp and hold on to it, dissect it or dismiss it.

In more perilous circumstances, where threat and loss are factors, souls may experience distressing emotions of a similarly all-consuming nature.

When out in a great storm, for example, caught up in a wildfire or close to an avalanche, a person may experience extreme fear, terror, anguish and grief. Even when reading about great destructive natural events such as earthquakes, tsunamis and volcanic eruptions, or seeing television images of them, the strongest feelings of rage, sorrow and powerlessness can well up.

Consider the phrases, 'To be filled with awe', 'To be ecstatic with joy', 'To feel choked right up', 'To be paralysed with fear', and 'To be racked with tears'. What do they signify? They mean, above all, that the person is alive and responding at a profound and unpremeditated level to events beyond their control, beyond (at that instant) even the grasp of their intellect. The everyday ego is overwhelmed, and these phrases describe strong emotions that often arise at pivotal, life-changing moments, whether seemingly either for better or worse. They are therefore central to, and afford important clues about, the psychology of spirituality.

Painful emotions are associated with attachment, threat and loss. They include bewilderment (confusion), doubt (hopelessness), anxiety (fear, terror, dread), anger (rage), recrimination (shame and guilt) and sadness (grief and sorrow). When healed, these are transformed into more pleasurable feelings, including clarity, certainty (hope), calm (serenity, wonder), acquiescence (acceptance, awe, reverence, gratitude), self-esteem (self-worth and innocence, purity) and joy (happiness, delight, ecstasy, rapture).

When attachments and aversions are relinquished, desires fade, to be replaced with emotions of satisfaction and contentment. To repeat, healing turns into a greater process, that of personal growth. A more secure equanimity and greater emotional resilience prevail after recovery, giving people greater freedom and energy to engage with their lives and to face future dangers.

SACRED UNIVERSALITY

Spirituality is inclusive and unifying. Each person is part of and pervaded by the sacred, by the spiritual dimension. It applies to everyone, including those who do not believe in God, a higher being, named or unnamed, or a spiritual realm or dimension of existence. No one is exempt.

Poetically speaking, the spiritual dimension is a divine realm. The word 'religion' has Latin roots in common with a word meaning 'to bind'. (Think of 'ligature', a tie or binding.) Similarly, the Sanskrit word 'yoga' is related to the idea of a yoke, also a type of binding. Many authorities refer to four types of yoga, each representing a major path of spiritual development.[17]

---

17 Originally associated with Hinduism, these four are: hatha yoga (postural physical exercises), bhakti yoga (devotional practice), jnana yoga (wisdom seeking) and karma yoga (giving, the exercise of compassion). See www.hinduwebsite.com/yoga.asp, accessed 9 June 2010. Also Fontana, D. (2003) *Psychology, Religion and Spirituality*. Oxford: BPS Blackwell, pp.62–79. Fontana includes raja yoga (control of the mind)

These words, 'religion' and 'yoga', both emphasize the seamless, spiritual connections between each one of us and the divine, also through these sacred connections to each other, to nature and to the physical universe.

This accounts for the profound and spiritual nature of 'non-separateness', of 'interbeing', and the associated principle of reciprocity according to which thoughts, words and actions intending either good or harm, either to another person or to nature, rebound accordingly on oneself. The effects may be subtle and hard to detect, but traditional wisdom has it that they are cumulative, and that payback occurs in spiritual time (kairos), rather than clock time (chronos).

HUMAN STORIES

Human stories entertain and educate us from childhood onwards. Attempts to introduce the psychology of spirituality must ring true with people's real life experiences. For these reasons, a number of illustrative stories will be recounted in the following chapters.

Summary points

1. *Spirituality is not an object for analysis*
It is better considered as an adventure or theme park to explore, offering both learning opportunities and playful excitement.

2. *Joy and wonder*
Children often experience and exhibit joy and wonder spontaneously. These may be facets of adult spirituality too.

3. *What goes round comes around*
Challenges are often repeated, slightly differently each time, throughout life. Thoughts, words and actions – helpful and harmful – have consequences: 'You reap what you sow.'

4. *Meaning and purpose in life (and death)*
Spirituality is concerned with motivation, with finding a deep-seated source of meaning and purpose in life, especially during hardship, through a journey that continues in stages of increasing maturity throughout life and in the face of death.

5. *God, religions, belief and faith*
Religion and spirituality are linked, yet can be distinguished from one another. The various names given to God are highly charged, but have different

meanings and significance for different people. Belief involves attachment to a thought or idea. Faith, based on spiritual wisdom and awareness, going deeper than belief, is one of the principal goals of the spiritual journey.

6. *Love, holism and the double nature of time*
The true self identifies with the sacred whole of creation, but the everyday ego retains a dualistic distinction between self and not-self, between self and other, emphasizing opposites. Holistic appreciation considers opposites as depending upon and defining one another. Chronos is linear clock time. Kairos, 'God's time', is unmeasurable and allows events to coincide meaningfully in a spiritual way.

7. *An inner source of knowledge*
A source of essential knowledge already lies within each person, accessible through intuition. The term 'mystic' is usually reserved for people who are adept in terms of spiritual awareness, who understand the value of contemplation and have received the blessings of wisdom. Their knowledge is about how to be and behave, concerns the consequences of unity of body, mind and spirit, and respects the benefits of promoting harmony.

8. *Contemporary spirituality*
Contemporary spirituality does not need to depend upon the language of one or another religion or other type of wisdom tradition. It recognizes five seamlessly interrelated dimensions that cover the whole of human experience: physical, biological, psychological, social and spiritual. The spiritual dimension creates, informs and inhabits the others. The emotions are vital to a sense of being alive, to having a sense of purpose and meaning. They are therefore often mediators of spiritual awareness, a bridge to cognition (thought), sensory perception and the impulse to act and speech (and to refrain from action and speech).

9. *Universality and reciprocity*
Reciprocity depends on sacred connections people have to each other, to nature and to the physical universe through its basically holistic quality. Payback occurs in kairos (spiritual time) rather than chronos (clock time). Human stories both entertain and educate, and the best will be true to life.

Exercises and questions for personal reflection and as a basis for group discussion:

1. Have you ever been to an adventure park, museum or similar holiday attraction, either as a child or as an adult accompanying one or more children? What were the good things? What was not so good? What

was the balance between enjoyment and education? Did you learn anything about yourself?

2. Imagine yourself as a very young child on a merry-go-round, watching out gleefully for your parents each time you circle, waving hello and goodbye. Think too of yourself as an adult, watching your child recede and return. Feel the connectedness, and note how something changes each time – a facial expression or a gesture; everything is similar but not quite the same.

3. Do you think of your life as a kind of journey or pilgrimage? Do certain kinds of challenge seem to be repeated? Do your thoughts, words and actions (or occasions when you have failed to act) keep returning to mind in a way that allows you to mull over the consequences, good or bad?

4. What gives you a special sense of meaning and purpose in life? (Think, for example, in terms of people, places, possessions, activities, experiences, ideas and ideologies.)

5. Do you agree that spirituality and religion, while linked, can be distinguished from one another? Do you think that everyone is affected by a spiritual dimension?

6. Do you ever find yourself contemplating the big issues of life and death, serious illness, war, famine and so on, trying to make sense of them? Do you think about God? Do you, on the other hand, automatically dismiss God and the idea of God? Do you sometimes feel caught in the middle between the idea that there is a God and that there isn't one? Could it be that the problem arises from 'either/or' thinking, whereas 'both/and' thinking might be more helpful?

7. Do you hold to the beliefs of any particular religion? Do you follow any religious practices? If not, are you aware of a personal spirituality, even though it may not fit into established structures and belief systems? Discuss this with someone whose advice and opinions you trust.

8. Read the vignette again. Think about it. Again, seek discussion about it with someone whose advice and opinions you trust.

Chapter 3

THE RELEVANCE OF SPIRITUALITY

Spirituality neglected

Contemporary psychologist, David Fontana, emphasizes that religion has inspired many noble acts of self-sacrifice and altruism, stimulated great art and architecture, motivated people to develop moral and ethical systems, and, through its institutions, been a guardian and force behind learning, commerce and other major activities, with a remarkable legacy of universities, schools, hospitals and social welfare.[1]

Against this, he does not deny that religion has historically served as an ultra-conservative and repressive influence, has led to social and cultural divisions, and been the excuse for barbaric warfare, torture and executions. At the individual level, it has resulted in psychological hardship and damage, a source of exaggerated guilt, fear and anxiety. Dogmatic teaching on ways of thinking and behaving, Fontana reports, have hindered educational development, led to rigid and punitive parental styles, justified unfair and pernicious social stratification, led to unnatural and repressive attitudes towards the body and sexual relations, and hindered creative expression.

Fontana concludes: 'Religious traditions of thought and behaviour thus undeniably provide a richness of material well-nigh impossible to find in any other area of human activity.'[2] He notes, however, the neglect of the psychology of religion and spirituality in academic circles until recently, and lists four main reasons:

---

1   See Fontana, D. (2003) *Psychology, Religion and Spirituality*. Oxford: BPS Blackwell.
2   *Ibid.*, p.2.

1. Religion and spirituality appear contrary to the teachings of science.

2. Religion has actively opposed the progress of scientific thinking; for example, in the case of Charles Darwin's theory of evolution.

3. Psychologists of religion and spirituality with the ability to glean knowledge from the complex mix of other disciplines (such as history, philosophy, theology and the creative arts), and the patterns of thought in which they are embedded, are rare. In addition, first-hand experience of meditation and mature contemplation, accompanied by the capacity to tolerate ambiguity and contradiction within the material being studied, is also uncommon.

4. The study of religion and spirituality present major methodological problems regarding the inner experiences of others that are not directly observable.

Changing attitudes – new organizations

These reasons for the neglect of spirituality by psychologists and others represent challenges and opportunities, rather than outright obstacles; and attitudes have been changing. Evidence for the relevance of spiritual and religious factors in a wide range of areas of human interest has been growing apace, as has the personal conviction of many scientists and those who apply science, such as healthcare and mental healthcare professionals.

Apollo 14 astronaut, Edgar Mitchell, experienced an epiphany in 1971 as he sat in the tiny space capsule returning from the moon. He saw planet earth floating freely in the vastness of space and was captivated by a profound sense of universal connectedness. He later said, 'The presence of divinity became almost palpable, and I knew that life in the universe was not just an accident based on random processes... The knowledge came to me directly.'

This spiritual insight caused him, in 1973, to found the Institute of Noetic Sciences in California. According to the publicity,[3] maintaining a commitment to scientific rigour while exploring phenomena that have been largely overlooked by mainstream science, the Institute 'conducts and sponsors research into the potentials and powers of consciousness – including perceptions, beliefs, attention, intention, and intuition'.

In the same year a comparable organization, the Scientific and Medical Network,[4] was established in England. This is now a large and vigorous,

---

3   See www.noetic.org (accessed 20 May 2010) where the quotation from Edgar Mitchell may also be found.
4   See www.scimednet.org, accessed 20 May 2010.

UK-based, international organization, publishing a regular journal and holding local, national and international meetings and conferences.

The aims of the Network are:

- to explore approaches to earth and community which emphasize a spiritual and holistic approach

- to provide a safe forum for the critical and open-minded discussion of ideas that go beyond the conventional paradigm

- to integrate intuitive insights with rational analysis

- to challenge the adequacy of scientific materialism as an exclusive basis for knowledge and values.

The John Templeton Foundation is a third influential organization in bringing spiritual matters to the fore. It was established in 1987, its mission being: 'To serve as a philanthropic catalyst for discovery in areas engaging life's biggest questions that range from explorations into the laws of nature and the universe to questions on the nature of love, gratitude, forgiveness and creativity.'[5]

Sir John Templeton's commitment to rigorous scientific research and related, cutting-edge scholarship is reflected in the Foundation's motto: 'How little we know, how eager to learn', which exemplifies the Foundation's support for open-minded inquiry and the hope of advancing human progress through breakthrough discoveries.

Changing attitudes – developments in mental healthcare
PROFESSIONAL ORGANIZATIONS

Psychiatrists have led the way in the UK in acknowledging spiritual and religious factors in the field of health and mental health. A small number of psychiatrists got together after a series of chance encounters at meetings of the Scientific and Medical Network during the 1990s. They set about establishing the 'Spirituality and Psychiatry' Special Interest Group (or 'Spirituality SIG')[6] within the Royal College of Psychiatrists. The SIG was officially formed by 120 psychiatrists in 1999 and now – open only to members and fellows of the Royal College (and those in training) – it has over 2500 psychiatrist members. The SIG is responsible for a public information leaflet on 'Spirituality and Mental Health' published by the Royal College.[7]

---

5   See www.templeton.org, accessed 20 May 2010.
6   See www.rcpsych.ac.uk/spirit, accessed 20 May 2010.
7   See www.rcpsych.ac.uk/mentalhealthinformation/therapies/spiritualityandmentalhealth.aspx, accessed 20 May 2010.

Its members organize conferences, and also publish newsletters and articles that are available to the public via its web pages.

Similarly, the British Psychological Society, the representative body for about 45,000 psychologists in the UK, has both a 'Transpersonal' section and a 'Holistic' Special Interest Group, founded in recent years.

These professional bodies are instrumental in the holistic (or 'bio-psycho-socio-spiritual') model becoming increasingly established in the context of mental healthcare. Professor John Swinton's landmark publication, the book *Spirituality and Mental Health Care*,[8] has also contributed significantly towards this paradigm shift.

PATIENTS' VIEWS ABOUT SPIRITUAL NEEDS

In the late 1990s, an experienced mental health nurse, Mary Nathan, conducted some qualitative research, interviewing psychiatric hospital patients about their spiritual needs.[9] Patients wanted a number of things in this context, as follows:

1. To feel safe and secure.

2. To be treated with respect and dignity, allowing them to develop a feeling of belonging, of being valued and trusted.

3. To have access to an environment for purposeful activity such as creative art, structured work and the enjoyment of nature.

4. To be given time to express their thoughts and feelings to sympathetic and concerned members of staff.

5. To have the opportunity, and receive encouragement, to make sense of and derive meaning from their experiences, including their illness experiences.

6. To have permission and be encouraged to develop a relationship with God or the Absolute (however they might conceive whatever is sacred).

In addition, patients elsewhere have asked for time, a place and privacy in which to pray and worship, also the opportunity to explore religious and spiritual matters. Patients appreciate encouragement in deepening their faith, allowing them to feel increasingly universally connected and, in some cases, forgiven.

---

8   Swinton, J. (2001) *Spirituality and Mental Health: Rediscovering a 'Forgotten' Dimension.* London: Jessica Kingsley Publishers.
9   Nathan, M. (1997) 'A Study of Spiritual Care in Mental Health Practice: Patients' and Nurses' Perceptions.' MSc thesis. Enfield: Middlesex University.

PATIENTS' VIEWS ABOUT THE BENEFITS OF SPIRITUAL CARE

Mary Nathan's patients also listed the benefits of receiving this quality of care. In terms of their illnesses, patients described recovery as being faster and easier, attributing this first to an improved ability to accept and grieve for losses, and second to an environment conducive to developing their strong points and maximizing their personal potential (see Vignette – Brenda).

Vignette – Brenda

Brenda developed schizophrenia during her mid teens. She began hallucinating, with unpleasant voices criticizing, taunting and insulting her. She also developed persecutory delusions, believing that family members had recruited the police to spy on her and bring about her downfall. She was constantly distracted by her symptoms and unable to concentrate on even relatively simple tasks. This led to neglect of her appearance and disturbances of behaviour. She began using alcohol and street drugs in an attempt to self-medicate for her problems.

As a result of her illness, which was not fully assessed and treated for several years, Brenda's education was interrupted. Her family were unable to cope and she became temporarily homeless before a spell in hospital, from which she absconded, was followed by placements in a series of bed-sits and other unsuitable placements. Eventually, in her mid-twenties, Brenda accepted psychiatric hospital care and medication which controlled the worst of her symptoms. As her mental health began to recover, she was able to discuss with her primary nurse not only her illness but also its consequences in terms of losses.

Brenda realized that failing to complete her schooling meant that she could not go on to higher education, or even obtain low-level employment. She could not earn money, and was immensely disadvantaged as a result, with very limited control of her life, even if she had not been mentally ill. She also recognized that her appearance and behaviour made it unlikely that she would meet a suitable male partner, marry, set up home and have children as her two sisters had already done. Education, employment, partnership and parenthood are sources of meaning and purpose for the majority of people in Brenda's culture. With her symptoms under improved control, facing these losses – not having what she once wished for and expected to have – was a necessary part and process in her recovery and rehabilitation. Brenda mentioned that, having been raised a Christian, she had always maintained some kind of prayer life, even when she was most ill. She had begged God often to release her from the voices, and asked many times why she had been singled out for this trial. She admitted having been angry with God, and frightened of going to hell after death. Now, knowing that, like many others, she had been the victim of an illness – schizophrenia – rather than the cause of her own downfall through sin, her faith was being restored. Her prayer life had started to provide her with valuable access to a renewed sense of self-worth, and thereby the courage, hope and inner strength she needed to weather future crises and maximize her potential during the recovery period.

Brenda also spoke about a new-found sympathy with others in difficult circumstances, and said she wanted to do something useful. She began voluntary work in a home for frail elderly people, and further boosted her self-esteem in this way.

Patients also reported that a spiritual dimension to mental healthcare helped improve their self-esteem and confidence, giving them a morale-boosting sense of being once again in better control of their lives. They described improved relationships, not only with family members, friends, carers and other acquaintances, but also – and importantly for some – with God. On the whole, they were less confused, less fearful, less angry, less guilty and less ashamed. They were altogether more relaxed about life. In addition, some patients said they had found a new sense of meaning and had experienced a reawakening of hope, resulting in peace of mind that enabled them to live with, endure and continue seeking solutions to problems not yet resolved.

Whereas some professionals would call key points listed in the preceding section as simply good healthcare practice, Mary Nathan made it clear[10] that the patients she interviewed emphasized strongly the spiritual dimension as critically important, identifying staff with spiritual sensibilities as more sympathetic and therefore more helpful than those with a less spiritual world view, less able therefore to take such a deep personal interest in providing the spiritual components of care.

Changing attitudes – developments in general healthcare
PUBLICATIONS
The impressive *Handbook of Religion and Health*[11] was published in 2001, offering critical, comprehensive and systematic analysis of more than 1200 published studies and 400 research reviews about both the positive and

10 In a personal communication with the author.
11 Koenig, H., McCullough, M. and Larson, D. (2001) *Handbook of Religion and Health*. Oxford: Oxford University Press.

negative effects of religion and spirituality on health and mental health in all age groups.[12]

In the foreword, epidemiologist Dr Jeff Levin calls this book 'a signal achievement in the history of medicine'. He wrote:

> Today, the epidemiology of religion and the larger field of clinical research on religion and spirituality are well established in the scientific world and in the public consciousness... For the first time, in one place, empirical research findings that support the existence of a protective or preventive effect of religious involvement are comprehensively reviewed and critiqued... The relationship between religion and health, on average and at the population level, is overwhelmingly positive.[13]

About 80 per cent of studies revealed beneficial effects, while only 5 per cent showed harmful effects. A more recent book, edited by Plante and Thoresen, while also suggesting possible mechanisms, points to similar conclusions.[14]

Another relevant and comprehensive book, *Handbook of the Psychology of Religion and Spirituality*,[15] was published in 2005. In the preface, the editors Paloutzian and Park wrote:

> From time to time, in any area of enquiry, the accumulated knowledge progresses to such a degree that a new level of maturity becomes identifiable. The psychology of religion is at this stage now. We see it reflected in the nature of the research questions asked, the range of topics investigated, the sophistication of the research methods used, the adequacy of the theoretical advancements to account for and integrate the increasing body of data, and the connections between research in the psychology of religion and scholarship in other areas of psychology and allied fields.[16]

This strongly implies that the four problems raised by Fontana have already been bypassed while others, related to research, have been addressed and are being overcome. Academic reservations are beginning to evaporate. Practical healthcare experience also adds persuasively to this research.

---

12 An updated version of the Handbook, to include a decade of new research, will be published in 2011.

13 *Ibid.*, pp.vii–viii.

14 Plante, T. and Thoresen, C. (eds) (2007) *Spirit, Science and Health: How the Spiritual Mind Fuels Physical Wellness.* Westport, CT: Praeger.

15 Paloutzian, R and Park, C. (eds) (2005) *Handbook of the Psychology of Religion and Spirituality.* New York, NY: Guilford Press.

16 *Ibid.*, p.xi.

PRACTICAL EXPERIENCE OF SPIRITUALITY AND HEALTHCARE

Neely and Minford[17] describe a 39-year-old patient facing extensive surgery for a major illness who, when interviewed, held no specific religious or spiritual beliefs, but who did not think this detrimental in her life. Nevertheless, she did suffer from depression, and at times felt alone and had difficulty coping. The effects of her illness, rendering her housebound, exacerbated the depression; and the patient described drawing strength from her family and from a charitable organization set up to assist people with her kind of illness. Forming new friendships and connections through the association helped her 're-find' herself and enabled her to cope better. She reported discovering a new source of inner strength and a new appreciation for life, aided too by music and complementary health therapies.

Neely and Minford comment that this attempt to assess and evaluate the patient's spirituality allowed the interviewer to gain a deeper understanding of the patient, identifying both stressors and coping strategies. Despite the absence of any specific or overt spiritual content, her sense of identity and the sources of meaning in her life were highly bound up with her illness. She derived a meaningful sense of well-being and belonging in the context of family initially, but also found her true, spiritual self again mainly through the charitable association and related connections.

The same authors described a second interviewee, a 68-year-old woman also due for surgery who described a strong religious faith that she applied every day, both by praying and attending religious services. The patient explained that her faith was very important to her during illness and helped her cope. She found prayer beneficial, strengthening her for the operation to come. She could discuss spiritual matters with her own priest, but was delighted to be asked if the healthcare team could be of any help. A visit by the hospital chaplain was soon arranged.

In both cases, information was elicited by enquiry into the patients' spiritual life that would not have emerged otherwise using a more mechanistic approach to the surgical problem. The attitude change is from an illness model to a health model, involving questions about what is healthy in this patient, what are her strengths and assets – so that they can be enhanced and recruited in combating illness, during recovery and rehabilitation, and for further prevention – as well as what has gone wrong.

As Neely and Minford also state, 'A patient needs to be treated as a "whole person" and not just as a condition or disease. A whole person has physical, emotional and spiritual dimensions which interact with each other and account for personal well-being.'[18] This is the 'bio-psycho-socio-spiritual',

---

17 Neely, E. and Minford, D. (2009) 'FAITH: Spiritual history-taking made easy.' *The Clinical Teacher* 6, 3, 181–185.
18 Ibid., p.181.

'person-centred' or 'holistic' approach that is increasingly being welcomed by patients and their carers, and to which professional staff are now turning.

Teaching spirituality
NEW MEDICAL SCHOOL – NEW IDEAS
Brighton and Sussex Medical School opened to students for the first time in autumn 2003, allowing for a measure of innovation in the curriculum. During the third year, students were asked to take four eight-week, half-day per week modules, selecting from a choice of over 50 of the possible 'Student Selected Components' (SSCs) on offer. The author was invited to teach an SSC on 'Spirituality and Healthcare', and did so four times, twice during each of the academic years 2005/6 and 2006/7.[19]

THE SSC STUDENTS
Twenty-seven students (8 male and 19 female) participated in four cohorts of six, ten, four and seven. The group size for each course depended mainly on student choice. Attendance levels were high, no student attending fewer than five sessions.

The religious and spiritual backgrounds of the students varied. Ten identified themselves as Christian from different denominations and varying degrees of involvement. There were three Hindus, two Muslims, two Buddhists, one Sikh, one 'sceptic' and one atheist. Of those with no formal affiliation, four thought of themselves as 'spiritual' or 'seeking', and three said they were not spiritual or religious in any way.

THE FIRST TEACHING SESSION
The first session began with each student saying something about their reasons for choosing this training module. Some were frank about wanting a 'soft option', a subject they perceived as not involving much hard work and rote learning. They had not thought very deeply about attending, but considered that the subject 'might be interesting'.[20]

The more openly religious students reported a natural desire to integrate their faith with their chosen profession. The remainder felt attracted to the topic, but found it difficult to put their interest into words. One student, for example, said that both her parents were doctors and atheists who had

---

19 Culliford, L. (2009) 'Teaching spirituality and health care to third-year medical students.' *The Clinical Teacher 6*, 1, 22–7.

20 One student, who had not been given her choice of module and had been selected for the spirituality SSC at short notice, made it clear from the outset that she did not want to be there or to participate. Her attendance level was poor and her final written comment after the course was, 'Spirituality wasn't really my thing.'

tried to persuade her about the nonexistence of God and denied a spiritual dimension to human experience. Her reason for attending the SSC was, 'I just felt there had to more to it than that.'

One or two students had felt supported by spiritual experiences during episodes of illness themselves, and expressed the wish to explore these episodes and their significance in more detail in a sympathetic setting.

Discussion between the students was encouraged, and the topic shifted towards the question, 'What is spirituality?' Students were asked to list words they associated with the two words 'religion' and 'spirituality'. The two lists were then examined. A relationship between the two was identified, but so too were distinctions. Students considered that religion involves social structures, with doctrines based on scripture, formal worship involving both words and music (liturgy), often a hierarchical priesthood, and special buildings: churches, convents, monasteries, mosques, gurdwaras, synagogues, and temples. Spirituality was considered more uniquely personal while, at the same time, being universally recognizable.

MEDITATION (MINDFULNESS) TRAINING

After a refreshment break, allowing students to interact with each other and continue informal discussion, they were invited to take up a comfortable, upright sitting posture and close or almost close their eyes. They were asked to take a few breaths while focusing their minds on each in and out breath. Next, under guidance, they performed a 'body scan', slowly moving the focus of consciousness to the crown of the head, and from there gradually down throughout the body, taking several minutes to do so before returning to the crown equally slowly and deliberately. They were then asked to focus on their breathing again for a few minutes.

On the first occasion, this meditation exercise, which was to be repeated most weeks, lasted only six to eight minutes. Eventually, the 'mindfulness of breathing' component was extended, the exercise lasting up to 20 minutes in total. It is similar to an exercise developed and described by Jon Kabat-Zinn,[21] a key part of the highly successful 'Program of the Stress Reduction Clinic at the University of Massachusetts Medical Center'.

More than half of the students had previous experience of meditation practice. None found it difficult or problematic in any way. It served to introduce students to the idea that meditation can be useful to a wide range of patients. It also introduced the topic of 'spiritual skills', and the idea that meditation can be good for healthcare practitioners too.

---

21 See Kabat-Zinn, J. (1990) *Full Catastrophe Living: Using the Wisdom of your Body and Mind to Face Stress, Pain and Illness.* New York, NY: Delta, pp.76–8.

Feedback at the end of the first session was good on all four occasions. Students responded well to the invitation to get personally involved by speaking about themselves, their cultural and religious background and their motives for taking the course. They appreciated the discussion, and the introduction of a brief guided meditation, linking it to the development of spiritual skills.

THE FOLLOWING WEEKS

The spirituality SSC was taught using three main headings or categories: knowledge, skills and attitudes/values. The knowledge component concerned the epidemiology of religion and spirituality in connection with health and mental health. This was based on three books: *The Handbook of Religion and Health*,[22] a shorter introduction to the subject by Harold Koenig, one of the Handbook's authors,[23] and on seven 'theosomatic' principles described by Jeff Levin.[24]

Research in general medical and surgical settings has consistently shown that assessing spiritual needs, supporting the patient's beliefs, validating religious distress, and making appropriate referrals have benefits in a wide range of physical and mental illnesses. The benefits include enhancing the patient's ability to cope, improving the doctor–patient relationship, boosting compliance with treatment, and increasing community-based support.

Positive results, such as faster and more complete recovery from illness, greater capacity for enduring continuing distress and disability, and improved satisfaction with medical care, do not depend on which religious or spiritual tradition a patient follows. However, 5–10 per cent of studies show that religion and spirituality may also be harmful to health and mental health.[25] It is important for students to be advised of both positive and negative aspects.

In week three, students were also taught about assessing patients' spiritual needs, or 'taking a spiritual history'.[26] There are a number of published protocols for doing this.[27] The students, however, were not asked to use a pre-prepared formula or questionnaire. They were simply instructed, either singly or in pairs, to 'have a conversation' with one or two patients of their own choice. During the SSC, students were on assignment to a range of hospital departments, and tended to choose patients they encountered in the ordinary

---

22 See footnote 11.
23 Koenig, H. (2002) *Spirituality in Patient Care: Why, How, When and What.* Philadelphia, PA: Templeton Foundation Press. (All students were provided with a copy of this book.)
24 See Levin, J. (2001) *God, Faith and Health: Exploring the Spirituality-Healing Connection.* Chichester: John Wiley and Sons, pp.13 –14. (2005/6 students were provided with a copy of this book.)
25 See footnote 11.
26 See Appendix 1: Taking a Spiritual History.
27 See Culliford, L. (2007) 'Taking a spiritual history.' *Advances in Psychiatric Treatment 13,* 3, 212–19.

course of those assignments. Medical, surgical and psychiatric patients were interviewed in this way.

The students were armed with just two types of question. The first was, 'Do you think of yourself as religious or spiritual in any way?' A positive response led to the follow-up question, 'Please explain and tell me about that.' Afterwards, or immediately in the case of a negative reply, the second question was, 'What helps you most when things go badly wrong (such as when you are ill)?' Students were encouraged to discover where their patient turned for strength, hope and support. They were looking for sources of both inner strength and external help, both practical and emotional.

The following week involved student feedback after interviewing patients in this way. It was often a breakthrough week for them, in terms of generating their enthusiasm for the subject, as they gave their accounts and listened to each other's.

One student later wrote:

> I was surprised that all of us managed to take quite detailed histories, even from patients who initially felt uncomfortable about what we were doing.

Another commented:

> One lady was initially very resistant, stating that she did not really have any religious or spiritual beliefs. However, the interview ultimately revealed much about what gave this lady meaning and purpose in her life, and ended up being one of the most in depth spiritual histories taken in the group.

A third reported:

> I found that, in asking about my patient's spiritual beliefs, I immediately strengthened the rapport I was beginning to build with him; a useful thing to develop in all clinical situations.

Other student comments included: 'The woman I spoke to opened my eyes to how much some patients enjoy talking about their spiritual beliefs.' 'It was one of the most harmonious and friendly encounters I have ever had with another individual.' 'We both left feeling like we had really made a difference to this lady. By simply talking about her spiritual views, we had made her happy.'

Another week, students met an experienced educator and counsellor who described experiencing, surviving and benefiting from an episode of

psychosis requiring hospital care, describing it as 'a spiritual breakthrough'.[28]
Students commented later:

> Nikki's story made me feel that spirituality is definitely something
> very tangible.

> I gained such an insight into spiritual growth through hearing
> [her] story, and was reminded not only of the ability for spiritual
> growth [to occur] through adversity, but also the power of a
> healthy spiritual life to lead to good physical, psychological and
> social well-being.

> The first thing I noticed was that Nikki seemed to be so at peace,
> and so comfortable with who she was. Instead of fighting her
> symptoms, she embraced her experience and her life has been
> transformed. This brought me a whole new perspective on mental
> illness, and personally it gave me hope.

> I was fascinated... I couldn't help thinking, 'What illness did
> she have?' It is evident that the emerging medical science has
> left no room for the role of spirituality and mysticism. When
> someone provides an account of seemingly psychotic symptoms,
> spiritual emergence is not seen as a differential diagnosis. Spiritual
> emergence can be seen as a natural process of human development.

The students were given time in the penultimate week to prepare a report
on the SSC, as required by the Medical School authorities. They were asked
to make it personal and reflective, and in the final week came together to
share their written thoughts and other comments on the course as part of
furthering a general discussion about the relevance of spirituality to medicine.
The following remarks are taken from students' written reports.

On the relevance of the subject:

> This SSC has thoroughly challenged any misconceptions I had
> about religion and spirituality and its relation to healthcare.

> Before this SSC my response [on the relevance of spirituality]
> would have been, 'It is someone's religion and has *no* role in
> modern medicine.' Since starting this SSC my view of spirituality
> and its role has changed quite dramatically.

> I assumed that spirituality was deep seated in strongly held religious
> belief and therefore automatically dismissed it. To my surprise,

---

28 For a description and commentary on the experience, see Slade, N. and Culliford, L. (2004)
    'Heavenbound.' In Barker, P. and Buchanan-Barker, P. (eds) *Spirituality and Mental Health:
    Breakthrough.* London: Whurr Books.

many of the patients reported that spirituality and religion have a very large bearing on helping them through difficult times and dealing with physical and mental illness.

Additional comments included:

I used to think that there is no place in today's scientific and evidence-based medicine for religion. We should deal with the patient's illness first. Now, however, I believe that this view is, for want of a better word, 'blinkered'.

Our failure to recognize the importance of spirituality to our patients is doing them a great disservice and denying them access to the optimum resources they need to heal.

Religion and spirituality provide patients and their families with a sense of acceptance of illness and hope of a better future.

My personal experience of integrating spirituality into my clinical skills and history taking has been nothing but positive. It allowed the patients to embrace their feelings and be able to express some of their most personal views about the meaning of life, the meaning of being well, of being ill, and also how they feel about death.

I was surprised by the number of patients who had spiritual beliefs, and how these altered their mood and ability to cope.

EPIDEMIOLOGY
On the subject of epidemiology (the study of factors affecting the incidence, manifestation, prevention and recovery from ill-health) one student wrote: 'I was unaware of the vast amount of literature pertaining to the area of spirituality and healthcare, and have been overwhelmed not only by the amount but also the degree to which spirituality and health are linked.'

MEDICAL SCHOOL TEACHING
The following comments reflected the disappointment and concern expressed by students at the omission of teaching on spirituality from the general curriculum.

I have received very little teaching outside this SSC on the effects religion and spirituality have on an individual's healthcare, and it has led me to believe that it is a subject neglected in undergraduate medical education.

We have been taught about a holistic approach to medicine. Although I had listened, I don't feel that it was until this SSC – and in particular when we started taking spiritual histories – that I really understood.

SPIRITUAL SKILLS TRAINING

Students wrote about their responses to meditation and spiritual skills training as follows:

It really is amazing how connected a person can feel when they restrict their conscious thought. Shortly after starting, I started to feel the breeze and hear the sounds coming in through the window. I sensed the light warming the room, and almost felt light-headed from what I can only describe as the *richness* of what I was perceiving.

I have become more aware of my own spirituality throughout the SSC, and in actively being aware of spiritual values and skills, I can ensure that I am addressing my own well-being in a holistic fashion.

I have enjoyed talking about and learning more about spiritual skills, which seem highly relevant to being a medical student.

PERSONAL EXPERIENCES OF ILLNESS

A few students had experience of either mental or physical illness, and wrote of their positive reactions to the SSC from this perspective.

These last few years have seen me fighting my own battle against mental illness. I started my SSC as a sceptic. My mind has been opened. I have been left wondering, but more importantly I have been given hope.

In 2003, I experienced an exacerbation of my [physical illness] to such an extent that I ended up in hospital for the most traumatic two weeks of my life. I felt extremely angry…especially at God. I began to think… Why me? Now my outlook towards doctors has changed completely. I look back and think how angry they made me feel at the time. Now, I am absolutely grateful to them for what they did. Their efforts in caring for me and treating me so well inspired and motivated my determination to become a doctor. I knew I was going to study medicine regardless of anything else.

SSC EVALUATION

As indicated by these comments, satisfaction levels among the students were high. One student, for example, wrote, 'Thank you for such a thought-provoking and soul-searching SSC.' The satisfaction score on the students' feedback forms was 78 per cent. More detailed analysis of the students' reports revealed a number of frequently occurring themes (see Box 3.1). Most students wrote statements of the 'before' and 'after' type. Negative or critical comments were very few.

Box 3.1: Themes from SSC student reports

1. *Before:* Spirituality was equated exclusively with religion.
   After: Distinctions were clear between the two: a person's spirituality was no longer considered dependent on religious affiliation, conviction or practice.

2. *Before:* Neither religion nor spirituality were thought to have a place in modern, scientific, evidence-based medicine.
   After: Spirituality is important, and patients' spirituality should be assessed routinely.

3. *Before:* Students were hesitant to discuss spirituality with their teachers or colleagues.
   After: They preferred being more open, feeling equipped to discuss the subject.

4. *Before:* Students were unsure about taking a spiritual history.
   After: They uniformly expressed confidence in being able to do this.

5. *Before:* Students were uncertain about the value of taking a spiritual history.
   After: Students considered that all healthcare staff in training should learn to do this, so that appropriate steps can be initiated to meet patients' spiritual needs where possible.

6. *Before:* Students had minimal knowledge of the epidemiology of spiritual/religious factors affecting health or illness.
   After: Students demonstrated a satisfactory general overview of the epidemiology.

7. Although the 'holistic' or 'bio-psycho-social' approach to healthcare dominated the rhetoric of teaching, students expressed concern that religion/spirituality had in practice been neglected.

---

8. The idea that people continue to grow spiritually through life, especially through adversity, resonated positively with several students.

9. Students reported that taking spiritual histories alone seemed to benefit patients.

10. Several students mentioned the inspiring effect of meeting and holding a discussion with the external tutor.

11. Some students reported previously neglecting their own spiritual development and having doubts about its relevance, particularly in medicine. Several later expressed their gratitude and relief, saying the SSC had rekindled optimism in their search, finding new importance for it in their chosen career.

CONCLUSIONS

The wide range of students' religious and spiritual backgrounds served to emphasize the universality of spirituality as they explored a complex subject together entirely harmoniously, with respect for and genuine interest in each others' religious, spiritual and philosophical backgrounds. Teaching them was a rewarding experience, and the exercise proves the subject to be both relevant and teachable.

Summary points

1. *Changing attitudes*
Spirituality has been neglected in academic circles and clinical practice until recently, but attitudes are changing due to both new evidence and life-changing personal experiences.

2. *Science is not the whole story*
Organizations have been established that challenge the adequacy of scientific materialism as an exclusive basis for knowledge and values.

3. *Patients' spiritual needs are clearer*
Developments in mental healthcare have led to clarification of patients' spiritual needs, and the benefits of providing for them, emphasizing a 'holistic' or whole-person approach that helps people develop self-esteem, inner strengths, courage and hope, as well as improved relationships and general spiritual maturity.

4. *Spirituality is important for health*

Developments in general healthcare, based on extensive and persuasive published evidence, acknowledge the relevance of the spiritual dimension in all clinical settings, even when patients do not consider themselves particularly religious or spiritual.

5. *Spirituality can be taught*

Medical students respond well to teaching about spirituality in terms of knowledge (epidemiology), skills and attitudes/values.

Exercises and questions for personal reflection and as a basis for group discussion:

1. In what ways do you think religion has influenced the culture you grew up in, both for better and for worse?

2. How would you distinguish religion and spirituality from one another? Try carrying out the exercise completed by the medical students, listing words and ideas you associate with religion under one heading, and those you associate with spirituality under another.

3. Look up the websites of the Scientific and Medical Network, the 'Spirituality and Psychiatry' SIG of the Royal College of Psychiatrists, and the John Templeton Foundation to investigate further their basic philosophies and agendas.

4. Read the vignette again. Think about it. Discuss it with someone.

Chapter 4

THE LITERATURE ON PSYCHOLOGY AND SPIRITUALITY

19th- and 20th-century pioneers

William James, asserting that there is something within people that seeks meaning in life beyond everyday concerns, was the first significant writer on the subject of psychology and spirituality. Brief accounts of four additional pioneers in the field, all influenced by James, are included because their ideas echo and confirm each other, and still provide useful guidance.

Evelyn Underhill, Pierre Teilhard de Chardin, Carl Jung and Aldous Huxley differ from each other in both their backgrounds and approaches to the subject, making the consistency and complementarity of their ideas particularly noteworthy. They were independent thinkers, whose writings often appear idiosyncratic and lacking in scientific rigour. They have therefore been undervalued in some quarters.

WILLIAM JAMES (1842–1910)

James first published his highly influential book, *The Varieties of Religious Experience*[1] in 1902. His even-handedness, plus a naturalistic style of observation and description, ensured a degree of compatibility with the aims and methods of the science of his time. Purists, however, considered his work too religious, and it did not therefore give rise to much further psychological

---

1   James, W. (1982) *The Varieties of Religious Experience: A Study in Human Nature.* London: Penguin American Library Edition.

research. Theologians, on the other hand, found it too psychological to influence religious enquiry.

Despite these early reservations, James is now considered one of the founders of modern psychology. He had a background in medicine and philosophy, and thought of himself as a pathfinder, applying the scientific methods of the time, observation and analysis. To justify his enquiry, he wrote: 'To the psychologist, the religious propensities of man must be at least as interesting as any other of the facts pertaining to his mental constitution'.[2]

James used the following broad definition of 'religion' (consistent also with the term 'spirituality'): 'The feelings, acts and experiences of individual men [people] in their solitude, so far as they apprehend themselves to stand in relation to whatever they may consider the divine'.[3]

After almost 500 pages given over to description and definition of deeply personal experiences – under headings including 'healthy-mindedness', 'the sick soul', 'conversion', 'saintliness', 'mysticism' and 'repentance' – James has a short chapter of 'Conclusions', which he summarizes as follows:[4]

1. The visible world is part of a more spiritual universe from which it draws its chief significance.

2. Union or harmony with that higher universe is our true end.

3. Prayer or inner communion with the spirit thereof is a process wherein work is really done, and spiritual energy flows in and produces effects, psychological and material, within the phenomenal world.

4. Religion brings a new zest, which adds itself like a gift to life, taking the form either of lyrical enchantment or of appeal to earnestness and heroism.

5. It brings an assurance of safety and a temper of peace, and, in relation to others, a preponderance of loving affections.

The people of his time may not have been ready to embrace these ideas fully. James's work linking psychology and religion was new, impressive and influential, but was not taken up directly in academic circles. Other writers were to discover similar obstacles to gaining widespread acceptance.

EVELYN UNDERHILL (1875–1941)

William James once wrote that he had, 'No living sense of commerce with a God.' He added that he envied those who did, 'For I know that the addition

---

2   *Ibid.*, p.2.
3   *Ibid.* Quoted by Martin Marty in the Introduction, p.xxi.
4   *Ibid.*, pp.485–6.

of such a sense would help me greatly.'[5] He spoke of having grown out of Christianity, and did not favour religious organizations, but did recognize within himself what he called 'a mystical germ' substantial enough 'to withstand all purely atheistic criticism'. Evelyn Underhill, on the other hand, was a prominent and devout Anglo-Catholic, whose life is still commemorated annually by the Church of England.

Born in Wolverhampton, Underhill studied history and botany at London's King's College. She was also well informed on physics, philosophy, theology and the psychology of her day. She wrote over 30 books, both under her own name and using the pseudonym John Cordelier. Originally agnostic in her views, she became increasingly interested in Christian spirituality, publishing her book *Mysticism*[6] in 1911.

Where James sought objectivity, Underhill was less scientific in her approach. She expressed differences with James, based on her educational background and her own spiritual experiences. She was more personally engaged with her subject. As a consequence, her writing comes across with great passion and enthusiasm, and a unique kind of authority.

Underhill emphasized faith development. According to her lengthy volume, spiritual growth occurs in the following sequence: 'awakening of self', 'purgation', 'illumination', 'dark night of the soul' and 'the unitive life'. In 1936, the author crystallized her thinking in a series of four radio broadcasts, later revised and expanded for publication.[7] At 96 pages, *The Spiritual Life* is a much shorter and more accessible book than *Mysticism*. In it Underhill wrote,

> Beneath the surface of life, which generally contents us, there are unsuspected deeps and great spiritual forces that condition and control our small lives. Some people are, or become, sensitive to the pressure of these forces... The rest of us easily ignore the evidence for this whole realm of experience.[8]

Underhill said that people remain unaware of the spiritual dimension, both because it is interior and concealed, and because they are busily engaged with more obvious and external everyday matters. Like James, she concludes, nevertheless: 'No psychology that fails to take account of [spiritual forces] can claim to be complete.' Poetically, she suggests that meaning and coherence

---

5   *Ibid.* Quoted by Martin Marty in the Introduction, p.xxiv.
6   Underhill, E. (1999) *Mysticism: A Study of the Nature and Development of Man's Spiritual Consciousness,* 2nd rev. edn. Oxford: Oneworld Publications.
7   Underhill, E. (1999) *The Spiritual Life: Great Spiritual Truths for Everyday Life. Consciousness.* Oxford: Oneworld Publications.
8   *Ibid,* p.16.

come into people's scattered lives only 'when we lift our eyes from the crowded by-pass to the eternal hills'.

'Spiritual life,' she wrote, 'means the willed correspondence of the little human spirit with the Infinite Spirit; its feeding upon Him, its growth towards perfect union with Him.'[9] Note that emphasis on the word 'willed' implies choice and responsibility. According to Underhill, such a will is created through the 'awakening of self' that appears when a person first encounters and feels affected by some form of spiritual experience; by means of an epiphany, when 'something happens'.

Underhill speaks of two realities that people ideally relate to simultaneously: the personal, practical and worldly, on the one hand, and the universal, mystical and divine on the other. These are, she insists, linked inseparably in and through human communion with God. Most conflicts and difficulties people encounter, she suggests, 'come from trying to deal with the spiritual and practical aspects of our life separately instead of realizing them as parts of one whole'.[10]

There are countless ways that growth towards perfect union can occur, Underhill says. Often it is through adversity, 'under conditions that seem like the very frustration of life, of progress'.[11]

This is an important idea, but what can be done to ease our passage and promote spiritual growth? Underhill claimed that earlier spiritual writers recommended two activities to be undertaken regularly: 'mortification' and prayer. She admitted that these terms might put her readers off, and translated them as 'dealing with ourselves' and 'attending to God'. Now, we might re-translate them as 'honest self-enquiry' and 'meditation' (or 'mindfulness'). Both are forms of disciplined, personal spiritual practice.

Underhill cautions readers against a common misunderstanding. Rather than a peculiar or extreme form of piety, she says, the spiritual life is about living unselfishly in the world, subordinating all interests to what she calls the 'fact' that each person is part of spiritual reality and has a unique role to play in this divine order.

The task, as Underhill puts it, is to accept this fact fully, to acquiesce to it and co-operate with God. 'We are the agents of the Creative Spirit in this world. Real advance in the spiritual life,' she says, 'means accepting this vocation with all it involves.'[12] She stresses that people must be willing to face adversity, and can do so with confidence.

Her ideas are compatible with William James's conclusions that harmony with a higher universe (or divine realm) is our true end, and that prayer is a

9   *Ibid.*, pp.22–3.
10   *Ibid.*, p.27.
11   *Ibid.*, pp.23–4.
12   *Ibid.*, p.61.

process wherein work is done, allowing spiritual energy to flow and produce effects within the phenomenal world.

People today may not choose to call that with which they communicate through meditation God, but that need not deter someone from looking into what Evelyn Underhill writes as a source of wisdom. For 'God' read 'the Absolute', 'a higher power' or 'the seamless totality of being'; whatever seems appropriate to help grasp – if not agree with – what she is trying to convey.

PIERRE TEILHARD DE CHARDIN (1881–1955)

Like Evelyn Underhill, Pierre Teilhard de Chardin was an actively religious person. He was a French Jesuit priest whose written work was rejected in his lifetime by Roman Catholic authorities. His defining books, *The Divine Milieu*,[13] an essay on the interior life (written in 1927) and *The Phenomenon of Man*,[14] an evolutionary alternative to the traditional creation story of the Book of Genesis (written in 1938), were only published after his death.[15]

Initially a teacher of physics and chemistry, Teilhard became a distinguished palaeontologist and geologist. In 1929, he was famously involved in the discovery of *homo erectus*, a forbear of our species *homo sapiens*, in a cave in China. Given his scientific training and experiences searching and excavating in the field, it is understandable that he thought that religion and science, 'must necessarily meet at some pole of common vision'.[16]

Setting out to explore this intersection, he developed the idea of the universe as God's 'evolutionary creation'. According to de Chardin, this universe, bringing love of God and love of the earth together, consists of unified 'spirit-matter', and is evolving towards the spiritual fulfilment of consciousness and human personality at what he called 'Point Omega'.

In summarizing Teilhard's observations and reasoning, it would be easy to make errors of oversimplification. In terms of psychology, however, the following quotations give a useful indication of his conclusions:

> Love alone is capable of uniting living beings in such a way as to complete and fulfil them, for it alone takes them and joins them by what is deepest in themselves.

13 Teilhard de Chardin, P. (1964) *Le Milieu Divin (The Divine Milieu): An Essay on the Interior Life.* London: Collins, Fontana Books.

14 Teilhard de Chardin, P. with Huxley, J. (2008) *The Phenomenon of Man.* London: Harper Perennial 2008. Huxley, listed as co-author, assisted in getting the English version published.

15 His life and work are accessibly summarized by Amir Aczel (2007) in *The Jesuit and the Skull: Teilhard de Chardin, Evolution, and the Search for Peking Man.* New York, NY: Riverhead.

16 All quotes from Teilhard in this section are taken from www.teilhard.org.uk, accessed 21 May 2010.

All we need is to imagine our ability to love developing until it embraces the totality of men and the earth… A universal love is not only psychologically possible; it is the only complete and final way in which we are able to love.

Teilhard's contributions extend the ideas of James and Underhill from the personal to the collective, from individual spiritual growth to the psychological and spiritual evolution of humanity. Carl Jung also decisively linked the personal with the collective.

CARL JUNG (1875–1961)

Jung was a Swiss psychiatrist and philosopher. Although the son of a Christian minister, like James he was interested in but did not support organized religion. Many of his ideas are relatively well known.[17] He wrote extensively throughout a long life and, like Teilhard, developed a forward-looking psychology incorporating ideas about human spirituality. A translated collection of his essays is called, *Modern Man in Search of a Soul*.[18]

Jung took an interest in the spiritual lives and development of his patients, and made links with the symbols and myths of many cultures, including aboriginal cultures, observing widespread similarities. His theories about 'archetypes' and 'the collective unconscious' grew from these observations.

Briefly, Jung described adults according to two main 'psychological types': introvert and extrovert. In addition, he said that people habitually orientate themselves in the world – and to their inner worlds – in one of four principal ways: through 'sensation', 'thinking', 'feeling' or 'intuition'. This leads to eight possible combinations, to the idea of 'extroverted intuitive' types, for example, or 'introverted feeling' types.

Jung makes it clear that he refers to the conscious rather than the unconscious mind in making this classification. The conscious mind is the domain of the 'ego', the conscious personal 'I'. It is instructive to look at how, according to Jung, this limited self-awareness comes to relate first to the personal unconscious and then to the collective or universal.

Jung calls the personal unconscious 'the shadow'. Every conscious ego has its unconscious shadow. The term represents all the drives, desires and aversions at odds with social standards and peer pressures, and therefore made unacceptable to each person's ideal personality. It includes everything concerning themselves that people are ashamed of and do not want to know about. The shadow is therefore hidden in everyday life behind a kind of mask, which Jung called the 'persona' (see Vignette – Jack).

17　See, for example, Frieda Fordham's (1953) short and very readable book, *An Introduction to Jung's Psychology*. London: Penguin Books.

18　Jung, C. G. (1933) *Modern Man in Search of a Soul*. London: Routledge and Kegan Paul.

Vignette – Jack

A young man, still attending school, spoke with a London accent that seemed 'not right for the character that he was attempting to inhabit', according to his teacher. He appeared very inhibited and, as they were talking, the teacher suggested he revert to the regional accent from where he lived as a boy. There was an immediate transformation. After a few seconds, tears were falling down his face. Using his new voice, he was suddenly conveying emotion.

It then transpired that the youth's family had split up when he was a child. He moved with his mother to a rough part of London and was bullied into disguising, then abandoning, his regional accent, taking on a new hard persona, a new but false personality, as a defence against the relentless persecution from his peers. David Hay, an expert on children's psychology, later commented, 'The boy had been forced into membership of a "tribe" that did not represent his true self.'[19]

The way forward is for each ego gradually to become aware of and face its shadow, to accept and integrate its distressing components. As with the young man in the vignette, there may well be the cathartic release of tears during this process. When reconnection with one's true nature is achieved and firmly established, the persona can (either abruptly or usually more gradually) be discarded.

The narrow personal ego expands in this way into what Jung called 'the Self', and it is this that communicates with the collective unconscious. Other terms that we can recognize as broadly compatible with Jung's 'Self' include 'true self', 'higher self', 'psycho-spiritual self', 'spiritual self' and 'soul'.[20]

The Self, according to Jung, is a much less inhibited version of each person than the ego. It appears far more relaxed and natural to others. In dreams, he reports, the archetype of the Self often appears as a magical or golden child.

Communication between Jung's Self and the collective unconscious is mediated, he says, through 'archetypes' shared by all members of humanity, whatever their personal history or cultural background. They are discovered particularly in art, symbols (including religious symbols), myths (including tribal and cultural myths) and in dreams.

The archetypes include a feminine principle called 'anima', and a corresponding masculine principle called 'animus'. The Self has access to both, bringing balance to the personality. Women can assume male characteristics

---

19 David Hay wrote about this story in *The Spirit of the Child* (rev. edn, 2006) co-written with Rebecca Nye. London: Jessica Kingsley Publishers.

20 'Higher self' (used in contrast with 'lower self' or 'personal self') is the term favoured, for example, by psychotherapist Robert Assagioli, the founder of psychosynthesis.

when necessary. Similarly, men can take on female attributes. The yin-yang principle of wholeness is thereby maintained.[21]

The 'great mother' (embodying aspects of yin) and the 'old wise man' (embodying aspects of yang) are two more influential archetypes described by Jung to explain how personal growth, what he called 'individuation', might occur. The 'great mother' (or 'earth woman') is endowed with an infinite capacity for loving and nurturing, for helping and protecting, prepared to wear herself out for the benefit of others. The old wise man is thought of as the archetype of meaning, the embodiment of power and wisdom. He can appear, for example in a dream, as a king, a hero, a healer or a saviour.

When influenced by these archetypes, Jung warns of the risk of thinking of oneself as indispensable, and of everyone around as helpless and dependent. This can lead to deceiving oneself into feeling godlike, omniscient and invincible, and to a kind of tyrant mentality, suppressing destructively the personalities of other people. This is the dangerous illusion of pride (*hubris*). Downfall (*nemesis*), humiliation and disillusion are certain to follow. To avoid causing and experiencing distress, says Jung, humility and a willingness to follow, rather than to dictate, are required. There are echoes of Evelyn Underhill's thoughts here.

Importantly, according to Jung, the Self involves a person's awareness of his or her unique nature, and of having an intimate relationship with everything, with all life – not only people but with animals and plants too – and with the inanimate, with the entire cosmos.

The archetype representing this wholeness, one of the world's oldest religious symbols, is the 'mandala'. The Sanskrit word refers to a mystical or magic circle, with radial and concentric elements, sometimes including square shapes, arranged about a central point, like this:

Jung found such images appearing in the dreams of his patients, often accompanied by powerful feelings of peace and harmony. He noticed that

21   In Taoism, 'yin' is the feminine principle and 'yang' is the masculine.

his patients' mandalas rarely contained images of a deity. His conclusion was that, for the people of his time, the place of God seemed to have been taken by a unified vision of mankind.

ALDOUS HUXLEY (1894–1963)

Aldous Huxley was the grandson of Thomas Henry Huxley, an eminent zoologist at the time of Charles Darwin with whom he collaborated. Two of Aldous's brothers became leading biologists in their turn, so his background in science was strong.

Like William James, Huxley seems to have been schooled within a Christian background, the tenets of which he outgrew. It was intended that Aldous himself would study medicine, but he was prevented by an eye complaint in his late teens that left him nearly blind for more than two years. Instead, he studied English Literature at Oxford University, then his path turned to writing.

Huxley moved to the United States in 1937 where he was introduced to 'Vedanta', a relatively modern school of Hinduism, and agreed to write an introduction to a new translation of the great Hindu scripture, *Bhagavad-Gita*, translated by Swami Prabhavananda and the English writer, Christopher Isherwood.[22] Here, Huxley referred to the 'Perennial Philosophy' of humankind, first written down more than 25 centuries earlier. With almost scientific precision, he enumerated its four fundamental doctrinal principles:[23]

1. The world of matter and of individualized consciousness is the manifestation of a Divine Ground within which all partial realities have their being, and apart from which they would be nonexistent.

2. Human beings are capable not only of knowing *about* the Divine Ground by inference; they can also realize its existence by a direct intuition, superior to discursive reasoning. This immediate knowledge unites the knower with the known.

3. Man possesses a double nature, a phenomenal ego and an eternal Self, which is the inner man, the Spirit, the spark of divinity within the soul. It is possible for a man, if he so desires, to identify himself with the spirit and therefore with the Divine Ground, which is of the same or like nature with the spirit.

22 *Bhagavad Gita: The Song of God* (1944) Trans. S. Prabhavananda and C. Isherwood. Hollywood, CA: Vedanta Press.
23 *Ibid.*, 4th edn (1987), p.7.

4. Man's life on earth has only one end and purpose: to identify himself with the eternal Self and so to come to intuitive knowledge of the Divine Ground.

Huxley suggests that this Perennial Philosophy is consistent with great truths espoused by the world's major religions, and describes the *Bhagavad-Gita* as one of the most systematic scriptural statements of that philosophy.

These four principles will help further unravel the psychology of spirituality. There are close comparisons with James's conclusions. The third point from the Perennial Philosophy echoes Jung's description of the relationship between 'ego' and 'Self', and the fourth indicates the possibility of spiritual growth throughout life. Similar ideas recur in the works of more recent authors on psychology and spirituality too, with the emergence of the new psycho-spiritual paradigm referred to in the Preface. (see before p.9).

20th- and 21st-century writers

James Fowler, whose ideas we will be examining and developing in Part 2, gives credit as major influences to three important researchers and authors: Jean Piaget, Erik Erikson and Lawrence Kohlberg.

JEAN PIAGET (1896–1980)

Piaget was Swiss. Studying children over a long period, he came to describe how they experience and make sense of the world. He put forward a comprehensive theory of cognitive development involving four stages between birth and adolescence, as follows:[24]

1. *Sensorimotor stage* (birth to 2 years): children experience the world through movement and the five senses.

2. *Pre-operational stage* (2 to 7 years): strong egocentrism initially, weakening later; unable to use logical thought processes.

3. *Concrete operational stage* (7 to 11 years): no longer egocentric, children can think logically with practical aids and remain very literal or 'concrete' in their thinking.

4. *Formal operational stage* (after 11 years): children can easily think logically, and develop the capacity for abstract thinking.

These observations on child development have been broadly accepted as accurate, informing and influencing education and child-rearing practices for

---

24 Piaget, J. and Inhelder, B. (1972) *The Psychology of the Child.* New York, NY: Basic Books.

decades; but they do not directly address the topic of children's spirituality, and do not therefore give a complete picture.

ERIK ERIKSON (1902–1994)

Erikson was born in Germany of Danish parents. He came to psychology after studying art, training as a psychoanalyst in Vienna before moving to the USA. His writing and teaching led him in due course to major prominence in the field of psychoanalysis.

Erikson built on Sigmund Freud's ideas covering the period from birth to adolescence, reducing Freud's emphasis on sexual development and extending his theories throughout adulthood into old age. Erikson eventually described an eight-stage life cycle, consisting of a series of crises, challenges or conflicts. He also attached a lasting virtue to successful transition through each of his stages as follows:[25]

1. *Infant stage:* seeking balance between 'basic trust' versus 'mistrust'. How reliable is the child's experience of caregivers? Trust is necessary, but to be too trusting can lead to the dangers of gullibility. (Lasting virtue: Hope)

2. *Toddler stage:* a crisis period of 'autonomy' versus 'shame and doubt'. The child explores the world, needing boundaries that are neither too restrictive nor too lenient for the optimal outcome. (Lasting virtue: Will)

3. *Kindergarten (pre-school) stage:* a crisis period of 'initiative' versus 'guilt'. The child plans and achieves things independently, thriving on appropriate encouragement and praise, reacting negatively to excessive prohibition and punishment. (Lasting virtue: Purpose)

4. *Pre-puberty stage:* a crisis period of 'industry' versus 'inferiority'. The child compares themself to others at home, in the classroom and playground, recognizing disparities. (Lasting virtue: Competence)

5. *Teenager stage:* a crisis period of 'identity' versus 'role confusion'. The young person faces deeply personal questions of the type: 'Who am I?' 'How do I fit in?' 'What does life have in store for me?' There may be too much pressure to conform, or insufficient guidance with inadequate numbers and types of role model. (Lasting virtue: Fidelity)

6. *Young adult stage:* a crisis period of 'intimacy' versus 'isolation'. The young adult faces questions like: 'What will I do with my life?' 'Do I want a life-partner?' 'What kind of person will that be?' (Lasting virtue: Love)

25   Erikson, E. (1982) *The Life Cycle Completed.* New York, NY and London: W.W. Norton.

7. *Mid-life stage:* a crisis period of 'generativity' versus 'stagnation'. The adult person appraises his or her lifestyle, the consequences of decisions made hitherto, of accomplishments and failures. Attending to the welfare of the younger generation is a source of satisfaction. Failing to do so sets up a sense of stagnation. (Lasting virtue: Caring)

8. *Old age stage:* a crisis period of 'integrity' versus 'despair'. Facing death and reflecting on the past, the older person looks for coherence, patterns and meaning from what they have lived through. Where these are missing, dissatisfaction can lead to despair. (Lasting virtue: Wisdom)

During the first crisis period, for example, an infant in a stable, loving and caring environment – where needs for food, warmth, cleanliness, attention and affection are quickly perceived and met – is more likely to develop a general attitude of trust, and a strong inclination towards hope. According to Erikson, should this persist into the second and later stages, it would be a favourable outcome. In a harsher and less reliable environment, the infant is more likely to experience mistrust as a lasting psychological feature, and to be more of a stranger to hope; yet all is not lost, because Erikson makes clear that corrective experiences can occur during later stages to restore earlier disadvantages.

Excessive mistrust will predispose a person to isolation and the risk of paranoid tendencies. Erikson also pointed out, however, that some capacity for mistrust is advantageous in life. It helps avoid being over-trusting, at risk of exploitation by others. Trust and mistrust are like light and dark, like yang and yin in the Taoist symbol. They likewise never reach a standstill. The question, 'to trust or not to trust?' always remains open. Things can change. And so it is with Erikson's other paired crisis outcomes such as industry versus inferiority, identity versus role confusion and integrity versus despair. Life isn't over till it's over. Many find hope in these thoughts.

There is limited discussion in Erikson's body of work about human spirituality.[26] Nevertheless, it can be thought of as definitely including spiritual insights. His vision of the life cycle, for instance, is entirely holistic, particularly given its consistent consideration of each person as an individual in the context of family and society. Note also the emphasis on facing adversity, challenges and crises, and the possibility of achieving virtues like fidelity, love and wisdom.

---

26 See, for example, Erikson, E. (1950, 1963) *Childhood and Society*; (1968) *Identity, Youth and Crisis*; (1959) *Identity and the Life Cycle* and (1982) *The Life Cycle Completed*, all published by W. W. Norton (New York and London).

Personal anecdote – learning about trust

I was taught about Erikson's life cycle in my mid-twenties, and it has had a powerful influence on me since.

After qualifying as a doctor and completing one year in the UK National Health Service, I travelled to New Zealand to further my training and experience, unsure of what branch of medicine to follow. After six months in a surgical post in the North Island, I obtained a six-month training post in psychiatry in Christchurch. Service duties were comparatively light. The employing authorities were commendably keen to emphasize learning, without undue distraction from a heavy and stressful workload. We tended to spend a lot of time with a relatively small number of patients, as well as in lectures, workshops, tutorials and in the library.

One of the two professors in the psychiatry department, on sabbatical from Harvard, was also a trained anthropologist and expert on Erikson. Each week we read up about and discussed in sequence the eight stages or crises of the life cycle. Always, thereafter, I saw my patients in the context of this journey they were making through life. I recognized the critical importance of the circumstances of their birth, especially in terms of family background, quality of parenting, birth order, number of siblings and so on.

More than this, I recognized too the importance of basic trust between people, and how this so often plays out in terms of autonomy versus control. It happened that the other professor in the department was a psychotherapist who insisted (even though I was only to be in post there for six months until my visa expired) that I took on a patient for twice-weekly therapy sessions under supervision. This taught me how to listen to the patient, to recognize what she was not saying as well as what she did say, and to remember that, at the beginning, she was unlikely to trust me and that this mistrust would affect things in a number of ways, especially over the issue of control. The ideal would be to share decision making. Sometimes I would take the lead, and sometimes the patient was given control, but the aim was to reach agreement when possible.

For example, the patient came early to several appointments, but learned that I would always keep to time. After that, she always came late, until, without reproach, I brought it to her attention and we discussed the matter. She then saw it was in her interests to arrive on time.

I controlled the timing of the beginning and ending of therapy sessions, but said she was free to discuss whatever topic she wished during them. Sometimes she asked for guidance, perhaps by enquiring if I had any questions for her. Once, when she expressed an objection to my sitting behind a desk writing notes, I changed my behaviour. Instructed to do so by my clinical supervisor, in following sessions I sat in a chair directly opposite the patient without the desk intervening. I also gave up on the notes, recording the sessions from memory afterwards. This proved to be something of a turning point. It clearly encouraged the patient that I had appreciated her discomfort and adapted the situation. She expressed relief that I was not insisting on continuing as before; and she was much more forthcoming and to the point in therapy thereafter.

This patient, in her thirties, was having problems in her marital relationship. She blamed herself for the aloof and emotionally cold behaviour of her husband. She hoped that they would get along better, to the point where they might consider starting a family together; but she was too inhibited to discuss the matter with him.

One day, she mentioned that her husband would be away for a few days. She said she expected to feel lonely, especially in the evenings. She reminded me that I had a record of her address, and seemed to want to say that I could relieve her loneliness by paying her a night-time visit. Of course, this would have been wrong, the breaking of strong professional boundaries. It would have been damaging to the patient exactly because it would have been a betrayal of trust. My supervisor – also a woman – explained how vulnerable to masculine, and specifically sexual, dominance this patient had become in her life. This was her core problem. She could not find equality in partnership – except now, deliberately so, in therapy. It was my task to model a new experience for her, a relationship of trust and mutuality of control, a partnership; albeit in this instance a highly structured, professional one.

The patient responded. At a later session she said she had not been lonely but had enjoyed the time on her own, finding things to do for her own satisfaction, free from the critical eye and cruel tongue of her husband. She began to realize that she had choices within the relationship. It was difficult for her when the time came for me to leave New Zealand and end her treatment, but she coped well with the separation. She made it clear that she had benefited, gaining in self-confidence and feeling generally happier. She expressed her thanks, and said that she had decided to use my departure as another learning experience.

I was grateful to my patient in turn. As her treatment was going on, alongside the rest of my training, I was learning and growing too. In this context, it was a great help to discover Erikson's life cycle. It gave me the opportunity to chart my place in young adult life and the trajectory I had embarked upon.

As part of my identity, if I wanted to continue a career in medicine, it was clear that I would have to be a trustworthy person. I would have to be consciously honest in my speech, forthright and dependable in my actions, otherwise I would only be adopting a persona. I already knew deep within, according to my truest self, that I did not want to dissemble, to play a part. I could see the falsehood in that, and how others would inevitably suffer from it. I was not yet sure though that I could find the virtue it would require to adhere to my ideals.

I was growing conscious that I needed to face and integrate my shadow. I had still to indulge and let go some attachments and aversions, and find healing for a number of emotional wounds, in order to grow spiritually and to mature. Awareness of this need in myself helped me to recognize it in others too, almost instantly and intuitively, when I met them; and this eventually made me want to help people even more. My life's meaning, from which I was gaining both a powerful sense of purpose and the power to carry it out, was becoming clearer. I was being guided firmly onto the track of my future professional career.

LAWRENCE KOHLBERG (1927–1987)

Kohlberg's work on child development was equally relevant to an understanding of human spirituality. His contribution was influenced by Piaget, extending his theories of cognitive development by observing how children at different ages reacted to moral dilemmas.

Kohlberg identified six stages, each more adequate than the last at handling a problem in which both of two alternative courses of action could be criticized on moral or ethical grounds. For example, stealing is usually considered wrong. Can it be condoned if a person's family is starving? Allowing your family to starve is also usually considered wrong.

Kohlberg's six stages of moral development are divided into three levels, with two stages in each, as follows:[27]

Level 1. *Pre-conventional*

(a) obedience and punishment driven

(b) self-interest driven

Level 2. *Conventional*

(a) interpersonal accord and conformity driven

(b) authority and social order obedience driven

---

27   Power, C., Higgins, A. and Kohlberg, L. (1991) *Lawrence Kohlberg's Approach to Moral Education.* New York, NY: Columbia University Press.

Level 3. *Post-conventional*

   (a) social contract driven

   (b) universal ethical principles driven

Kohlberg therefore outlined a course towards moral maturity, compatible with ideas about spiritual maturity consistent with the psycho-spiritual paradigm that forms the substance of this book. To give an idea of the range, his Stage 1 (Level 1.a) is driven by obedience and punishment-avoidance. According to this, actions are considered by young children as wrong if they get punished, not otherwise. The more severe the punishment, the worse the child considers the act to be.

By contrast, Stage 5 (Level 3.a) recognizes that people come to hold different opinions and values. This requires moral dilemmas to be resolved according to majority decisions and compromise.

Kohlberg's Stage 6 (Level 3.b) goes even further. It depends on abstract reasoning about what is right, considering ethical problems in terms of justice rather than law. The role of consensus may also be challenged. An individual who has reached Kohlberg's Stage 6 may feel bound to act in a certain way, even against the decisions of others. The implication will be that such a person is guided by some inner moral compass, hearkening to the true, spiritual self.

Conclusion

The writers discussed in this chapter set the scene for contemporary authors and researchers in the fields of psychology and psychiatry to consider anew the topic of spirituality. Once the 'forgotten dimension' of mental healthcare, it is now giving birth to a new paradigm, which is the subject of Chapter 5.

Summary points

1. *Pioneer William James*

James, now considered one of the founders of modern psychology, published *The Varieties of Religious Experience* in 1902, concluding that the visible world is part of a more spiritual universe, something within which people seek meaning in life accordingly.

2. *Other writers on spirituality*

From different backgrounds, the writers Evelyn Underhill, Pierre Teilhard de Chardin, Carl Jung and Aldous Huxley, came to comparable conclusions. Teilhard and Jung in particular linked the personal to the collective, associating individual spiritual growth with the psychological and spiritual evolution of humanity.

3. *Personal development charted*

Later writers, Jean Piaget, Erik Erikson and Lawrence Kohlberg, each charted different aspects of personal development from infancy, through childhood and adolescence into adulthood and old age, setting the scene for a new paradigm of psychology and spirituality, and for James Fowler's stages of faith.

4. *A personal anecdote*

The anecdote tells how useful Erikson's life cycle ideas were to the author as a young adult.

Exercises and questions for personal reflection and as a basis for group discussion:

1. Read through again the five conclusions of William James and the four points of Huxley's Perennial Philosophy. Do you agree with some and not others? Do you consider that people's lives have only one end and purpose? Discuss these questions with someone else.

2. How does the idea that life proceeds in a series of recognizable stages, such as those described by Erikson, strike you? What do you think the main tasks are during adolescence, young adulthood, middle age and for the elderly? How active do you think a person should be in acknowledging and addressing the different challenges? Might it not be better to be relatively passive and allow your destiny to unfold naturally?

3. Think about Jung's ideas regarding the ego, its shadow and the persona (or 'mask') used to face the world and hide or disguise a person's true nature. Do you understand what he is getting at? If so, try explaining it to someone else. If not, think and read up about it some more. Try getting someone who does understand it to explain it to you.

4. Read the vignette again. Have you ever (or can you think of someone else who has) either deliberately or unconsciously (at the time) copied the speech and behavioural characteristics of a group in order to be part of it? Was this successful? Think of the consequences, both beneficial and harmful. What were they? Discuss this with someone you trust.

Chapter 5

PARADIGM SHIFT: CHALLENGING CURRENT THEORY AND PRACTICE

What is a paradigm shift?

A paradigm is a way of seeing or construing the world which underlies the theories, operating principles, rules and methodologies of science during a particular period of history. Such a model incorporates values, assumptions and beliefs accepted by the scientific community and by those engaged in applying science, such as in the fields of health and social care. A paradigm shift involves a major conceptual change in both theory and practice. It is necessarily a development or extension of what has gone before.

Spirit and psyche: a psychotherapist's view

Like John Swinton[1] and David Fontana,[2] Victor Schermer is a leading contemporary proponent of a major shift in psychology to incorporate a spiritual dimension.[3] A writer and practising psychotherapist, he describes himself as, 'both by nature and nurture an incorrigible skeptic and a scientifically-minded, humanistically inclined individual'.[4]

---

1   See Swinton, J. (2001) *Spirituality and Mental Health Care: Rediscovering a Forgotten Dimension.* London: Jessica Kingsley Publishers.
2   See Fontana, D. (2003) *Psychology, Religion and Spirituality.* Oxford: BPS Blackwell.
3   Schermer, V. L. (2003) *Spirit and Psyche: A New Paradigm for Psychology, Psychoanalysis and Psychotherapy,* New York and London: Jessica Kingsley Publishers.
4   *Ibid.,* pp.21–2.

He says that, like most working psychologists for many years, he deliberately kept spiritual ideas apart from his work, research and therapy with patients. He describes how the discipline of psychology was built around the idea of more complex phenomena being explained in terms of those that are simpler: the mind, for example, in terms of biology. Similarly, it involved explaining later development in terms of earlier: such as adult life seen as a function of infancy and childhood.

In favour of this, Schermer points out that such reductionism has led to many insights and applications, helping people better to perceive themselves in the context both of biological and cultural evolution. He stresses how reluctant he was to change his thinking, which was based on the conviction that belief in God amounted to 'metaphysical speculation' and had no place in a scientific approach to psychology. He thought democratic principles should apply to keep psychology and faith (or lack of it) apart; also that treatments should be based on universal methods and theories that transcend religion and culture.

Introducing a new paradigm

Victor Schermer states that these arguments have served well since the 19th century, when psychology, psychiatry and psychotherapy separated themselves from philosophy and theology as separate disciplines based on empirical research. But, in response to a renaissance of spirituality in contemporary culture, a growing interest in meditation, Eastern philosophies and traditions, and developments in complementary medicine, he now insists a new paradigm is overdue.

To demonstrate his point about the evolution of ideas, Schermer gives the example of classical and modern physics. Classical physics was based, for instance, on a belief that measurement of time was independent of the observer. Modern physics, in contrast, says that the velocity and location of the observer have an important effect on the measurement of time. A new level of understanding, a new paradigm, is therefore involved. Similarly, the new 'psycho-spiritual' paradigm in psychology assumes that religious and spiritual explanations of experiences and behaviours are now required, whereas in the past they were excluded.

Schermer's own change of heart involved confronting a five-point challenge. Before this, as for many, secular 'object relations' theory and 'self-psychology' provided him with rich, convincing and useful frameworks and theoretical reference points. He says he did not think it appropriate to impose his own beliefs or scepticism on his patients.

This type of standpoint remains the norm for many professionals involved in healthcare and mental healthcare. Nevertheless, however detached and isolated one may be, others would call it impossible completely to withhold or disguise one's true thoughts and feelings about religion and spirituality from either patients or colleagues.

Five challenges
ONE
Schermer seems to have understood this, identifying the first challenge to his 'therapeutic agnosticism' as arising out of extensive work he undertook in the field of addictions treatment. This was strongly influenced by the principles of Alcoholics Anonymous and the recommended '12-step' method that is now used in many forms of addiction.[5] The second and third of the 12 steps involve the statements:

> We came to believe that a Power greater than ourselves could restore us to sanity.

> We made a decision to turn our will and our lives over to the care of God as we understood Him.

Schermer writes:

> I witnessed significant healing of patients with substance misuse disorders and trauma occur through means which, while they did not require a supernatural explanation, could only be described as spiritual in the sense of a significant change in beliefs, attitudes and personality which involved higher consciousness and/or faith in God.[6]

He witnessed deeply and persistently disturbed people develop 'full, rich, ethical and socially-oriented lives'. No sufficient explanation for these recoveries was possible, he says, using the former, secular paradigm.

Schermer comments:

> The differences in outcomes between the AA-based approach and the traditional techniques were astonishing to me. It led me to question everything I had learned in my graduate studies and psychoanalytic training. I haven't jettisoned the latter…but found I needed to add a dimension to my understanding'.[7]

He adds that the changes in the patients were great enough for anyone to see without subtle statistical tests. These changes included: renewed family life, a sense of hope and faith, improved self-esteem, restored careers, access to a

---

5   See www.alcoholics-anonymous.org, accessed 22 May 2010.
6   Schermer, *ibid.*, pp.24–5.
7   *Ibid.*, p.33.

greater range of feelings and an increased ability to establish intimacy with others.

One of the key therapeutic factors was called 'spiritual awakening', the specifics of which varied from patient to patient. 'While spirituality appeared to be an essential ingredient,' writes Schermer, 'the spiritual path was an individual matter. Thus, I concluded that the spirituality necessary for healing was not identical with any specific religion or professed set of beliefs, but rather a set of qualities that could be developed within any individual who sought them.'[8]

TWO

Schermer's second challenge came from a simultaneous new fascination with Eastern thought, meditation and states of consciousness. He does not elaborate on this point, except to say that he discussed these subjects with other, favourably disposed therapists.

THREE

His third challenge resulted from published research[9] offering rigorous empirical evidence for the health benefits of spiritual practices.

FOUR

As a group and family therapist, Schermer learned about systems theories and the importance of context, which called into question the sufficiency of more straightforward cause and effect models for human emotion, motivation and behaviour.

Quoting other contemporary authors Frank Capra,[10] Ken Wilber[11] and Gary Zukav,[12] Schermer writes:

> If we examine biological, social and ecological systems in widening circles of interaction, we move beyond simple causal connections to the spiritual depth of biological, social and ecological processes. Similarities can be found among spiritual teachings, living systems theories, modern relativity, quantum and chaos/complexity theories, all of which go well beyond ordinary

---

8 *Ibid.*, p.35.
9 Such as that collected in Koenig, H., McCullough, M. and Larson, D. (2001) *Handbook of Religion and Health.* Oxford: Oxford University Press.
10 Capra, F. (1975) *The Tao of Physics.* Boston, MA: Shambhala and (1997) *The Web of Life: A New Understanding of Living Systems.* New York, NY: Doubleday.
11 Wilber, K. (1998) *The Marriage of Sense and Soul: Integrating Science and Religion.* New York, NY: Random House.
12 Zukav, G. (1979) *The Dancing Wu-Li Masters.* New York, NY: William Morrow.

cause–effect relationships to the realms of paradox, mystery and realities beyond the senses.[13]

FIVE

Finally, Schermer reports how the work of a psychoanalyst, Wilfred Bion, brought together for him the several diverse spheres of influence in which he had become interested.[14] Beginning with philosophy and the study of scientific method, Bion developed an astonishingly coherent rationale for linking spirituality to object-relations theory that ultimately led to a mystical view of the mental life.[15]

CONSEQUENCES – THE PSYCHO-SPIRITUAL PARADIGM

The consequences of the shift in Schermer's attitude to his own work are detailed in his book. His aim, he states, has been to develop a 'psychospiritual paradigm' that brings spiritual understanding into conjunction with science-based ideas regarding the mind and its development.[16] The new paradigm, he says, will offer a way of thinking about and doing psychology, psychoanalysis and psychotherapy which integrates spiritual principles with psychological models of the mind and behavior'.[17]

Schermer insists that a key premise of the paradigm is the unity of body, mind and spirit. Echoing James, Underhill, Huxley and others, he says, 'We are all possessed of a divinity within. It is inherent in human nature to have valid experiences that transcend mundane reality.'[18]

Spirituality, he says, involves,

> A capacity and a motivation for living fully within the context of being and faith, based upon an urge to experience infinitude and something or some One beyond the confines of our everyday perceptions of ourselves and the world. That is, spirituality is that aspect of our psyche which is always reaching for union with the mysterious and the beyond.[19]

---

13 Schermer, V. L. (2003) *Spirit and Psyche: A New Paradigm for Psychology, Psychoanalysis and Psychotherapy*, New York and London: Jessica Kingsley Publishers, p.25.

14 Wilfred Bion (1897–1979) was a British psychoanalyst and pioneer in group dynamics. He was associated with the Tavistock group of psychologists who founded London's Tavistock Institute of Human Relations. He was President of the British Psychoanalytical Society from 1962 to 1965.

15 Schermer, *ibid.* pp.25–6.

16 *Ibid.*, p.26.

17 *Ibid.*, p.26.

18 *Ibid.*, p.29.

19 Ibid., p.29.

Schermer devotes a full chapter to this inner core of human experience, calling it the 'psychospiritual self'.[20]

He stresses that spirituality is not external or peripheral; saying that it is not a system of beliefs, but rather a quality of living, being and experiencing which involves an awareness of the infinite, the ineffable and the indescribable. He says it is not an 'add-on' to our basic drives and energies, but an integral part of them, informing and structuring them. Rather than a mere religious doctrine or pursuit, or a supplement to our basic needs, he describes spirituality as defining both our existence and our essence.

According to the new paradigm, Schermer says:

> It becomes possible to raise questions, formulate hypotheses and develop treatment strategies, so that we begin to think of the psychospiritual as a legitimate and systematic area of investigation and practice, rather than a potpourri of personal testimonies, miracle cures, and research that is fascinating but uncoordinated.[21]

Many authorities are now in agreement with this.

THE NEXT STEP – A 'PRISTINE EGO'

There seems to reside in the newborn, 'a component of self which possesses a purity, wholeness, untarnished innocence and spontaneity'.[22] Schermer borrows a term from the doyen of British child psychotherapy, Donald Winnicott, and calls this component the 'pristine ego', describing it as the 'developmental seed' of the spiritual self, that part of each person capable of spiritual awareness.

The pristine ego is a theoretical construct, a short-lived, yin-yang wholeness. According to Schermer, 'Tragically, yet central to all spiritual development, this pristine state of being quickly finds itself inundated with conflicts and anxieties'.[23] This early infant ego soon perceives and identifies with its body, feels pain, discomfort, frustration, abandonment, emptiness and insatiability. It soon therefore splits, experiencing itself as helpless and dependent (yin) one minute, all-powerful and all-knowing (yang) the next.

These initial struggles are defining moments for the spiritual self, which now seeks to maintain its unspoiled, pristine essence while at the same time surviving and growing in a body, in time and space.

Needs associated with survival and desire come to the fore; matters necessarily involving attachment, threat and actual loss, matters that are

---

20   The simpler terms 'spiritual self' or 'true self' will be used in this book.
21   *Ibid.*, pp.108–9.
22   *Ibid.*, p.115.
23   Ibid., p.116

constantly at the heart of human psychology. The pristine ego, the forerunner of the spiritual self, is pitted from the outset against the body-bound, earth-bound, time-bound ego of desire and survival. However, in the form of the spiritual self, its indivisible, holistic nature remains inviolable, however masked or otherwise hidden.

Personal ego and spiritual self, bound together like two light particles emanating from the same source: this is a theme to be followed as we examine and develop the ideas of another pioneering psychologist, James Fowler.

Before we do, here are a few additional thought-provoking ideas from Schermer, who says that separation of mind and body is a kind of spiritual malaise afflicting our world. Divorcing mind from spirit leaves people estranged from themselves, each other and their origins. This division, he says, is a source of the collective neuroses and psychoses of humanity.

This is a big statement from a psychotherapist, an immense and direct challenge to the old paradigm that ignores the spiritual dimension. It could be construed as destructive, but Schermer also offers hope and a remedy: knowing that spirit, matter and energy are one, he says, is liberating and leads to wholeness. The mind/body continuum contains both the inevitability of suffering and death and the ultimate source of joy and vitality. Here we have yin and yang in proximity once again.

This is a genuinely new and vital step ahead for psychological theory, comparable to Einstein standing on Newton's shoulders, looking towards much farther horizons. The earlier theoretical framework of academic psychology is correct within limits, but must now be considered incomplete. Even for the traditionalist and the sceptic, knowledge and experience of the new paradigm is required to avoid being overtaken by history.

James Fowler
BACKGROUND

James Fowler did not describe his work as foreshadowing or contributing to a new paradigm, but hindsight allows us to view it that way. The son of a Christian minister, raised in North Carolina, Fowler studied divinity and went on to teach the subject at Harvard University. He was later appointed Professor of Theology at Emory University in Atlanta, retiring from the post in 2005.

He once wrote about recalling being taught theology as an adult as though he had never been through childhood, and this seemed wrong to him. He objected that it ignored the fact that powerful images of God and other spiritual experiences had occurred to him before he was five. This conviction spurred him on throughout his academic career to develop a way of understanding people's lifelong development of faith. It had formerly been the custom for psychologists and theologians to concentrate on people's intellectual beliefs. Fowler felt it important to go further and include the whole of human experience, so he developed a theory based on three sets of well-established ideas (those of Piaget, Erikson and Kohlberg) before putting it to rigorous experimental test.

FOWLER ON FAITH

Fowler describes 'faith' as a universal feature of human living, calling it the most fundamental category in the human quest for relation to transcendence. 'Faith' here equates with the comparable term 'spirituality'. According to Fowler, this is a universal feature of human living, recognizably similar everywhere, despite the remarkable variety of forms and contents of religious practices and belief.

In all major religious traditions, according to Fowler, faith involves an alignment of the will and resting of the heart in accordance with a vision of transcendent value and power, making this one's ultimate concern. It is 'an orientation of the total person, giving purpose and goal to one's hopes and strivings, thoughts and actions'.[24]

In the light of these comments, there can be no doubt that a person's attention to faith or spirituality (or relative neglect of these) will be a major influence on their psychology; on their emotions, as well as on their thoughts, words and actions. Depending on the degree of spiritual development attained, the nature and degree of such influence will vary with time throughout a person's life. Fowler's stages help us understand this.

FOWLER'S SYNTHESIS

Fowler describes the basis of his theories through a fictional conversation he wrote, as if between four people: a convener (himself), Piaget, Erikson and Kohlberg. The conversation, he says, is held in a spirit of 'playful seriousness and serious playfulness'.[25] It has an introduction, and is then divided into sections on Infancy, Early Childhood, Childhood, Adolescence, and Adulthood.

In the following chapters, Fowler outlines how the theory of faith development grew from a creative synthesis of ideas already summarized in this conversation, together with additional ideas from the work of other authors.[26] He then outlines each of the six stages, beginning with a brief description of 'Infancy and Undifferentiated Faith' that precedes Faith Stage 1.

---

24   Fowler, J. (1981, 1995) *Stages of Faith: The Psychology of Human Development and the Quest for Meaning.* San Francisco, CA: HarperSanFrancisco, p.14.
25   *Ibid.* (1995) p.41.
26   Fowler notes a particular debt to Paul Tillich, Richard Niebuhr and Daniel Levinson.

RESEARCH METHODS

Fowler's descriptions of the stages cover 13 to 15 pages for each.[27] They are illustrated by excerpts from research interviews conducted by the author and his collaborators. These interviews lasted from two to two-and-a-half hours (shorter for children), and were conducted in and around Atlanta, Boston, Chicago and Toronto on 359 subjects between 1972 and 1981. Topics were covered under four headings: 'Life review', 'Life-shaping experiences and relationships', 'Present values and commitments', and 'Religion'. These interviews were recorded and transcribed in full for analysis.[28]

RESEARCH RESULTS

Fowler insisted that his stages were not to be understood as an achievement scale. They were not to be used either to evaluate the worth of people, or as educational or therapeutic goals towards which to hurry or pressurize people.

Having made that clear, he reported his group as finding 23 people at Faith Stage 1 (all but one age 6 years or under); 25 were at Stage 2 (all but one between 7 and 12); 86 were at Stage 3, 89 at Stage 4, 25 at Stage 5, and just one at Stage 6. The remaining 110 cases in the interview sample were described as being in 'intermediate' stages.

COMMENT ON THE RESULTS

There is a problem in deciding on a set of categories and then interviewing people to see if they fit them, in the hope of establishing support for a theory. This is an example of circular thinking. In addition, although evenly divided by sex and age group, the sample was mainly white and at least 85 per cent Christian, with about 11 per cent Jewish.

It is difficult to say, then, that these results satisfactorily confirm Fowler's theory of stages of faith development. For example, no evidence is provided for his statement about faith being 'a universal feature of human living', because only a few world faiths are represented. People with agnostic, atheist and humanist beliefs and lifestyles are also excluded. The high proportion of people in intermediate stages is also a problem that the theories, and Fowler's book, insufficiently explain.

From a scientific perspective, therefore, Fowler's results are flawed. They prove little; but this does not mean they are worthless. More sophisticated modern research methods may yet give them weight. Furthermore, descriptively, to explain people to themselves and each other, they are extremely useful. For this reason, Fowler's theories have been widely acclaimed and continue to be

---

27 Except Stage 3, which is significantly longer.
28 Fowler (1995) *ibid.*, pp.307–12.

taught in theological colleges and elsewhere. As a detailed bridge in helping to understand spirituality in terms of psychology, they are unparalleled.

Spirituality is deeply personal and essentially subjective. It is difficult for a person to report spiritual experiences accurately, and it is difficult for another person to interpret such a description with objectivity in a way that is meaningful and does it justice. Any well-considered account of such experiences, and the way they develop through life, is of value. It helps if the interpreter, acknowledging a degree of subjectivity, has had a similar experience and can relate positively to it, that is if the interviewee's account somehow 'rings true'.

This resonance is important. If the accounts of Fowler's stages ring true with readers, a consensus builds that gradually increases both their truthfulness (validity) and their usefulness. This may not be a strictly scientific approach. Nevertheless, the experiment is worth the attempt. It is also persuasive when descriptions, such as those of Fowler, are consistent with those from other sources.

Summary points

1. *Shifting the paradigm*
A paradigm is a way of construing the world which underlies the theories, principles and methodologies of science during a particular period of history. A paradigm shift is necessarily a development of what has gone before.

2. *Contemporary authors on spirituality*
John Swinton, David Fontana and Victor Schermer are leading proponents of a new 'psycho-spiritual' paradigm for psychology.

3. *Schermer's views*
Schermer explains his personal reasons for adopting the paradigm, describing five challenges to his former way of thinking. He says spirituality is not an 'add-on' to our basic drives and energies, but an integral part, informing and structuring them.

4. *Challenges to the 'pristine ego'*
These begin in infancy and represent defining moments for the spiritual self, which seeks to maintain its unspoiled nature while at the same time surviving and growing in a human body, in time and space.

5. *Another pioneer thinker*

James Fowler also thought of faith (spirituality) as involving an orientation of the total person. It gives purpose and direction to one's hopes and strivings, thoughts and actions.

6. *Fowler's theory*

Fowler developed and tested a theory involving six stages of faith, based on the ideas of Piaget, Erikson and Kohlberg. Although the numerical results of his research are questionable, Fowler's descriptive accounts of the stages are very useful.

Exercises and questions for personal reflection and as a basis for group discussion:

1. 'A paradigm is a model that incorporates values, assumptions and beliefs accepted by the scientific community.' Think about this statement. Do you agree with it? Alternatively, do you think that science is designed to be 'objective' in such a complete way that it removes the necessity for assumptions and beliefs, offering people a uniform set of 'rational' values based on its findings? Discuss this with someone you respect who does not necessarily fully agree with you.

2. Both Schermer and Fowler indicate two conflicting elements in the newborn:

   (a) a pristine ego, seeking to retain its unspoiled spiritual nature as a spiritual self that promotes the maturity of the individual throughout life

   (b) a body-bound consciousness, subject from early on to anxiety and distress through feeling pain, discomfort, frustration, abandonment, emptiness and insatiability.

   Do you agree that divorcing the body-mind from spiritual self could leave people estranged from themselves, each other and their origins, and so be a source of the collective neuroses and psychoses of humanity? Please think about this now and bear the question in mind as you read on in this book.

3. Fowler says that faith is a universal feature of human living, recognizably similar everywhere, despite the remarkable variety of forms and contents of religious practices and belief. Does this ring true for you? To what extent have you knowledge of one faith tradition? (None, some, a moderate amount, much or an expert level?) How does this compare with your knowledge of other faiths? Try to find someone from another faith background to discuss this with.

PART 2

STAGES OF FAITH

'Something Happens'

Chapter 6

INTRODUCTION TO PART 2

Overview

Schermer writes of a 'spiritual malaise' resulting from the widespread divorcing of mind from spirit, of psychology from a spiritual dimension (see Chapter 5). This, he says, is an important factor in the collective neuroses and psychoses of humanity. Describing recovering patients with alcohol dependence, Schermer emphasizes in contrast that a spiritual factor has been responsible for beneficial changes, great enough for anyone to see.

At the personal level, we must therefore ask how the split – between a body-bound, earth-bound, time-bound, 'everyday ego', beset by desire and the imperative to survive, on the one hand, and a constant, unspoiled 'spiritual self' on the other – develops through the life cycle. We are also wise to ask how this split may be healed.

At the social level, the question arises as to how the separation between the everyday ego and the spiritual self in individuals results in forms of collective maladaptation and insanity, including widespread conflict. We are also wise to ask similarly what remedies may be applied to these social ills.

These are the questions addressed in Part 2, through an examination and extension of Fowler's six stages of faith. It will be necessary to look more closely than he did at the transition points between stages, also to consider more deliberately the interplay between personal and social psychology. We begin with a parable: a made-up story aimed at illustrating points of wisdom.

The tribe parable

Two men once lived with their tribe in a deep gorge, tucked into the slopes of a steep mountain range close by the ocean. The geography of the place was such that clouds and a dense layer of mist hung perpetually over the steep-sided valley. The people dwelling there seldom encountered direct sunlight, living out their lives in humidity, twilight and gloom.

A REVELATION

One day, one of the young men made his way to a high peak, and momentarily caught a glimpse of sunlight striking the rock-face. He felt its warmth on his skin. This was very rare, and the experience changed him. He began to question in his mind what had happened. When he asked others, including his parents and the tribal elders, they said it must have been a dream or an illusion; yet he knew himself to have been awake and in his right mind.

DOUBTS AND QUESTIONS

The certainty of the experience of sunlight stayed with him, and he found himself wondering if what the elders always taught and what the tribe believed could be mistaken in other ways. The rituals, directed by his tribe towards a deity they prized for keeping them hidden and safe in their cloud-covered valley, began to lose meaning for him. He began to prize clear-headed thinking over the tribe's routine practice of imbibing powerful narcotic intoxicants during their rituals.

PRESSURE TO STAY

The youth took to spending time alone, away from the tribal village, so that he could think for himself without interruption or distraction. He returned frequently to the hilltop where he had had his life-changing vision. Others in the tribe, especially from his family, noticed this change in behaviour, and began to encourage him to rejoin and recommit himself to group activities. The elder women said it was time for him to choose a wife. The men said he should be given his own dwelling and land, so he could start growing crops for himself. When he resisted, requesting patience, members of the tribe began thinking of him as strange. He was pressing uncomfortably against invisible and long-accepted boundaries of attitude and conduct.

THE DECISION TO LEAVE

Apart from one friend who stayed loyal, the young man felt increasing discomfort among his own people, and with it a rising curiosity for an explanation about his experience on the hilltop. He decided to make a journey. Whatever the risks, he felt he must take them or never again know inner peace. This had happened before. A man had left the tribe approximately once in every few decades, but none had ever returned.

TWO SET OFF

After much discussion, the young man managed to persuade his loyal friend to leave the security of the tribe and accompany him. Eventually, they set off on their pilgrimage, having to climb steeply, travelling inland over high passes through similar valleys for several days. The friend's disquiet grew with the distance travelled, intensifying until, during a fierce thunderstorm, his resolve gave way. He had grown terribly afraid, and now insisted on returning to the tribe where he was welcomed back with rejoicing.

ONE CONTINUES

Saddened, the first youth carried on, all the more determined to conquer his doubts and difficulties. Eventually, cresting a final peak, he came upon a watercourse flowing away from his tribal land towards the plain below. He followed it down, and by nightfall of the following day had reached even ground.

THE NEW COUNTRY

Waking the next morning, the traveller was struck by the clear sky, the dry air, the bright sunlight, the brilliance of the colours around him and the pleasant if unaccustomed force of the heat. It brought immediate joy to his heart, and a sense of validation, a calming of his earlier doubts and fears.

Travelling on, he met the local people. To his surprise and pleasure, they spoke a similar language and looked like his own people, although – the climate being warmer – their skins were a shade darker and they dressed differently, wearing more colourful clothing of lighter material. They offered him food, and he noticed some differences here too. There were delicious fruits growing locally that he had not seen or tasted before. There was a greater variety of crops, and animals had been domesticated for farming, rather than having to be hunted or trapped.

Above all, the youth noticed how much more cheerful the people he encountered were, compared with his own people. They were welcoming and friendly too. Their smiles made the young women seem to him more attractive. He could understand why no one ever went back to the dark valley from which he had come.

RESPONSIBILITY

Life was so much better in the bright daylight. The young man in exile from his own tribe found work on a farm, and felt increasingly comfortable there. Nevertheless, he remembered his family and friends. He felt a responsibility towards them. In due course, after several months, he made up his mind to return and tell them what he had found. He wanted to persuade some at least to follow him back, to take the risk of leaving the valley and share in a much better life.

THE RETURN
The young man said farewell to his new friends on the sunlit plain and retraced his steps. Fearless now, the return journey did not seem so hard. He simply followed the watercourse back up into the mountains, returning over the high passes to the cloud-covered valley of his tribe.

GREETED WITH MISTRUST
Among the first people he met was his former loyal friend. He was happy to see him, but his friend acted strangely, feeling ashamed at having abandoned him on the hillside. He was confused by the young man's joy. Expecting reproach, he barely recognized the smiling man in front of him. He was bewildered by the darker shade of his skin and his colourful clothing; and so he mistrusted his words.

'The sun shines every day on the plain,' the returning pilgrim was saying. 'Everyone is happy and content. There is so much life, so much vivid colour. The crops grow in abundance. The animals grow fat. There is enough for all to share. The people are very well fed, and they are very friendly. Life is much less of a struggle.'

REJECTION
He asked his friend to have courage and return to the plain with him, insisting that the journey was perfectly safe. 'Please join me,' he said. 'We will return later and together will persuade others to make the journey. Perhaps we can resettle everyone and be hailed as heroes.' But his friend was not persuaded by this entreaty and grew even firmer in his decision to stay. Later in life, this man became one of the tribal leaders in his turn, and was eventually acclaimed their chief.

The young man remained in the tribal valley for several weeks. He grew desperate to change his friend's mind, but he only noticed himself growing frustrated and gloomy again. His friend could not conceive of and believe in the existence of a sunlit country where people lived calm, happy lives of friendship and contentment. He remained convinced that he would be better off in familiar surroundings.

The young man also spoke to his parents, brothers and sisters, and was soon asked to go to speak to the tribal elders. In each case, the response was the same. No one wanted to make the journey over the mountains to the plain. Their minds were closed. 'That is not for us,' people told him. 'We have our ways, the ways of our ancestors. We belong here.'

FEELING INCREASINGLY ALIEN

Sometimes the young man pleaded with his relatives. Sometimes he grew impatient and angry with the intransigence of the elders. Sometimes he even began to doubt his own experience of the world outside the valley, and sometimes he felt saddened, guilty and ashamed at the distress he was causing others whom he loved. He did not want to leave them, but felt increasingly alien among them. He again began spending time alone. He was confused and bewildered. He needed more time, and freedom from distraction, to think.

Eventually the young man came to understand that, in his heart, he had outgrown his tribe and its ways. He could not convert any among them to see matters his way. He felt shunned by the elders, who remained steadfastly indifferent to the outside world and intolerant of his message. They seemed close to branding him an outcast, as someone dangerous, a polluter of ancient tribal wisdom.

CONSEQUENCES

Unable to identify fully with his people, the youth decided to leave his tribe once again, returning to the sunlit plain below. He never went back. He had, however, sown some powerful seeds. Although he was never to know it, his actions did have positive consequences. Tribal children from future generations heard the stories about a young man who left, returned with tales of wonder from the plain and went away again. Some were inspired to follow in his footsteps, to go to see for themselves.

Some of these, in turn, made their way back to the tribe to confirm the earlier reports of an easier and happier life to be had elsewhere. Others eventually followed. There was finally a great exodus from the valley, with large numbers of the tribe's people relocating and integrating with the communities on the plain, taking their animals with them. A remnant, comprising mainly older people left behind, withered quickly. In time, the shaded valley was left empty. Only a few carved totems and ruined stone buildings remained.

INTERPRETING THE PARABLE

This story will serve to illustrate many points as we discuss spiritual development over the following chapters.

It emphasizes, first, the strong interactions between individuals and the communal groups to which they belong.

Second, it exemplifies that attachments, threats and losses, and thus priorities and values, operate at both personal and group levels, and these may be at odds with each other. In this case, tribal attachments to traditional beliefs and practices were threatened by the young man's attachment to liberty and the prospect of an easier, happier way of life.

The third point that the story demonstrates is how a single experience (that of sunlight for the youth) can bring about a universal realignment of someone's thinking and way of being, can ignite a passionate quest for a new vision of reality, a new truth, setting them off on a kind of pilgrimage. This is the nature of spiritual awakening, at least for some people. For others, it is a more gradual process, like those future generations of the tribe, influenced little by little by folklore surrounding the first youth's adventures.

Finally, the story reveals several stages of individual development the young man has to go through to reach personal and spiritual maturity. During Fowler's 'conformist' Stage 3, for example, a person adheres to the culture, authority, values, belief system, rituals and other established behavioural practices of the family and communal group, in this case the tribe. Degrees of difference are tolerated, often encouraged, so that each new generation has a way of distinguishing itself from those that precede it. Nevertheless, as we will see later, there remains a degree of conformity about the new differences. Real challenges to the old order are much less well tolerated and are usually energetically resisted. The threat to long and strongly held attachments, and therefore to communal stability, is experienced as unacceptably great.

The significance for the individual is massive. The drive to belong to a group and retain the security this affords now appears to be in direct contrast to another powerful drive: to be more independent and think things through for oneself. Entering Fowler's 'individual' Faith Stage 4 involves recognizing this, and beginning to work out for oneself the ideal balance between the two. You are torn between exploring the new territory and staying behind where all is familiar and feels safe. This is not simply an academic exercise. A person has to travel around in the new country, genuinely to investigate its similarities and differences, and to live by the new conventions in different circumstances, rather than just think about what it might be like to go there.

Whatever the new environment is like, going into new territory involves loss. It involves leaving place, people and other attachments behind. The emotions of loss on occasions like this may include bewilderment, doubt, anxiety, anger, shame and guilt. Then sadness supervenes, heralding healing, recovery and a return to calm, confident, joyful, contented acceptance of the changes involved.

The people left behind also feel naturally aggrieved, and are subject to a similar set of painful emotions, but with less likelihood of relief. Living with small, partial certainties robs individuals and groups alike of the kind of holistic vision required for emotional healing and spiritual growth. Even religious groups are affected when their version of their faith is partial, therefore partisan and exclusive.

These are among the dangers of individuals and groups conforming in a blinkered way with each other, as they do in Stage 3. They come to be dominated by 'either/or', dualistic thinking, a way of being that divides people into 'us' and 'them', separating ideas, beliefs and practices into 'right' and 'wrong'. Conflict arises easily during Stage 3, both within and between groups. Anger (based on resistance) and fear (based on anxiety), directed at specific threatening people, ideas or other factors, are the frequently prevailing emotions. Doubt, bewilderment, shame, guilt and sorrow are less well tolerated, and usually therefore denied and repressed. Hidden and unresolved emotions like these are the basis of all neuroses.

Stage 3 is therefore best seen as a way-station rather than an endpoint on the spiritual journey. It is a kind of frontier that only relatively few cross completely. Stage 4, in consequence, involves mentally separating oneself from the larger group, beginning to take responsibility for one's own thoughts, words, actions and emotions.

Stage 4 can involve a lonely and difficult period, often prolonged for two main reasons. The first is that we often try, like the youth in the parable, to influence those we would rather not leave behind, to have them follow us in the development of our ideas and new life choices. Some spend many unhappy years in this half-in, half-out kind of limbo.

Second, we also often invest a great deal and travel far, so to speak, trying to discover a new group to which to conform that does not have the perceived faults of our former group. This desire, too, is often frustrated. However good one might feel about adopting, and being adopted by, a new group, a degree of alienation persists, a subtle, disquieting awareness that wholeness of self must involve something of what we have left behind, as well as the new goodness that we have discovered.[1]

Stage 4 is therefore a period of mixed thoughts and feelings, a time dominated by deep-seated ambivalence. The discomfort, due to a persisting dissonance between everyday ego and spiritual self, prompts and encourages the individual to continue to seek healing. We will examine this (using the example of Barack Obama's) in due course.

---

1   Tobias Jones, in his book *Utopian Dreams* (2007) London: Faber and Faber, goes in search of communities and associations formed to provide idealistic alternatives in England and Italy, giving a vivid description and his own impressions. They include: Damanhur (www.damanhur.org), Emmaus (www.emmaus.org.uk), Hartrigg Oaks (www.jrht.org.uk/Housing+and+care+services/ Retirement+living+and+support/Hartrigg+Oaks), Libera Terra (www.libera.it) Nomadelfia (www.nomadelfia.it) and Pilsdon Manor (www.pilsdon.org.uk), all accessed on 22 May 2010. While praising them generally, Jones finds none fully satisfactory.

Eventually, enabling a move forward towards and into Fowler's 'integration' Faith Stage 5, a second kind of spiritual awakening occurs, as it did to another person whose life is explored in a later chapter, holocaust victim and heroine Etty Hillesum. Again, either abruptly in some form of epiphany or more gradually, a person comes to recognize that, at the most profound level, separateness is an illusion. We are all one.

The key realization is that a person does not need to join this group or that group, based on these ideas, values, beliefs and practices or those, because we each already belong to a universal group: humanity at large. It is our true selves, our souls, which tell us incontrovertibly that this is so. We come to recognize that we are part of and inseparable from a spiritual reality that is holistic, holy, indivisible, divine, complete, perfectly whole.

That most people already have intuitive knowledge of this in childhood is discussed in the next chapter. During adulthood, the dissonance between everyday ego and spiritual self diminishes as the split between them is healed. We discover again that we are seamlessly and inseparably unified with nature and the cosmos, with each other, and with whatever it is that people refer to as God.

This often feels like a kind of homecoming, and marks the beginning of spiritual maturity. Stage 5 involves somehow reworking and re-evaluating our personal history, altering our values and behaviour to accommodate the new, holistic wisdom until, naturally embodying attitudes of compassion and wisdom, becoming natural healers and teachers, we may embark on Stage 6.

Different trajectories

The young man and his friend in the parable were on different trajectories of spiritual development.[2] The friend, whose courage failed and whose allegiance to the tribe ultimately outweighed his loyalty to his ally, was attached to conformity and afraid of change. Dissonance within him between his everyday ego and a spiritual self that was fully identified with tribal culture grew stronger the further his thoughts and actions took him from the tribal village. New experiences brought on discomfort. As a result of both biological and social conditioning, he lacked the capacity for individuation. He was unable to break free.

The youth, on the other hand, had an unusual spark of independence. For him, after the first awakening experience of sunshine, personal-spiritual dissonance arose more strongly when he failed to think and act independently of the tribal group. Nevertheless, he was pulled both ways and experienced strong ambivalence for a while.

---

2   See figure 1.1, p.29.

Despite breaking away, some loyalty remained that compelled him to return, to try to convert the tribe to his new understanding of the wider world outside the valley. This is the transition zone between Stages 3 and 4. He needed to accept the losses involved, to grieve and let go of his tribal past; then he was free to move on and find his future in the sunlit valley across the mountains. Accepting the people of the plain as both similar to, but also different from those of his own tribe, he was able to integrate with them successfully. He was well on the way to Stage 5.

VALUES

The split between mind and spirit can also be seen to play itself out in terms of two contrasting sets of values at work in contemporary society. Wherever people live on the planet, and in whatever fashion, all are affected by the global economy and the values embedded within it.

This set of values, driven by the profit motive and the laws of supply and demand, is essentially materialistic, even mercenary. The values are also divisive, result in the development of self-interest groups and pit people into competition with each other. They have a tendency to involve sequences of short-term and opportunistic projects, rather than carefully planned, robust and enduring endeavours. They are the expedient values of the everyday ego, aiming simply to survive and flourish while facing both threats and opportunities.

The other, contrasting set of values at work in the world is that of spiritual values associated with the true self, the soul. At the deepest level of a person's 'psyche', seamless communication with the Absolute, with the divine realm of the spirit, informs us of ultimately undeniable and vital links with each other, with nature, the planet and the cosmos. The values arising from even glimpses of this reality are imbued with both wisdom and compassion.

These two go together, because wisdom without compassion is false, and compassion without wisdom can lead to exhaustion. Combining compassion and wisdom produces an attitude of mature and selfless love, the actions of which are based firmly on the golden rule of doing to others only what we would wish done to ourselves.

Some of the spiritual values, virtues or attributes arising from mature love, from wisdom and compassion are listed in Box 6.1:

Box 6.1: Some spiritual values

Honesty	Discernment
Trust	Humility
Kindness	Courage
Generosity	Compassion
Tolerance	Wisdom
Patience	Beauty
Perseverance	Hope

It is easy to see how complete honesty and unbounded generosity might undermine the efforts of those interested in economic profits – from the advertising and sale of goods, for example. People will argue that wealth creation can benefit everyone, and there is an element of truth here when material benefit alone is considered. However, if some are being exploited for the benefit of others, spiritual values are being compromised. Think about low-paid labourers and factory hands in far-off places. Think too about consumers enticed into spending on what may not be essential for them at the expense of more basic goods and services: housing, food, clothing, healthcare and education, for example.

It seems fair to say, then, that worldly or material values, driven by the demands of the global economy, are potentially constructive, especially when moderated and balanced by spiritual values. It is when they override and dominate spiritual values that they become a force for harm and destruction. Here is the root cause of conflict, hardship, war, famine and all the other man-made evils besetting a humanity still, in many ways, passing through collective adolescence.

We have yet to learn to mature in faith, to grow spiritually; and in the following chapters the journey for each individual is mapped out through six stages, beginning with childhood.

The more people in each generation make this journey successfully, discovering the joy, serenity and contentment to be experienced, and the more who reach the later stages and spontaneously begin teaching and healing others, the sooner will humanity pass through its painful adolescent passage to achieve a more mature, much easier and happier future. The world is so destined to become a better place.

People will have to ensure that spiritual values inform and prevail over material values, learning first how to achieve this in their own lives. In other words we all need to develop spiritual skills, and to do so by engaging regularly in spiritual (not necessarily religious) practices.

Summary points

1. *Questions*

Divorcing mind from spirit leaves people estranged from themselves, each other and their origins, giving rise to questions to be examined at personal and social levels; how does this split develop through the life cycle, and how may it be healed? How does self-dissonance in individuals result in collective malaise and conflict? What remedies may be applied to social ills of this type?

2. *Parable*

A parable describes a youth breaking free from his tribe and its attachments to place, people and culture, discovering a new, easier and happier life elsewhere.

3. *Interpretation*

Interpretation of the parable is discussed in four ways. Strong interactions are noted between individuals and communal groups. Attachments operating at both personal and group levels may be at odds with each other. A single experience can bring about a universal realignment of someone's thinking and way of being. The parable reveals important aspects of Stages 3, 4 and 5 faith development.

4. *Further comments*

The adventurous youth and his more hesitant friend are compared. For the friend, dissonance grew the further his thoughts and actions took him from his tribe and tribal traditions. For the youth, discomfort grew when he failed to think and act independently.

5. *Worldly and spiritual values*

Materialistic, economic values are potentially beneficial but ultimately divisive, in contrast to spiritual values like honesty and generosity. The ideal is for the latter to prevail over and inform the former; then the people of the world – currently going through a kind of adolescence – could enjoy better, happier, easier lives.

Exercises and questions for personal reflection and as a basis for group discussion:

1. Reflect on the statement, 'Divorcing mind from spirit leaves people estranged from themselves, each other and their origins.' What do you make of this? Do you think there might be a spiritual dimension to world problems? Discuss your thoughts with someone else.

2. Think about the people you live among, relate to and interact with at local, national and international levels. Do you consider there to

be communities and cultural groupings, some that you belong to and others you don't? How are they similar to tribal groups, and how do they differ? Can you think of a very exclusive group or club, holding to a strong set of rules, values or traditions? How might it feel to be an insider? Or an outsider?

3. Think about the young man in the parable. Are you more like him, adventurous and free-thinking? Or are you more of a traditionalist, like his friend? What are the advantages of each attitude? What type of situation or experience might turn a traditionalist into a free-thinker?

4. Make sure you understand the section on values. Read it again if necessary. Can you think of examples from your own experience where profit-driven, short-term expediency (based on material values) overruled more compassionate concerns (based on spiritual values) for those affected? Rehearse in your own mind (and/or in conversation with someone else) the discussions that arose, the advantages and disadvantages of going ahead with a project from which some would gain and others suffer. Look at it from both sides, and try really hard to put yourself in the place of those who were going to lose out. How much is that usually allowed to influence what happens?

Chapter 7

CHILDHOOD SPIRITUALITY

Children are spiritual beings

John, a six-year-old, speaking to researcher Rebecca Nye told her how he 'sees' God:

> With my mind and with my eyes. Sometimes I feel that…I am in a place with God in heaven and I'm talking to him… And there's room for us all in God. He's… God's…well, he is in all of us… He's in everything that's around us. He's that microphone. He's that book. He's even… He's sticks. He's paint. He's everything around us…inside our heart…heaven.[1]

John is remarkable in using a language that speaks directly about God, but his profound awareness of a sacred and unified reality is not unique among children. Educators and researchers are discovering that it is commonplace for very young people to have rich and varied spiritual lives.

American psychologist Tobin Hart described children as 'natural contemplatives'. He tells, for example, of eight-year-old Miranda at the beach one day with her father who watched her stand for 90 minutes up to her waist in the sea, swaying with the tide. She said to her dad immediately afterwards, 'I was the water… I was the water. I love it and it loves me. I don't know how else to say it.'[2]

---

1 Hay, D. and Nye, R. (2006) *The Spirit of the Child* (rev. edn). London: Jessica Kingsley Publishers, p.102. (Hay wrote eight of the chapters. Nye wrote the other two. First published in 1998.)
2 Hart, T. (2003) *The Secret Spiritual World of Children*. Maui: Inner Ocean, p.47. As I was preparing to write this chapter, one rainy morning I saw something similar. A small boy was waiting for his mother outside a building, apparently transfixed with wonder at the raindrops falling on his upturned hands. Totally absorbed by the experience, nothing else seemed to matter to him in that moment.

Adams, Hyde and Woolley also stress that spirituality is integral to every child's life.[3] They add that it is a part often invisible to the adult world and not always sufficiently valued or nurtured. Hay and Nye come to similar conclusions.

Why children's spirituality is important

According to Brendan Hyde, a member of the Australian College of Educators and another researcher in the field, children's spirituality is important because it underpins altruistic and ethical behaviour throughout life.[4] He relates the story of Tam, a young girl, who notices that a younger boy, George, is unable to reach the tap of a drinking fountain in a playground. When her teacher approaches and asks if she is coming inside, Tam says she is, but says too that she thinks she should get a small chair for George to stand on as he cannot reach the tap to get a drink. Having been in a similar situation before, Tam is relating to George in his difficulty. Her natural compassionate desire to help him has been aroused.

Children's spirituality is important too, Hyde states, as a basis for finding enduring meaning, purpose and connectedness throughout life. Giving the example of a young boy, Jake, faced with the death of his beloved pet dog (who wonders spontaneously if maybe Scamper's spirit is somehow alive in one of the pups newly born in a house down the street), Hyde suggests how aspects of children's spirituality may help them when losses and other forms of adversity are encountered. This is especially noteworthy for workers in the field of paediatric medicine, including palliative childcare. As Bluebond-Langner makes clear, spiritual matters are important to children who develop serious illnesses, and such children often keep their experiences private, often as a way of trying to protect their parents.[5]

Hyde summarizes that children's spiritual awareness needs to be discovered, acknowledged and nurtured if they are to grow into holistic people who are not only cognitively, but also socially, emotionally and spiritually, developed.[6] As we will see later, this could have wide-ranging social consequences.

---

3   Adams, K., Hyde, B. and Woolley, R. (2008) *The Spiritual Dimension of Childhood*. London: Jessica Kingsley Publishers, p.9.

4   Hyde, B. (2008) *Children and Spirituality: Searching for Meaning and Connectedness.* London: Jessica Kingsley Publishers, p.19.

5   Bluebond-Langner, M. (1980) *The Private Worlds of Dying Children*. Princeton, NJ: Princeton University Press.

6   Hyde, *ibid.*, p.20.

Research into childhood spirituality
ERRONEOUS EARLY IDEAS
Educational psychologist Ronald Goldman, working in the 1960s, found that children had difficulty understanding religious narratives, particularly the text of the Bible. As a result of his limited investigations, he proposed that direct sensations of the divine were practically unknown in children.[7] His views, although incorrect, were barely questioned and remained highly influential for many years.

According to David Hay, Goldman made the same mistake as many educational psychologists by maintaining a strong cognitive bias in his research. He was wrong to assume spiritual awareness always to be extraordinary and equated with mystical ecstasy, rather than considering it possibly normal, an ordinary aspect of young children's everyday experience.[8]

Another researcher who also considered it mistaken to give priority to intellectual operations in the attempt to understand children's spirituality was American child psychiatrist Robert Coles. Hay cites a large-scale study undertaken by Coles over many years at Harvard University in which Coles reported on numerous conversations with children from many different countries and cultural backgrounds.[9] He insisted on listening to what the children said without laying his own interpretation on their narratives. As a result, he began thinking of spiritual awareness as a universal human attribute, and this observation provoked Hay to set out (with Nye, his research assistant) to examine how, from childhood, spirituality might be rooted in normal human awareness.

THE DECLINE OF SPIRITUAL AWARENESS IN LATE CHILDHOOD
Some important and rather disquieting evidence was already available. Maria Bindl in 1965, for example, produced over 8000 drawings on religious themes by Christian schoolchildren aged from 3 to 18 years.[10] Her methods have been criticized, but her findings remain interesting because she appears to have identified a four-part developmental sequence:

1. *A naïve relatedness to the 'Wholly Other' (God)*
   God is experienced simply, in an 'I–Thou' relationship.

---

7   Goldman, R. (1964) *Religious Thinking from Childhood to Adolescence.* London: Routledge and Kegan Paul.
8   Hay, D. and Nye, R. (2006) *The Spirit of the Child* (rev. edn). London: Jessica Kingsley Publishers, p.50.
9   Coles, R. (1992) *The Spiritual Life of Children.* London: HarperCollins.
10 Maria Bindl's original paper in German is quoted by Hay and Nye (2006) *The Spirit of the Child*, pp.55–6.

2. *A decline in spontaneous spiritual experiences*
Reason displaces fantasy and the powerful experience of the 'Wholly Other' begins to fade.

3. *A narcissistic reversion towards one's own self*
Awareness of the 'Wholly Other' is closed off by self-preoccupation.

4. *A consciously striven for relation to transcendence*
This return occurs in the later teenage years, but only in some cases.

According to Hay,[11] Bindl's findings in Germany were supported by those of Leslie Francis in England published in 1987, and those of Kalevi Tamminen in Finland, published in 1991. Both demonstrated high levels of religious or spiritual interest up to the age of eight years (Francis) or 12 years (Tamminen), followed by a steep decline.

This drop-off appears to reflect contradictory educational influences coinciding, for example, with a child's first serious introduction to the traditions of science, often also accompanied by overt religious scepticism.

Hay offers the conjecture that the 'blotting out' of spirituality is culturally mediated, adding that intellectualist theories of religion need to be complemented by a similarly strong interest in the nature of spiritual awareness. There is a distinction, he points out, between 'knowledge about' naturally occurring phenomena (which is intellectual) and 'direct knowledge of' these (which is holistic). Both, he insists, are of value.

A PROBLEM OF LANGUAGE

In a Western, technologically sophisticated and industrialized society, children quickly pick up on cues provided by adults and their peers about the use of specifically religious language and imagery. This is widely discouraged in secular culture, and there is strong pressure on children to conform.

This proved a problem for researchers like Clive and Jane Erricker who, in the 1990s,[12] pointed out the difficulty of identifying an immutable spirituality in children in a social context where normal spiritual or religious language is either absent, suppressed or repressed because of problems of plausibility in a modern, scientific culture.

A SOLUTION

In search of a solution, Hay and Nye again stress the importance of letting children speak for themselves, and allowing them to do so in an environment

---

11   Hay and Nye, *ibid.*, pp. 55–7.
12   Erricker, C. and Erricker, J. (1996) 'Where Angels Fear to Tread: Discovering Children's Spirituality.' In R. Best (ed.) *Education, Spirituality and the Whole Child.* London; Cassell, pp. 184–95.

where they can describe their experiences and express their inner worlds without fear of criticism or ridicule. Hay specifically warns against underestimating the difficulty of providing a safe setting like this. He also warns of a problem common to researchers into spirituality at all ages: the 'myth of objectivity'.

Spirituality is deeply subjective, and a detached attitude towards the object of this type of qualitative social research is bound to be problematic. By way of remedy, Hay calls it necessary for the researcher to engage 'mindfully', employing 'total awareness'. Only this high degree of focus can then, he says, provide an instrument engaged in understanding and interpreting the information that emerges as a result of the bond created with the child.[13]

To gain the best chance of understanding and interpreting the children in the study accurately, Rebecca Nye therefore deliberately adopted a near-meditative approach, her aim being to reduce to a minimum the amount of distraction from inner prompts and desires, from subtle expectations and wishes for certain kinds of responses from the child being interviewed.

To ensure that she was not encountered as a total stranger, Nye also spent a half-day as a helper in each of the school classes from which the children she was to interview were drawn, and attended the schools' assemblies.

HAY AND NYE'S RESEARCH
The study involved 38 children of either six to seven years (18 children), or 10 to 11 years (20 children), from two English primary schools. There were equal numbers of boys and girls in each group. Both groups contained seven boys and seven girls with no religious affiliation. There was a Muslim girl in each group, and two Muslim boys in the older group. The remaining children (three in each group) were Christian (Church of England two; Roman Catholic one).

Nye had up to three meetings with each child, and each tape-recorded conversation lasted about half an hour. She collected each child from their classroom and took them back afterwards, allowing for a brief, friendly chat before and after the research conversation.

Rebecca Nye later emphasized the children's willingness and enthusiasm to talk with an adult they hardly knew, describing this as a sign of their generosity of spirit. She added that, in almost every case, something more was present. She somehow had the repeated sense that a child's unique spirituality was being expressed in how and what they spoke about. 'Something more

---

13 Hay and Nye, *ibid.*, p.97. This echoes contemporary advice on taking a spiritual history from adults, which 'involves engaging with the other person as an equal and listening empathically'. See Appendix 1.

was present,' Nye reported.[14] 'Something happened': something of a special and spiritual nature.

Nye noted that the expression of each child's spirituality had a markedly individual character, reflecting their unique disposition or personality. It was therefore possible to identify a kind of personal 'signature' for each of the children that pertained to their spirituality.[15] This was illustrated with reference to two of the children in the study: Ruth and Tim.

RUTH (AGE SIX)

Ruth had a profound sense of wonder and delight. Happy and articulate, she described attending Anglican Sunday School as boring, but she also imagined heaven as: 'a mist of perfume, with gold walls, and a rainbow stretched over God's throne'. She said it was pervaded by a lovely smell, 'Like the smell that you get when you wake up on a dull winter morning, and then when you go to sleep, and you wake up, the birds are chirping, and the last drops of snow are melting away, and the treetops shimmering in the breeze, and it's a spring morning.' Then she added, 'It's not a season at all, not really, because it's just a day in delight, every day.'

Nye remarks that Ruth's imaginative response, drawing on nature, her senses and an appreciation of the mysterious transformations that occur in life, pervaded many of her comments in other 'non-religious' contexts. For example, she said, 'I like nature… [Why?] Just because I like it. I don't know. And it's so beautiful to be in the world.'

Nye adds that Ruth resembled many of her peers in other respects, for instance in struggling with ideas about death and the afterlife. Like others, she tended to draw on cinematic types of fantasy to construe and explain a sense of mystery. She showed some deference to parental world-view ideas, but these were decidedly subordinate to her unique and individual spirituality at this stage.[16]

TIM (AGE TEN)

Tim's family rejected any religious affiliation, and he likewise. Despite this, he spoke spontaneously on themes broadly linked to religious matters, such as animal reincarnation, polytheism, afterlife, morality and free will.

According to Nye, the distinctive characteristic that coloured Tim's discussions was a sense of inner struggle. His allusions to the spiritual were framed as conflicting hypotheses representing a special kind of mental work.

---

14   Hay and Nye, *ibid.*, p.92.
15   *Ibid.*, p.94.
16   *Ibid.*, pp.94–5.

This framework of discomfort and struggle also characterized his sense of wonder, awe, meaningfulness and mystery.

Tim appears to have engaged in two particular spiritual dilemmas without resolving them: 'Is there a single true God?' and, 'How can we cope with the mystery of infinity?' Nye remarks that his sense of inspiration was clear, but frustrated and struggling, rather than joyful. Tim was also concerned about a similar problem regarding the efficacy or otherwise of prayer, saying that it gets annoying trying to think about because he couldn't find the answer. He worried that his brain was going to get scrambled.[17]

Tim thought of spirituality as 'a feeling of being emotionally moved', and told Rebecca Nye that he might have had 'a lot' of experiences when younger of something like God's guiding, an influence shaping his life. His spirituality was clearly marked at this stage in his life, though, by an insistence on wrestling mentally and thinking things through for himself, despite the emotional pain associated with feeling frustrated. He received no guidance from his family or elsewhere. He also readily described unusual experiences and feelings he had had when visiting churches and sacred sites, and when thinking his thoughts alone at night; but he was deriving little comfort from these. Could he have already reached Faith Stage 4?

OTHER CHILDREN

Nye states clearly that Ruth and Tim were not at all exceptional cases in the context of the whole research sample. Other children were equally forthcoming and thoughtful at times, also reticent or flippant at other times. One distinction she noted was that the older children demonstrated an ability to reflect more intentionally on their thoughts, feelings and experiences than those in the younger group.

Several children also seemed to have given up their use of religious language and spiritual imagery.[18] The biblical language at their disposal apparently failed to capture the inherent complexity and mystery the children wanted to convey, and the attempt was therefore discarded. Instead, their spiritual awareness still intact, they turned to other means of expression.

One six-year-old's sense of mystery, for example, focused more on the incomprehensibility of human nature than on any questions about God; and a ten-year-old preferred to concentrate on the messages he had in dreams (using the symbolic language of the unconscious) when relating thoughts about ultimate meaning.

---

17 *Ibid.*, p.96.
18 *Ibid.*, p.104.

RELATIONAL CONSCIOUSNESS

In commenting on the research material, over 1000 typed pages of transcribed interviews, Nye admits that while it was moving and impressive to encounter the quality of such material in children so young, there was no obvious rationale for labelling it as 'spirituality' per se. She said her intuition that these passages were representative of children's spirituality had to be justified in another way.[19]

In due course, she and David Hay were able to identify a common thread: the core category of 'relational consciousness'. They established two main aspects for this category, as follows:[20]

1. Children demonstrated an unusual level of consciousness or perceptiveness, compared with other passages of conversation spoken by that child.

2. The conversation was expressed in terms of four types of relationship:

   (a) to things

   (b) to other people

   (c) to the child himself or herself

   (d) to God.

The research authors comment regarding 'relational consciousness' that a distinctly reflective type of consciousness is involved; also that the child involved demonstrated some degree of awareness of the remarkable or 'extra-ordinary' nature of his or her own mental activity in certain contexts.

The sense of being objectively aware of themselves as 'subject' seemed particularly important. According to Nye, it was often this apparently *objective* insight into their *subjective* response that fostered a new dimension of understanding, meaning and experience.

Varieties of children's spiritual experiences

Adams, Hyde and Woolley summarize the varieties of children's spiritual experiences under the headings: moments of awe and wonder, the afterlife, ultimate questions, religious experience and the darker side of spiritual experience.[21]

---

19   *Ibid.*, p.105.
20   *Ibid.*, p.109.
21   Adams, Hyde and Woolley, *ibid.*, pp.60–70.

MOMENTS OF REVERENCE, AWE AND WONDER

Young children, like Miranda in Hart's account mentioned earlier, are constantly experiencing and expressing wonder, showing fascination, asking questions, and are curious to see, touch, taste and smell everything around them.

Canadian academic, Daniel Scott, gathered 22 adults' recollections of spiritual experiences from childhood and adolescence.[22] He noted how often the accounts had been kept secret, accompanied by a claim that they had never been told before to anyone.

One woman, Joyce, spoke of a night when she was three and her older brother took her outside to see a full moon. She recalled being astonished by its utter beauty and glimmering light. Hearing from her sibling about the relationship between the earth, the moon and the sun, Joyce felt a strong sense of connection with these three magnificent balls out in space, feeling throughout her life that she had been given a precious gift which, in her own words, 'had fed, warmed and amazed' her since that night.[23]

Adams, Hyde and Woolley note that children are particularly quick to take notice not only of nature, but also to marvel at and feel inspired by it. They also say some children have sensory experiences not available to adults. Hyde describes a nine-year-old, Lisa, who was able to see auras, lights seeming to shine around people.[24] Tobin Hart's own daughter, at age six, had similar experiences, seeing shapes and colours around both people and objects.[25]

THE AFTERLIFE

A number of researchers have remarked on children's curiosity and fascination with death and questions about a possible afterlife. Jake wondering about the spirit of his dog Scamper exemplifies this. But some children, although strongly discouraged from discussing it and often frankly disbelieved or ignored, seem to have direct experience of the dead. For example, Adams, Hyde and Woolley describe a woman, Jean, asking her six-year-old son Paul where he has been, and being surprised by his reply that he had been 'sitting on the stairs talking to Grandma'. Paul's grandmother had died some months before.[26]

Some aspects of children's spirituality clearly remain mysterious, with research throwing up more questions at this stage than it answers. Another story of Tobin Hart's concerns 18-month-old Sydney, living in a Victorian

22 Scott, D. (2004) 'Retrospective spiritual narratives: Exploring recalled childhood and adolescent spiritual experiences.' *International Journal of Children's Spirituality* 9, 1, 67–79.
23 *Ibid.*, p.75.
24 Hyde, *ibid.*, pp.14–15.
25 Hart, *ibid.*, p.123.
26 Adams, Hyde and Woolley, *ibid.*, p.63.

house in the USA, who regularly stared at a rocking chair in the house as if it were moving back and forth. Watching it like this, she would often point and say, 'Lady!' There was no sign of fear or distress, and when she later saw a photograph of someone for the first time, as if in recognition, she pointed and shouted excitedly, 'Lady!' The picture was of Sydney's great-grandmother who had lived in the house 20 years before Sydney was born.[27]

ULTIMATE QUESTIONS

Children can be expected to ask adults about death and what might lie beyond. According to Hyde, they do so as a way of weaving threads of meaning to connect with those who have died, and often link this with other deep, philosophical questions that help them explore their meaning and purpose in life.

Hart describes children as natural philosophers, often seeking to know why the human race exists, whether there is life before physical birth or after death, why people suffer, why war and poverty exist, and whether or not there is a God.[28] Many are able to develop a positive identity and sense of purpose through awareness of being part of something far greater than themselves. The questions they raise, in other words, and the experiences they have, strongly relate to their relationship with self, others, the world and sometimes also a 'transcendent other' or God.[29]

RELIGIOUS EXPERIENCE

Some children's spirituality is strongly informed and flavoured by the faith context of the family and culture to which they belong. Nevertheless, they often retain a personal element or 'signature' in terms of spiritual expression.

Robert Coles tells of Habib, a 12-year-old Muslim boy from Tunisia who spoke eloquently of his connection to Allah who, when he heard the call to prayer, would stop everything and say to Allah, 'I am only this one boy, but I believe in you.'[30] He had a special relationship with the wind, describing his conviction that Allah 'hears prayers and answers them through the wind'.[31]

Adams, Hyde and Woolley make the point that children's spiritual experiences do not have to be religious in nature. Nevertheless, children from a variety of different faith backgrounds may use religious language to describe their spiritual experiences, and it is as well to take this into account.

27   Hart, *ibid.*, p.133.
28   Hart, *ibid.*, p.91.
29   Adams, Hyde and Woolley, *ibid.*, p.66.
30   Coles, R. (1990) *The Spiritual Life of Children*. London: Harper Collins, p.199.
31   Tibetan Buddhists share a similar idea, hanging auspicious coloured flags with prayers inscribed on them from trees and buildings, allowing the winds to waft them away over the earth and into the realm of the spirit.

Gaining a good level of knowledge and appreciation of their particular faith will help understand the children's experiences in more depth.

THE DARKER SIDE OF SPIRITUAL EXPERIENCE

Hay and Nye's report of their case example, Tim, makes it clear that for some children spiritual experiences can be difficult. There may be negative associations that give rise to conflicting thoughts and painful emotions: the bewilderment and doubt of uncertainty, and the anger of frustration.

There may also be fear to the point of terror, such as when nine-year-old Joe saw his uncle's ghost.[32] These darker moments may in time either be reconsidered positively or forgotten. Months later, for example, Joe was able to explain that his uncle had come to protect rather than frighten him. But they may conversely contribute to a more lasting negative effect on children's mental life, on their thoughts, emotions and behaviour.

Starting life's spiritual journey
THE DAMPENING OF SPIRITUAL AWARENESS

Given the evidence of researchers from Maria Bindl onwards, there is a strong suggestion that the majority of children have a vivid spiritual dimension to their experiences, on a more or less everyday basis, until they are 10, 12 or a little older. It is then discouraged, particularly in Western, secularized, industrial and technological cultures, through the powerful conditioning influences of families, teachers and peer groups.

As a result of this dampening, awareness of and preoccupation with the spiritual dimension both fade and disappear. Receiving limited encouragement and having no adequate language of expression, many children's capacity for spiritual awareness atrophies very significantly (but not necessarily completely). In a minority, however, something of it persists to provoke conscious attempts at rekindling during adolescence or later.

EARLY TRAJECTORIES OF SPIRITUAL DEVELOPMENT

These observations are consistent with ideas mentioned in earlier chapters about the 'pristine ego' of the newborn. Immediately facing challenges for survival in the struggle for everyday necessities, a split soon develops between the everyday ego and the spiritual self. Those children with strong initial spiritual experiences, who retain a potent 'relational consciousness' (to use Hay and Nye's term) into adolescence and later life, can be said to follow a low trajectory of spiritual development. Should they encounter very

---

32 Adams, Hyde and Woolley, p.69.

strong discouragement, even these spiritually well-grounded children might experience displacement to a higher trajectory, as the split or dissonance between everyday ego and spiritual self is forced wider (see Chapter 1, Figure 1.1, p.29).

In contrast, according to this aspect of the 'psycho-spiritual' paradigm under discussion, those children who have weak early levels of spiritual awareness and expression begin their lives on a higher trajectory. However, they do not necessarily stay there if, for example, they encounter and are influenced by teachers skilled at nurturing the rudiments of spiritual sensitivity that remain at the core of their being, even when apparently well masked or forgotten. The religious traditions of a number of faiths hold strongly that the spiritual self, the human soul, cannot be completely extinguished.[33]

Fowler on children
COMPARING FOWLER'S WORK WITH MORE RECENT RESEARCH

James Fowler, ignoring the period of infancy when a child is not yet sufficiently self-aware, divided children's spirituality into Faith Stages 1 and 2 (see Chapter 1, Box 1.2, p.23). Fowler did not have the benefit of the more recent research. His 1981 account of children's spirituality draws on the cognitive insights of Jean Piaget as well as interviews conducted by his own research group. There is, however, a satisfying degree of coherence between Fowler's conclusions and those of more recent authors.

STAGE I

Fowler reports 'egocentric' Faith Stage 1 as lasting between ages two and six years,[34] a period during which children exhibit endless curiosity and fascination with the world about them, asking many 'what' and 'why' questions. Fowler says that this is the stage of first self-awareness, adding that the 'self-aware' child is egocentric as regards the perspective of others.[35]

---

33 Here is how the Christian monk, Thomas Merton, put it after a profound spiritual experience in March 1958: 'At the center of our being is a point of nothingness which is untouched by sin and by illusion, a point of pure truth, a point or spark which belongs entirely to God…from which God disposes of our lives, which is inaccessible to the fantasies of our own mind or the brutalities of our own will. This little point of nothingness…is so to speak His name written in us… It is like a pure diamond, blazing with the invisible light of heaven. It is in everybody, and if we could see it we would see these billions of points of light coming together in the face and blaze of a sun that would make all the darkness and cruelty of life vanish completely.' Thomas Merton (1915–1968). The quotation is from *Conjectures of a Guilty Bystander* (1966) New York, NY: Doubleday, pp.140–2.

34 Fowler's research interviews started with four-year-olds.

35 Fowler, J. (1981) *Stages of Faith*. San Francisco, CA: HarperCollins, p.133.

He also notes that by the third or fourth year children have developed an often preoccupying fear of death, particularly fear of the death of a parent.[36] He suggests that the emergent strength of this stage is the birth of imagination, the ability to unify and grasp the 'experience-world' in powerful images and as presented in stories that register the child's intuitive understandings and feelings toward the ultimate conditions of existence.[37]

Fowler makes no mention of a 'pristine ego', but the intuitive understandings he refers to seem consistent with the promptings of a 'spiritual self'. He does not say what happens to children who remain in Stage 1 into adulthood, except to remark that this is very rare. Such people, though, are likely to retain an unrealistic sense of omnipotence, and therefore either endure much repeated frustration or discover – through a combination of both threat and charm – to bend the ways of those around them in their service. Tyrants and dictators may well fit this description.

STAGE 2

At the 'conditioning' stage, Fowler offers a different explanation for the fading of spiritual awareness and change in the preoccupations of children. He remarks that, in contrast with the pre-schooler, the ten-year-old constructs a more orderly, temporally linear and dependable world.[38]

Tobin Hart calls children natural philosophers and contemplatives. Fowler, noting the capacity of older children for inductive and deductive reasoning, says that the ten-year-old has become 'a young empiricist'. He states that these children work hard at sorting out the real from the make-believe, and insist on demonstration or proof for claims of fact.

There appears to be a contradiction here, but it is not necessarily so, for empiricists are philosophers too; and Fowler adds that the child does not cease to be imaginative or capable of a highly developed fantasy life. What happens, he says, is that the products of imagination are more confined to the world of play.

He does not appear to recognize that young children may not be totally narcissistic. As in the case described earlier of Tam, wanting to help George reach the playground tap, they are capable of empathy, of imagining themselves in the predicaments of others, responding accordingly.

The kind of cognitive or intellectual developments affecting older children, first proposed by Piaget, render children vulnerable to social conditioning. No longer egocentric, more aware of the existence, similarities and differences of others, eager to please and fit in, they have become increasingly subject

---

36   *Ibid.*, p. 130.
37   *Ibid.*, p. 134.
38   *Ibid.*, pp. 135–6.

to pressures and social taboos. These include those encouraging them to suppress and avoid discussing any spiritual insights and experiences; but young children might equally be impressed and influenced at this stage by guidance and examples concerning spiritual values such as kindness, tolerance, patience and honesty.

Fowler's view is that, between 6 and 12 years, children take on the stories, beliefs and observances that symbolize belonging to their community. Stories become their main method of giving unity and value to experience. However, these children tend to give literal interpretations to religious and historical narratives and the folk tales handed down according to myth and tradition. They are also literal in their understanding of moral rules and attitudes.

This can be inhibiting. Unlike the children interviewed by Rebecca Nye, most of Fowler's subjects were not able to step back from the flow of stories to formulate reflective, conceptual meanings. Meaning, for them, was thus both carried and 'trapped' in the narrative.[39]

Fowler observed that the limitations of literalness can result either in an overcontrolling, stilted perfectionism, or in its opposite, an abasing sense of badness, embraced because of mistreatment, neglect or the apparent disfavour of family and significant others.[40] Children who do not develop much beyond Stage 2 often therefore grow into adults who feel incomplete. They are needy for confirmation of their worth, both through continual praise (which they often mistrust) and personal obedience to tight, structured, even petty, rules and conventions. People remaining at this stage of development into adulthood are often those giving tyrants and dictators the backing they need to succeed in their quest for power.

This sense of incompleteness is among the predisposing factors for both mental ill health and, when widespread, for social malaise. There is a strong and entrenched dissonance between the two selves: personal and spiritual, when spiritual awareness has not been adequately fostered, or has even been actively discouraged.

Comment

There is an obvious need for further research, including longitudinal, qualitative research into the changes in experience and expression of spirituality among children, carried forward into adolescence and young adulthood. This will require a better grasp of the new paradigm under investigation. Yet, despite some inconsistencies, a relatively coherent account of children's spirituality

---

39   *Ibid.*, p.149.
40   *Ibid.*, p.150.

is already emerging. It prepares the way for understanding many aspects of adolescent and adult spirituality, to which we now turn our attention.

Summary points

1. *The importance of children's spirituality*
Although often invisible to the adult world, it is normal for children to have rich and varied spiritual lives. This is important, because it underpins altruistic and ethical behaviour, guiding children towards enduring meaning, purpose and connectedness throughout life.

2. *Where early investigators went wrong*
Research into childhood spirituality was wrongfooted in the 1960s by an intellectual bias, until researchers began listening to what children said without laying their own interpretation on their narratives.

3. *Spiritual experiences decline in later childhood*
A reduction in spiritual awareness and expression is normal among older children in industrialized societies, under pressure to conform to a secular world view, as they encounter religious scepticism and the traditions of science.

4. *Children's spirituality shares features but is unique to each*
Hay and Nye investigated 38 schoolchildren in two age groups, around six and ten years. They discovered that, although each child's spirituality was unique, a common thread (which they labelled 'relational consciousness') could also be detected.

5. *A new dimension of experience*
Older children reflect more intentionally on their thoughts, feelings and experiences. It was often an *objective* insight into their *subjective* responses that gave them a new dimension of understanding, meaning and experience.

6. *Varieties of children's spiritual experiences*
Children's spirituality involves moments of reverence, awe and wonder, concerns the afterlife and life's ultimate questions, includes religious experiences, and may also involve a darker side of spiritual experience.

7. *Mysteries remain, but the benefits are significant*
Some aspects of children's spirituality clearly remain mysterious, with research throwing up more questions at this stage than it answers. However, it is also clear that many children are able to develop a positive identity and

sense of purpose through awareness of being part of something far greater than themselves.

8. *Spirituality's darker side, and the advisability of knowing about religions*

Some children's spiritual experiences hold negative associations and can give rise to conflicting thoughts and painful emotions. A good level of knowledge and appreciation of a child's particular faith often assists in understanding the children's experiences in more depth.

9. *Overall support for a new paradigm*

James Fowler divided children's spirituality into Faith Stages 1 and 2, with findings reasonably consistent with other researchers, and supportive of a new psycho-spiritual paradigm.

Exercises and questions for personal reflection and as a basis for group discussion:

1. Spend some time reflecting on your own early childhood. What, for example, is your first memory? Can you recall a sense of wonder and delight, moments of total absorption in your own being and your surroundings? Did you have any early specifically religious experiences, related to your own (and your family's) faith background?

2. Did you at any time experience a darker side to spirituality, finding yourself struggling, and possibly feeling alone while doing so, with life's difficult questions?

3. In later childhood, do you remember a declining interest in spiritual experiences (of awe and wonder, or over a preoccupation with death, the afterlife and life's other ultimate questions)? Did this 'just happen', or do you remember being influenced by family members, teachers or others? Were you actively encouraged to accept a more scientific world view, and discouraged from religious or spiritual explanations about things?

4. Is there a family member (parent, grandparent or sibling) who remembers your childhood with whom you can discuss these matters, comparing your recollections? Try asking people of a different generation about their experiences, and about how they would answer these questions.

5. If you are a parent, a teacher or someone else in a position to listen to children sensitively, and to observe them unobtrusively, see if you can hear comments or observe behaviour attesting to a degree of spiritual awareness of the type described in the chapter. If you have children of your own, try asking them about their experiences without seeking to impose your own interpretations on them.

Chapter 8

BELONGING

The blessed and the rest

Some people retain a strong awareness of the spiritual dimension throughout life. The everyday ego and spiritual self of such a well-integrated person are always in close sympathy, making the trajectories of their spiritual journeys very low. Most maintain and strengthen their link to the Absolute through a disciplined routine of religious and spiritual practices.

The regimen might include regular worship, scripture reading and prayer, together with more secular spiritual practices such as engaging in charitable work, attending to nature, reading poetry and philosophy, and spending time alone in contemplation while gardening, perhaps, or going for long walks.

These are truly 'spiritual beings having human experiences',[1] running an accelerated course of spiritual development to Stage 6. Everyone benefits from their presence. They are conscious of the effects of the natural order according to which each person participates inseparably in the life of everyone else. Many such spiritually mature individuals go unrecognized; others come to be thought of as great leaders, heroes and saints.

Such people often speak unself-consciously of God, and poetically describe feeling the forces of heaven working in their favour. They call this 'grace', and feel themselves to be blessed. Most of us, however, do not experience life like this, except maybe once in a while. According to James Fowler's original survey, 77 per cent of people over 11 years were identified as being either in Faith Stage 3, in Stage 4 or between the two, and most of the remainder were close.[2]

---

1   This phrase has been attributed to Pierre Teilhard de Chardin: 'We are not human beings having spiritual experiences, but spiritual beings having human experiences.'
2   Fowler, *ibid.* About 6 per cent were in transition between Stages 2 and 3; almost 10 per cent were between Stages 4 and 5. According to the survey, fewer than 10 per cent of adults were in or between Faith Stages 5 and 6.

More and better surveys are required, including longitudinal studies, but for now we can say that almost four out of five adolescents and adults, living under the influence of Westernized consumer city culture, have not yet reached spiritual maturity. This chapter and the next will therefore concentrate on these two stages and the transition between them.

Before continuing, it is necessary to clarify that, according to the psycho-spiritual paradigm presented here, people advance along the different trajectories at different speeds. Development, especially after childhood, is not necessarily age-related. This explains how people fail (at least for a time) to progress beyond the earlier stages.

Failure to progress is about slowing down or being held back, rather than about lacking potential. Like fruit on a tree that needs water, warmth and sunlight for it to ripen, everyone can be expected to make progress when the right conditions prevail.[3]

Two opposing drives

The parable about the youth in Chapter 6 illustrates how, from adolescence onwards, people are motivated by two common, but apparently opposing, drives:

1. to belong to a group

2. to experience oneself as independent-minded, as a separate person.

Faith Stage 3 is dominated by the first of these. There is a premium on wanting to feel stable and safe.

The second drive takes precedence in the more adventurous Stage 4. It necessarily involves a degree of sacrifice, but provides many with their only pathway towards significant personal and spiritual maturity. It is possible to think and act independently while remaining broadly conformist *within* a group, but only inside limits set by the group. The less tolerant the group's attitudes and the more rigid its rules and belief system, the more difficult this will be.

As we will see, opposition between the two drives can only be fully resolved after relinquishing group membership, in Stages 5 and 6. This means that, for any group or tribe, a person may be deemed a hero by following either path. In the parable, the conservative friend is celebrated at the time. In addition, the free-thinking adventurer becomes a more lasting legend later, among future generations. Both did what was right for them, holding true to their inner self at the time.

---

3   In Hebrew and Aramaic, the word for 'evil' is said also to mean simply 'unripe'. This implies that maturity is possible, resulting in evil converting to good. This is a hopeful idea.

There are many parallels today, whereby traditionalists and innovators appear opposed to each other. Those sceptical about, and even alarmed by, the relevance of spirituality in health, mental health and social care, for example, strongly resist the 'psycho-spiritual' paradigm that is under development and actively supported by others.[4] The debate is healthy; and there are heroes, people of conscience, in both camps.

Faith Stage 3
GROUP CRITERIA IN GENERAL SOCIETY
In the 21st century, with the latest developments in communication and travel and the emergence of a global economy, general society is less well defined than in the past. People hold to a variety of groupings dependent on a range of criteria that include:

- gender
- nationality (nationality of origin and, where relevant, adopted nationality)
- place (current home and neighbourhood, as well as place of origin)
- race
- language (including accent or dialect)
- skin colour
- sexual orientation
- social class
- religious (or non-religious) affiliation
- political persuasion.

People tend to identify themselves as family members (parent, sibling, child, aunt, uncle and so on) and according to marital status, together with details from the above list. This is combined with other factors that are more specific or idiosyncratic, such as level of education, income and wealth, type of work,

---

4   Psychiatrists Rob Poole and Robert Higgo, for example, object to references to spirituality in mental health care, partly (and arguably erroneously) through equating spirituality firmly with religious beliefs. Proponents of the emerging 'psycho-spiritual' paradigm would see this limited interpretation as a false representation of the holistic principles involved. See, for example, Poole, R. and Higgo, R. (2010) 'Spirituality and the threat to therapeutic boundaries in psychiatric practice.' *Mental Health, Religion and Culture* (in press). The concluding sentence of their paper reads: 'We believe that the risks involved are serious, and that there is no option but to defend existing professional boundaries.' Not everyone agrees. For a full response, see Culliford, L. (2010) 'Beware! paradigm shift under way.' *Mental Health, Religion and Culture 13* (in press)

dress, diet, hobbies, preferences for music and media viewing, sports interests and teams followed. This all contributes to our 'persona'. It amounts to who we think we are and the person we present to the world.

In everyday life, the mind dominated by the everyday ego (the ego-mind) is unaware of the spiritual dimension, and therefore assumes that a list like this of material or worldly factors is sufficient. The ego-mind holds sway particularly during Faith Stage 3. For those who go beyond the conformist stage, the important distinction involves awareness that there is more to each individual than name, family, place, race, employment, status and so on: a spiritual dimension, a truer and more complete self, a soul.

In general society today, people tend to switch allegiances more readily than in the past, making it harder for individuals to establish themselves as members of any clearly defined group. Nevertheless, the impulse to do so, and to define others similarly according to these types of criteria, remains strong.

POLARIZATION

Assisting this tendency is the fact that, even though contemporary consumerist society is amorphous, its members are all subject to and expected to conform to a number of similarities of conditions and pressures: the rule of law, for example, national allegiances, and a set of mainly secular and consumerist values transmitted relentlessly into people's homes (and their minds) via advertising and the media.

Polarization and an oppositional attitude are common in a number of important arenas. They are embedded, for example, in the legal process, and in the party politics of democracy. In the USA there are two main political groups: Democrats and Republicans. In Great Britain there are three: Conservative, Labour and Liberal Democrats, with several smaller parties.[5] In other countries, there may be more political groups, but the principle is the same everywhere. Politics in a democracy is adversarial, and people are obliged to choose and vote for one group. In Australia, for example, a person can be fined for not registering to vote, and fined again for not actually voting in all three types of elections: local, state and federal (national). It is compulsory to take sides.

A degree of liberalism notwithstanding, these factors promote the kind of black and white, right and wrong, 'us and them', essentially self-seeking and partisan, 'tribal' mentality that prevails among people during Faith Stage 3.

---

5   These words are evocative and seem to reflect the two basic drives mentioned earlier in the chapter. 'Conservative' implies a reluctance to make changes. The conservative drive is to belong. 'Liberal' means unconfined, free-thinking and of generous character. The liberal drive is to become separate and whole in oneself, and to have others do likewise.

The challenge of this chapter for some readers will be to accept that such conformist thinking and behaviour, while offering many benefits, also has significant drawbacks.

In terms of spiritual development, Stage 3 is decidedly immature. Rather than being critical, a comment intended to indicate significant potential for growth. To get a clearer picture, we will examine both risks and rewards in the context of tribal and other close-knit communities.

NATURAL DRIVES AND SELF-INTEREST

For adolescents and young adults, life can be a struggle. Priorities turn naturally to matters of survival, to acquiring education, occupation, income, property, a home, a partner and family, and simultaneously to obtaining protection and relief from life's twists and turns; from discomfort, losses and the threat of loss. We seek security, stability and freedom from pain, often to the point of luxury. These are natural drives.

Self-interest tends therefore to dominate at Stage 3. We want what seems best for ourselves and those close to us, despite the fact – if we were to think about it – that this could be at the expense of others. We recognize a need for other people, people who will give guidance and help, people we feel we can trust; so it helps to join and feel part of a secure group.

The process of identification with others to form or join a group need not be problematic. We follow our inclinations. Other members are identified, and attachments (friendships, alliances and coalitions) made accordingly. To put it simply, 'I like you' often accords directly with, 'I *am* like you'.

Faith Stage 3 is less about people having individual spiritual experiences than about adherence to a group (however strictly or loosely defined) that gives its members a meaningful sense of identity and belonging.

Traditional tribes

Part of the resistance to spiritual growth depends on the argument that, until recently, ingrained patterns of self-preservation have served mankind well. The many benefits involved in belonging to a stable, close-knit group are exemplified by a number of tribal peoples, still to be found living in relatively isolated places around the world.

According to Bruce Parry and Mark McCrum,[6] the Babongo people of Gabon in Africa, for example, believe that they were the first people on earth. From a psychological perspective, this shows how belonging to a clan or

---

6   Parry, B. and McCrum, M. (2008) *Tribe: Adventures in a Changing World.* London: Penguin Books. See also www.bbc.co.uk/tribe/bruce/index.shtml, accessed 22 May 2010. Information about other tribes mentioned in this chapter come from the same source.

tribe can provide each member with an inviolable sense of identity, and be the principal basis from which to derive a deep sense of meaning and purpose.

A number of factors enable this, notably consistency of place, appearance, language, shared values, solidarity in resistance to threat, unique forms of belief and spiritual expression, and a timeless way of life. We can trace many similarities of attitude and behaviour predominant during Faith Stage 3 back to aboriginal cultures informing our past.

PLACE (TERRITORY)
Even nomadic tribes and peoples, such as the Mongolian Darhad, wander within boundaries, governed by terrain and other features of local geography. For herdspeople and hunter-gatherers, the limits of their territory will be governed by the range covered by the animals they depend upon. Their lives are intimately bound up with the land.

So it is also with forest peoples such as the Kombai from Papua New Guinea who, in contrast, may inhabit smaller, more circumscribed territories and be more stable in terms of place. But different tribes may live relatively close together, competing for food and natural resources. Such competition, which may be hostile, even deadly at times when resources are scarce, requires tribal people to be strict about territory. A stranger entering a Kombai clan's territory, for example, is viewed as an extreme threat, potentially to life itself.

APPEARANCE
Tribal people must also be readily able to identify members of their own group and distinguish outsiders. Appearance is therefore important. Members of tribes can often be distinguished by their natural facial and other physical features. Different tribes whose members are of similar physical appearance require other ways of separating themselves. Typical tribal dress and adornments, including jewellery, together with skin painting, scarring, other markings, piercings and tattoos, perform this function.

LANGUAGE
Tribes are also distinguishable in terms of the spoken word. Within separate tribes, particularly those with a more widely spoken language, new meanings for old words, and idiosyncratic pronunciations arise. Specific, highly distinguishable dialects are formed. New words and slang also appear.

VALUES
The values adhered to are those with the tribe at the centre, reflecting the need for conformity, coherence and inner harmony.

In times of plenty, tribal people can live together in joyful equanimity. In the face of any form of threat, for example from climatic conditions such as drought or flooding, tribal welfare holds sway over individual priorities. The Hamar people, who live in the Omo Valley of Southern Ethiopia, for example, share land and also pool their livestock and labour. Communal ownership and sharing serves to preserve the structure and emotional stability of the tribal group, as well as the resources. Independent mindedness is experienced as threatening, and so discouraged.

FACING THREATS

Where there is competition from other groups, an 'us and them' mentality begins to dominate tribal attitudes. This works in the group's favour by increasing its hostility to outsiders. A calm and cheerful nature is replaced in times of threat by anxiety and specific fears (of being attacked and displaced, even annihilated). Hatred is engendered towards members of other groups, anger arising easily, leading to clashes and violence, ultimately to warfare. In many cases, this aggression serves to protect the group, but it can also be risky, provoking clashes leading to losses, injuries and deaths.

SPIRITUAL EXPRESSION

The core identity of a tribal group unifies biological, psychological, social and spiritual dimensions. Spirituality is the essential element, the life-force that underpins and motivates human existence within the group.

Spiritual beliefs (also rituals and practices, the expression of those beliefs) serve to confirm, both to themselves and outsiders, who they are. The Hamar, for example, have a unique set of rituals to mark the passage of young men into adulthood. The Adi, subsistence farmers living in the foothills of the Himalayas, believe that spirits can cause illness, and have to be placated with offerings and incantations.

Spiritual expression by means of ritual, sometimes involving intoxicants (alcohol and hallucinogenic drugs) demonstrates and reinforces relations between the tribe and the spiritual realm. The Babongo, for example, use iboga, a drug that apparently allows people to see into their true selves, and vividly revisit the consequences of past actions.

In another case of spiritual expression and identity, the land occupied by Australian aboriginal people is itself deemed sacred. It is mystically revered in rituals involving story-telling, songs and dancing. For these and other tribal peoples, their sense of spiritual identity is mediated through sacred natural phenomena such as animals, also through ancestor spirits and deity figures. Totems and icons, powerful spiritual symbols, bear witness to this in many native cultures; and gods may be worshipped in the form of man-made effigies or 'idols'.

All forms of spiritual belief and expression serve to emphasize the uniqueness and supremely special nature of the tribe, giving its people the basis for their sense of self-worth. This, in turn, is a key to their vitality, even to the point of survival.

A TIMELESS WAY OF LIFE

Another special aspect of spirituality for many tribal cultures concerns attitudes to the passage of time. Rather than straightforwardly linear, it is experienced as rhythmic or cyclical. The year goes by according to seasons, and the months according to the lunar cycle. Weeks may be marked by a day kept special and sacred. This 'sabbath' mentality involves a day of rest and ritual. It is a day set aside for reflection and recuperation. It is a day of healing, and of preparation for immediate and longer term challenges. Additional 'holy days' (the origin of 'holidays') may be added for special occasions. Keeping such days is an inherently healthy practice.

The days and nights are reckoned in turn according to hours divided by the passage of the sun rising and bringing light, setting and leaving darkness. Among the Adi tribespeople, for example, the sun-moon deity Dionyi-Polo is worshipped in recognition of this. In some contemporary cultures, as in some forms of Hinduism and Sikhism, prayers and rituals accompany both passages of transition, at dawn and at dusk. Many Christians also make a point of praying in both the morning and evening. In other traditions, spiritual awareness is consciously attended to more frequently, with services of prayer or thanksgiving five or more times a day, as in Muslim, traditional Jewish and monastic Christian cultures.

The spiritual dimension of people's lives involves adapting them to kairos rather than chronos, and to the timeless rhythms of nature. Captured by the words of a well-known, poetic passage from the Old Testament book Ecclesiastes that begins, 'For everything there is a season, and a time for every matter under heaven', the polarities of existence are also highlighted here.[7] This is *both* yin *and* yang, the interplay of opposites contributing to the whole, fulfilling the holistic ideal of completeness and thus to perfection.

Powerful remnants of tribal mentality in contemporary society

In tribal society, group identity and a sense of belonging fulfil the most central spiritual needs of the people, adding meaning and purpose to their

---

7   Ecclesiastes 3: 1–8.

lives. In today's society, this remains true for many about belonging to a group. It might be a national group, a political group, a religious group, or a group of football or other sports team supporters. The word 'fan' comes from 'fanatic' and indicates the intensity of devotion involved. Whatever the nature of the group, a common feature is the high degree to which members invest in it their time, energies, thoughts and emotions. Investment of time, energy, thought and emotion is the hallmark of attachment.

The conditioning stage of later childhood prepares most adolescents for the conformist stage, conforming in terms of values, traditions, beliefs and practices, in other words in thoughts, words, appearance and behaviour. This can be a relatively smooth development, but the Stage 2 to Stage 3 transition period allows for considerable experimentation as adolescents try out different attitudes and lifestyles.

Social pressures operate within this search for an appropriate adult identity, and teenage rebellion has a conformist element too. Young people tend to follow trends (in clothes, music and politics, for example) keeping in step with their peers, however at odds they may seem to be with their parents' generation. They do things together in groups. Small-scale groupings behave as 'gangs', often in stark and continuous opposition to other gangs with which they clash regularly.

In the mid-1960s in Britain, for example, violent confrontations between two groups regularly made headline news. These were the 'Mods' and the 'Rockers'. Rockers rode motorcycles, wore black leather jackets, and preferred rock and roll music. Mods wore suits or suede, rode motor scooters, and preferred soul music, rhythm and blues. These groups were obliged to be antagonistic towards one another. They also helped to define each other, as being a Mod meant that you were definitely *not* a Rocker, and vice versa.

A few years later, Mods and Rockers had become much less prominent, to be replaced by new opposing groups: the 'Hippies' and the 'Skinheads'. There is a kind of repetition here: 'What goes round, comes around.' The groups change, but the psychology of polarization and rivalry between them is much the same.

LIKES AND DISLIKES

It is a drawback, then, that Faith Stage 3 is characterized by strong allegiances on the one hand, and by opposition to whatever does not seem harmonious with and within the group on the other. Attitudes of mistrust, suspicion, envy and resentment are common.

Conflict and rivalry are based upon ignorance of the principle of reciprocity in the other sense of 'What goes round, comes around': the sense of, 'Reaping what you sow' discussed in Chapter 2. Destructive attitudes and behaviour follow on from failure to seek and recognize similarities at the spiritual level that go deeper than the superficial and more obvious differences between people.

During adolescence, a person develops the strongest of attachments: to places, people, objects (including sacred objects) and to ideas (including beliefs). As with any kind of attachment, once formed they inevitably come under threat. A person holding on to such attachments must resist being overcome by the whole spectrum of painful emotions (see Chapter 1, Box 1.1, p.22), including anxiety, confusion and doubt, and will do so by force of will, by strength of conviction, however blind this may later turn out to be.

Intransigence often follows, along the lines of: 'We (in my group) are right and you (in your group) are wrong.' This is an example of 'either/or' thinking. Such fixed attitudes become the basis for zealotry, political totalitarianism and all forms of ideological fundamentalism where 'We are right' becomes 'We are *in* the right,' and 'Those who are not with us, are against us.'

A conformist group, that may hold together only weakly, strengthens whenever opposition (which may be real or only apparent) is perceived. This encourages group members (who may not ordinarily get along that well) to stick together in mutual support. The group sets itself to denounce and counter the threat, setting up the conditions for conflict. Anger and aggressive behaviour follow. Persecution and cruelty may not be far behind.

IDEALIZATION

In Stage 3, people tend not to be aware of how much they are 'idealizing' the group to which they feel they belong. This is an automatic and unconscious process, useful for survival in tribal days but increasingly problematic and inappropriate in the 21st century. Jung's account of personal development, involving tension between the conscious 'ego' and the unconscious 'shadow', is relevant here (see Chapter 4). In this case, the 'shadow' represents all beliefs, drives and desires at odds with the principles and standards of the group.

According to the strength of its members' conviction, the group cannot be called into question. It can do no wrong. As a group, the people have no option but to identify what is unacceptable as alien to them, and therefore as belonging only to outsiders. They do not own their shadowy aspects but cast or 'project' them on to other people and other groups. The problem is compounded when those from the other group do the same in reverse. This is the cause of many long-running feuds.

'Both/and' style, holistic thinking is not in favour with people during the conformist stage. Similarities between the groups (often extraordinarily strong and striking to third parties) are therefore frequently denied and ignored. There is a powerful element of tragedy here. The denial of everything about themselves that people are uncomfortable with, and its projection on to others, has been and remains the cause of untold human cruelty and distress; but it does not have to be so.

People at Faith Stage 3 can be highly sensitive to criticism and other forms of perceived opposition, and are likely to become increasingly entrenched in their views and protective behaviour when they meet it. They do not want to change their allegiances. They do not want to change anything. They do not want anything to change. But change is, paradoxically, one of life's constant features. All are capable of maturing in wisdom, and 'things happen' that will make at least some people change.

RISKS AND REWARDS OF GROUP COHESION

Cohesion means sticking together, and there is no doubt that competition between groups can help members of different groups, teams or organizations support each other, expand their abilities and improve their efficiency. There is increased co-operation between group members who share common goals of success and of 'beating the competition'. These two principles – competition and co-operation – go hand in hand. Naturally, though, where there are winners, there are also losers. People suffer.

People also suffer whenever the goal takes precedence over the well-being of individual group members. Material goals relate to success, wealth, fame and power, none of which can be shared or retained equally and fairly by all members of a group. Co-operation and cohesion may not last following failure, or even after a success when the need to co-operate is less strong. Group stability becomes vulnerable. Competition and discord, rivalries and factions may appear *within* the group. Unless hands of friendship continue to prevail, unless spiritual values are enacted, people inevitably suffer.

SPIRITUALLY MINDED GROUPS

The situation is not simple but complex. For example, groups based on *secular* principles can provide people with high levels of motivation, meaning and purpose, and so paradoxically fulfil their most central *spiritual* needs. There is therefore limited impetus within these groups for their members to change.

Some social groups go further, retaining a strong spiritual flavour, encouraging members to minimize the ego-self split by holding to spiritual values like honesty, kindness, patience, tolerance and compassion. This is admirable, but a problem remains.

The key feature of group conformity involves exclusion; emphasizing differences between those on the inside and those on the outside; and this fatally contravenes the holistic principle of 'interbeing' at the heart of spirituality. According to a popular proverb, 'Everyone's blood is red; everyone's tears are salty'.We are all alike, brothers and sisters, particularly in our propensity to suffer pain, physical and emotional. Everyone is capable of experiencing the same set of emotions. This means that even the most spiritually minded group goes against wisdom whenever discrimination and exclusion of others occurs. Such a group, often despite its professed aims and ideals, can still be the source of much human conflict and suffering.

In many ways, this is the core problem of humanity, of the almost seven billion people who share a single, vulnerable planet of limited resources. Division into self-interest groups provides the basis for conflict, threatening the stability and livelihood of everybody. These are truths that need spiritually informed remedies at personal, community and international level, and we shall look into the options in Part 3.

MARGINALIZING THE WEAK

The conformist mentality of Stage 3 operates powerfully, even among loosely cohesive groups, at both the larger level of general society and within many of the smaller groups that comprise that society. The need to stick together is often stronger, paradoxically, when the group is vulnerable and under external threat.

The psychological imperative here, fulfilling a vital spiritual need, is for each person to be able to feel, 'I belong', and 'My life matters'. This egocentricity results in the unfortunate but inevitable consequence of seeing some other people as 'not belonging', even expendable. In the context of larger society, many people are stigmatized and either marginalized or shunned completely as a result of this attitude of intolerance.

Although human rights are taken more seriously than before and matters have been improving, it remains true that the poor, the elderly and those, for example, with physical disabilities, long-term ill-health, learning difficulties and mental health problems, have less choice about belonging to general society in consumerist cultures than other people.

At one level, such people are not deemed sufficiently economically productive. At another, they may be marginalized and discriminated against because they are different, and their differences are threatening reminders to others of potential losses they also face but prefer to ignore.

THE POWER OF FEAR

The spiritual self, linked to a higher wisdom, retains awareness of self-seeking attitudes and behaviour and the social inequalities that result, while the everyday ego (intent on self-preservation and other material goals) strives to remain unconscious of such matters.

Here is the origin of conscience, the split between worldly ego and spiritual self. That the concept seems out of fashion currently, to the point of being mocked by some people, confirms the spiritually immature condition of general society today, dominated by Stage 3 thought processes involving partisanship and idealization.

When you consider yourself and those like you to be in the right most of the time, there is no place for a conscience. For this reason, while the self is open and knowing, the ego enforces a kind of anaesthesia on itself. It must remain unaware of its own pain, as well as the suffering of others. In particular, it must deny and ignore all feelings of responsibility for any suffering, usually seeking to blame others.

For those involved in the care of socially disadvantaged individuals, whether as professionals or as friends and relatives, understanding the nature and particularly the almost indomitable defensive power of Stage 3 conformist thinking at work may be helpful. It is a deeply ingrained, conditioned and largely unconscious form of self-preservation that will not respond to simple argument.

Fear and anger are natural reactions to life's struggles for survival, property, family and freedom from discomfort. It is natural to resist and fear losing what you have acquired, also the means for acquiring and retaining material benefits, especially if you have known disadvantage in the past and needed to work exhaustively to gain what you have.

It is also natural to be afraid that you will lose what you have not had to work for, to feel that somehow you do not deserve it and that it might disappear or be taken away. Either way, in addition to fear and anger, the painful emotions the ego seeks strenuously to avoid during Stage 3 are those associated with threat (including bewilderment and doubt) and loss (including guilt, shame and sorrow).

Living with a constant fear of loss is uncomfortable, even if it is only a vague and low intensity level of anxiety. Living a life motivated principally by fear and anger does not lead to contentment but to mistrust, envy and alienation from others. Others are seen as insufficiently helpful, or worse as potentially hostile competitors, and therefore as either indirectly or directly threatening to one's possessions and welfare.

Anxiety also breeds impatience. To live continuously in a state of hurry, pressure and general dissatisfaction, with fear and anger perpetually close to the surface, is to live an unhappy life, and one that inevitably also brings suffering to others. It is the lot of many. In this situation, during the conformist stage, people strive to remain oblivious to their own emotional pain. Many types of distraction are employed in the attempt.

DISTRACTIONS

There is a kind of logic to the obsessive pursuit of material benefits and worldly goals that appeals to many people during Stage 3. Wealth creation is seen as a boon to all. However, from a more spiritual perspective, this can be seen as a destructive kind of intoxication that prevents people from seeing the full consequences of their thoughts, words and actions.

Healthy ambition for moderate degrees of success in life can easily deteriorate into a form of infatuation with being 'the best', with gaining success, celebrity and material wealth. This is an immature and narcissistic vision. According to myth, Narcissus was a young man who fell in love with his own reflection in a pool of water. Narcissists are in thrall to their everyday egos, while oblivious to their shadows. It takes others to see and tell us about how we look from behind; but the narcissist is unresponsive to others. They are literally 'care-less' causers of suffering.[8]

Some organizations are equally self-serving. There are manufacturers, for example, which continue to exploit staff (for example with long hours, low pay and poor conditions), consume valuable, non-renewable resources (such as trees from rain forests and fossil fuels), and contribute to greenhouse gas emissions and global warming. The motive to stay in business and achieve financial profit while selling products to people who desire them remains uppermost, while other considerations take second place and are given relatively little attention. This bears thinking about, and is why the 'tribal' mentality of Stage 3 is no longer appropriate in today's global industrial society. It can ultimately lead to ruin, but there is a way forward (as we shall see in Part 3).

People who are able to distract themselves from and ignore human suffering by a near-total focus on adding to their material wealth or status, may eventually feel sated and dissatisfied. They may then turn towards other goals of high achievement, but can soon lose their appetite for these as well. Ageing and physical impairment may become factors, reducing their capacity for success or for enjoying it. They may continue to 'go through the motions', but be increasingly disgruntled and disillusioned. A stronger anaesthetic may be required to numb the painful experience.

Those who are less successful may similarly turn to numbing agents, cocooning themselves from the emotionally painful effects of life's harsh

---

8   Narcissus has a mythical counterpart, Echo. Echo is deeply attached and devoted to Narcissus, but he loves only himself and ignores her. She offers herself, is rejected, and in response feels both shame and sorrow. This is why she is always heard fading away.

realities. Seeking 'pleasure' is a common form of anaesthetizing distraction, which has similar natural limits involving either eventual satiety or physical incapacity.

Pleasures involving intoxicants (nicotine, alcohol and other so-called 'recreational' drugs) are extremely widespread in general society today. Furthermore, people often engage in them early in life, from their teenage years. Both consequent on and contributing to many social ills in a kind of vicious cycle, these substances usually have serious built-in health and economic implications, being destructive on the small scale (to health, human relationships, work ability, financial situation and so on) and in the wider social context. Other pleasures, involving gambling or sexual behaviour, for example, have similar destructive propensities. Many of these are addictive and hard for people to abandon.

DEATH ANXIETY AND THE THREAT OF ANNIHILATION

People have a need to avoid feeling the threat of loss, but it is an ultimately hopeless endeavour. It does not take much thought to recognize that, at the point of death, control over everything by way of material wealth and success a person has gained must be relinquished. This is the central cause of the fear at the heart of Stage 3, the only true remedy for which is a combination of faith, courage and hope. Few people at Stage 3 have genuinely faced the inevitability of their own death. It has not yet become a reality for them.

Personal anecdote – encounter with death
As a student in my first week on the wards at London's Guy's Hospital, I had to interview a man in his forties and familiarize myself with his case. He had lung cancer. When I saw him, he was having difficulty breathing. His skin had the dusky blue appearance showing that he was not getting enough oxygen into his blood. Underlying the carcinoma was chronic obstructive airways disease. He had repeatedly been exposed during his working life to lung irritants, possibly including asbestos (the dangers of which were only becoming apparent in the early 1970s). Previously an amateur boxing champion, he had lost much weight and was very weak lying in the bed. Beside him, visiting, were his wife and two young children. I examined the man after speaking to him for a few minutes about his symptoms. His chest was marked by dark black lines, inscribed by medical staff, the target for his radiotherapy. My naïve assumption was that this would work and he would get better.

I went to see this patient again the following day and learned more about his life. He had travelled the world in the Merchant Navy, and had married only when he finally came ashore, ten years earlier. I remember liking and respecting this man for his dignity, his uncomplaining attitude and strong family values. He stuck particularly in my mind because, when I came to the ward the following morning, I was told that he had died in the night. My thoughts went immediately to his wife and small children. What would become of them? Death, and its consequences, was now very real for them. It had suddenly become real for me too.

Medical students were not well trained for death. Our teachers then used shock tactics (as some still do). On our first day at medical school, long before we were allowed to meet living patients, we had to attend the dissection room where, in my case, 50 preserved human cadavers on tables awaited the dissection skills of 200 students, most of us aged 18. There was no discussion about who these people might have been. We were kept ignorant of any human associations, and were silently encouraged therefore simply to consider them as objects.

Neither was there any discussion of our thoughts and feelings on meeting death for the first time. The strong but unspoken message, both then and throughout our training, was that we should suppress and ignore personal sentiments. This, we understood, was the 'professional' approach. To do otherwise could only hinder our progress as doctors.

I do not remember questioning this at the time, but think now that it was a mistake and a valuable opportunity missed. About ten years later, I was in a group of about six people training to become psychiatrists when we were asked to recall that first day in the dissecting room and to be honest about the emotions we felt at the time.

Every one of us remembered strong feelings of anxiety, and some also of self-doubt, coupled with guilt towards the dead person whose body we were about to savage (as it felt at the time), tempered by the knowledge that each former owner had chosen deliberately to donate their remains in the interests of medicine. I remember also feeling angry at being put in this position without any warning or preparation. It affected me deeply for a long time. From being ignorant of death, I had become afraid of it, angry about it and good at masking my feelings. Was this what my teachers intended? Meeting the man with lung cancer and his family helped me begin also to feel sad about death. This, I feel, was the start for me of emotional healing and rehabilitation on the subject. For this, I remain grateful to that man, even though his name is forgotten.

The spiritual self knows that death may occur at any moment, 'as quick as intuition'. Fear of it is also the fear of complete personal annihilation, of meaninglessness. It is therefore, similarly, also the fear of any kind of mental illness, of any madness that brings powerful, painful and inconsistent emotional experiences, together with loss of control of one's thoughts and actions. It is, by extension, the fear too of whatever may threaten these, notably extreme hardship (such as poverty), injury and all forms of physical illness.

There is a kind of irony in the fact that worldly 'pleasures', particularly those that are dependency-inducing, are among the most direct causes of hardship, including physical and psychological ill-health.

MOVING FORWARD

People who feel trapped by their circumstances, whether sated by wealth and luxury or imprisoned by some form of addiction, eventually experience at least some impetus to move forward. The remedies are essentially spiritual in nature, involving acknowledgement of a higher power, for example, as in the 12-step method pioneered so successfully by Alcoholics Anonymous. The healing process of spiritual development involves being transformed rather than overwhelmed by experiencing, rather than avoiding, painful emotions. This is the work that begins in Faith Stage 4.

This work involves accepting the ultimate meaninglessness of personal aggrandizement and possessiveness, of considering only oneself as the generator and beneficiary of the material benefits accrued in one's life. It means accepting the principle of 'non-separateness' and acknowledging one's place as both beneficiary and contributor among the wider group of humanity. All this implies spiritual maturity. Acknowledgement of these assertions therefore marks movement forward away from Stage 3.

It becomes necessary to accept our similarities with other people that we had been excluding as different, finding favour in what we had previously considered worthless, allowing divisive 'us and them' attitudes and behaviours, like Echo, simply to fade away.

As spiritual maturity develops in increasing numbers of individuals, hope and courage grow, and general society will not remain so damagingly riven. A tipping point can be reached, so that more and more people find new meaning in selflessness and in working for the common good without any discrimination. Understanding the mechanism helps the developmental process of transformation, and we will be looking into this again in more detail in later chapters.

Summary points

1. *Most people are still developing spiritually*

Occasionally a person is born who retains a strong awareness of the spiritual dimension, but nearly four-fifths of people over 11 are in Faith Stage 3, Stage 4 or between the two.

2. *Age may not be a factor*
Spiritual development, especially after childhood, is not necessarily age-related. Failure to progress is often about slowing down or being held back, rather than about lacking potential.

3. *Competing impulses*
People are subject to competing impulses: to belong to a group, and to think and act independently. The former dominates Stage 3, the latter Stage 4. Opposition between the two drives explains much human conflict and suffering, and can only be fully resolved in Stages 5 and 6.

4. *Usual criteria for group membership*
In today's ill-defined general society, people tend to identify themselves as family members and according to marital status, together with details of gender, nationality, place, race, language, skin colour, type of work and other criteria. Oppositional attitudes prevail, and the urge to conform remains strong.

5. *Group spirituality*
Faith Stage 3 is less about people having individual spiritual experiences than about adherence to a group that gives its members a meaningful sense of purpose, identity and belonging.

6. *Successful tribal antecedents*
Ingrained patterns of self-preservation have served mankind well. The many benefits involved in belonging to a stable, close-knit group are exemplified by a number of tribal peoples.

7. *Success factors*
The success of tribes depends on factors including consistency of place, appearance, language, shared values, solidarity in resistance to threat, unique forms of belief and spiritual expression, and a timeless way of life. There are powerful remnants of tribal mentality in contemporary society.

8. *Destructive attitudes*
It is a drawback that Stage 3 is characterized by opposition to whatever does not fit with and within the group. Attitudes of mistrust, suspicion, envy and resentment are common. Destructive attitudes and behaviour follow failure to seek and recognize similarities that go deeper than the more obvious differences between people.

9. *The role of fear in Faith Stage 3*

The black and white, right and wrong, 'us and them' mentality of Faith Stage 3 results directly in the marginalizing and stigmatizing of the weak, the sick, the poor and others who seem economically underproductive. These self-seeking, partisan and 'tribal' attitudes are based mainly on fear of losing material gains, including wealth and status, and ultimately on the fear of death, of annihilation and meaninglessness. Fear and anger often go together, with destructive consequences.

10. *Distractions*

Many methods of distraction, reducing the impact of emotional pain, have serious health and economic implications, being destructive both on the small scale and in the wider social context.

11. *Eventual loss of illusions heralds growth*

Stage 4 begins when egocentric illusions are seen through and begin to be relinquished.

Exercises and questions for personal reflection and as a basis for group discussion:

1. Begin by identifying yourself according to family position(s) and marital status, then according to the list of criteria near the beginning of the chapter: gender, nationality, place, etc. Having done this, ask yourself again, 'Who am I?' and, 'What is my true nature?' Take your time over this. Be as complete in the answers you give yourself as you can.

2. What major group or groups do you identify with? What is your job? Are you a team player, content to belong to a political, religious or employment organization without 'making waves', without calling into question any of the beliefs, basic assumptions, values, aims, traditions, rules or regulations in operation?

3. Alternatively, do you consider yourself a relatively free-thinking agent *within* the groups or organizations you belong to?

4. Do you consider yourself to be fully independent-minded, free of any externally imposed constraints regarding thought and action? If so, what internal promptings and constraints operate to regulate your thoughts and behaviour? Are you motivated by a degree of self-interest, or do you think and act mainly in the interest of others? Do you consider yourself spiritually motivated in any way?

5. Have you experienced being part of a group or organization where competing or 'getting results' took precedence over the welfare of

individual members? Was there a difference in the atmosphere when the group was being successful from when it was struggling? Did splits occur? Did rivalries appear, or factions *within* the group? What was that like? Did it make you feel you wanted to leave? Discuss your thoughts and experiences with someone else.

Do not worry if you cannot answer these questions, or find any of them difficult. Try to keep them in mind as you read on through the next few chapters.

Chapter 9

SEARCHING

Transition
BECOMING AN ADULT

The 'individual' stage, Faith Stage 4, is notably about separating from the parent group and becoming an adult human being, thinking for yourself and taking responsibility for your words, actions and emotions. It is also about the search for a new setting in which to belong, and in which to find a genuine, rewarding and lasting sense of meaning and purpose. Although a period away may allow you to see things more clearly, it is not essential to move to another place. Either way, you will no longer identify yourself so completely with the group.

GROUPS UNDER PRESSURE

The transition from Stage 3 to Stage 4 may be smooth and gradual, but not necessarily. Things often seem to get worse (and may need to do so) before they can get better. An abrupt shift out of the comfort zone could begin when something happens to weaken both earlier illusions and any tendency to idealize the group to which we have belonged.

The original group may start to disintegrate as a result of external pressures and the threat of failure. Factions and rivalries form. There may be something that the group, working together, can do about it, taking the bigger picture into consideration (see Personal anecdote – avoiding conflict through understanding). Otherwise, it becomes necessary to think for oneself, and to begin struggling with personal differences from other members of the group, acknowledging disagreements over values, traditions, beliefs and practices, for example.

Similarly, leaving the territory, the home base of the primary group and going elsewhere for education, for example, may expose us to new experiences and ideas that call into question the assumptions, beliefs, practices and values we have held to hitherto. The choice before us is either to spend some time in reflection, evaluating and assimilating the new experiences, or with less forethought, to follow the crowd. This can be a painful and lonely time; however, the rewards may eventually be truly worthwhile.

Personal anecdote – avoiding conflict through understanding

In 1970, aged 20, I worked as a waiter in an eight-week summer camp in the USA. There were five of us, responsible for five tables each and for serving three meals a day to 12 children at each table. We also laid out crockery and cutlery, and cleared up after meals. I became friendly with the other waiters but, about five weeks in, friction started growing between us.

There were not enough knives and forks to go round, but none of us wanted any of 'our' children to go short. This was mainly through self-interest, as we were counting on tips from the kids and their families at the end of camp to supplement our meagre wages. We began arriving earlier before meals to get to the cutlery first. When this didn't work out, we began taking items from each others' tables to supplement our own supply. At each meal, some children lost out and, of course, started complaining. We waiters were no longer friends but rivals, and angry exchanges were increasingly common.

After a few days of unpleasant hostility and mistrust, someone eventually realized that we, the waiters, were in no way to blame for the problem. The children had been removing cutlery, especially knives, to take back to their huts. We called a truce and went to see the Camp Director. He grasped the situation instantly, and bundled three of us into his car for a drive to the nearest supermarket where he purchased a plentiful supply of new cutlery.

The problem was solved and we could be friends again, but it set me thinking about conflict between people, and how similarly it can arise when required resources (water, food, shelter, fuel, employment, education and so on) are in short supply. The community spirit of co-operation can quickly break down, to be replaced by hostile competition unless people grow wise and look at the bigger picture, then combine their knowledge and forces to remedy the situation. It was a lesson that stood me in good stead throughout life later, for example when working in small units or groups (such as hospital wards and community mental health teams) and in a larger organization like a National Health Service trust. People too often waste time, energy and emotional reserves through unnecessary and unproductive conflict in this way.

PROBLEMS WITH THE CULT OF PERSONALITY

In today's general society, the element encouraging conformity is strong, but so too is the so-called 'cult of personality', according to which, in seeking to stand out, people feel encouraged, even obliged, to reject many of the traditions of the past. The central preoccupation is with celebrity, gaining fame in a way that also seeks to retain a comfortable sense of security. Celebrity figures act as both scapegoats and champions for the larger group. Emphasizing 'personality' is not the same, however, as encouraging people to think for themselves and take responsibility.

Another aspect of the prevailing risk-avoidance culture involves the high value placed upon evidence provided by science and other forms of research. A problem arises, however, when people are asked to accept this *unquestioningly*, to defer to the knowledge and opinions of 'experts' (especially if they too are well-known personalities) and the 'science community'. Science is of great value, but caution is recommended because the evidence may be incomplete. Sometimes it is misinterpreted. Sometimes it is even corrupted and biased towards vested interests, becoming propaganda or 'spin', rather than knowledge. Furthermore, wisdom requires more than simple factual knowledge.

SKILLS, WISDOM AND GUIDANCE ARE NEEDED

As Chuang Tsu wrote, many years ago, 'First, there must be a true man; then there can be true knowledge'.[1] The cult of the personality reflects dissatisfaction with unthinking conformity, but does not promote true, spiritually mature individuality. For wisdom, certain experiences are necessary in addition. Certain skills are also required – spiritual skills – and, therefore, guidance. Such guidance may come from within, through the intuition of an attentive self in communication with the divine realm, the spiritual source of truth and wisdom. It may also come from external sources, human and written, from both teachers and books, and from other resources, such as the internet.

A key skill to acquire involves the acceptance and accommodation of threat and loss with equanimity. Moving from Faith Stage 3 towards Stage 4 involves giving up much that was cherished and valued. It involves letting go of rigid attachments. Generally speaking, it is harder to let go of attachments formed by conforming within a closely knit group than a less well defined one. The attachments (to beliefs and ideas, traditions, practices, places, people and values) are more extensive and stronger.

---

1 Chang Tsu (1974) *Inner Chapters*. Trans. Gia-Fu Feng and English, J. London: Wildwood House, p.113.

GOING INTO ORBIT AROUND THE PARENT GROUP

Some people do not leave their parent group behind completely, but go into a kind of ambivalent orbit around it, neither fully in nor out. This occurred for a time to the tribal youth in the parable related earlier, when he returned, told of his new experiences and tried to convert the tribe. Eventually, though, he was forced to grieve his losses and let go, moving on with his life. After breaking away, emotionally as well as physically, this was the continuing work for him of Stage 4, a time of potential isolation and loneliness.

However major an effort has been required, it is worth emphasizing that to enter Stage 4 does not mark an end-point but only another way-station on the journey of spiritual development. It is a new beginning, setting a new scene, providing us with a new platform and preparing us for a new kind of homecoming: integration and eventual entry into Stage 5.

A modern example – the Amish
BACKGROUND

Even successful groups generate some degree of discord. The Amish people, living in exclusive communities mainly around Pennsylvania and in Canada, came to the USA from Switzerland and South Germany in the early 18th century. This followed a religious split in the parent Mennonite church, a form of Protestant Christianity.

The Amish are well known for their plain attire, simple lifestyle and an opposition to using modern technology, preferring to use horse-drawn rather than motorized vehicles, for example, and disallowing televisions and telephones in their homes. Outsiders are not allowed to join, and they maintain a firm separation from mainstream society through strict interpretation of a passage of New Testament scripture.[2] This gives them a powerful sense of identity, and their certainty provides them with a potent and authoritative buffer against the risk of meaninglessness.

Stage 2 conditioning is powerful among the young, who are not exposed to contemporary cultural influences from outside. The majority of adult Amish community members therefore readily fit the criteria for Faith Stage 3: they are overwhelmingly conformist. The leaders of Amish communities do seem to appreciate that during adolescence some misbehaviour to test imposed limits is natural, so a degree of leniency is applied until the young individual makes a personal commitment to uphold the rules, usually between the ages of 16 and 25 when they undergo ritual baptism. After that, there are no exceptions.

---

2   'You are a chosen race, a royal priesthood, a holy nation, God's own people.' 1 Peter 2: 9.

THE OLD ORDER – A TRIBAL PEOPLE

The most traditional group, the 'Old Order' Amish, can be described as a successful community. This success is based upon a strong sense of personal and group identity, high moral principles and sincere reverence for scripture, God and the sacred. Their numbers are said to have increased by 50,000 (equivalent to 38%) in the eight years since 2000. However, the constraints of strict obedience to a formula for living within a strict religious organization do not feel comfortable for everybody.

The Amish have many characteristics of a tribal people, not only in their sense of their own divine significance, their dress and appearance, but also in their language and customs. They still speak an old form of German known as 'Pennsylvania Dutch'. The Old Order is led by male bishops and elders who ensure that members abide by a complex and detailed written set of rules that prescribe many aspects of daily living, including clothing. Members are not permitted to marry outside the group. There is no tolerance for any form of independent-mindedness or for any behaviour that does not conform to the rules and expectations of the group. Rule-breakers are asked to repent and change their ways. Those who persist find themselves shunned by the group for a period. Some are eventually excommunicated and required to leave.

To ensure conformity among the Old Order Amish, their Bible, written in an antique form of German that people no longer speak or understand, cannot (according to their rules) be translated into English. Neither is any English translation permitted to be acquired or read by members of the community. Scripture can only therefore be interpreted by the elders.

RULE-BREAKERS AND THEIR FATE

According to a recent television documentary,[3] to read and interpret scripture was the first non-negotiable rule broken by two Old Order Amish men, Ephraim and Jesse, compounded by them joining regularly with others from the wider Amish community in groups to study the English language Bible and sing English language hymns.

Both men were eventually excommunicated after refusing to repent and change their ways. They are now shunned by the community, members of which are no longer allowed to associate with them in any way. Both are attempting, with their wives and children, to continue to live according to Amish culture, while practising a more liberal, enlightened and authentic form of Christianity.

Their dissent from the order is based on a deep and powerful sense of personal conviction. It had become apparent to the men, from reading the

---

3   *Trouble in Amish Paradise* directed by Andrew Tait, produced by Ludo Graham; BBC 2, 18 February 2009.

Bible and reflecting on its message, that many of the strict rules of the Amish were not, as they had consistently been told, based on Holy Scripture. Some rules appeared particularly arbitrary and unnecessary, and the authority of the leaders of the community grew correspondingly weaker and questionable in their minds.

One of the men reported that he was not supposed to challenge the Elders' authority. He was just supposed to listen and agree to what they said without thinking. He said he could not do that. He explained that his excommunication did not directly follow from English Bible study, but from disobeying instructions. Disobedience to any rule or instruction from church officials would have had the same effect, even for a crime of theft or murder.

Neither man wanted to leave the community. After excommunication they remained living nearby with their wives and children. For a time they continued to attend religious services, despite being formally shunned, including by their own parents and other relatives (who would themselves have been excommunicated otherwise). They were not alone. It was made clear that a number of other families were similarly outcast but remaining in touch, trying to live by their Christian principles on the outside. As the documentary ended, the future for the two men and their immediate families remained unclear; however, their religious faith and personal conviction regarding their conduct seemed to be holding firm.

LOYALTY AND GROUP COHESION

Loyalty is a highly prized attribute in most human cultures, yet in the present global society, it is overdue for review. It is of relative but not absolute value, and there are occasions when it is wise and appropriate to set it aside.

Loyalty is automatically weakened when a person becomes aware of something deeply unsatisfactory about the group they have been identifying with and endeavouring to conform to during Stage 3. Illusions of infallibility are relinquished. This dissonance between person and group marks the onset of the transition towards Stage 4.

No criticism is implied of the Amish, an astonishing group of migrant survivors. Their tale is told here only to support the paradigm of psycho-spiritual development, and to demonstrate some of the drawbacks to rigid conformity.

The Amish know themselves to be under threat from external influences, so they are staunchly exclusive. This does not lead to conflict and the risk of destruction (as with more aggressive peoples), first, because contact with non-Amish people is kept to a minimum, and second, because they are deeply pacifist by both inclination and practice.

We do not know how many members leave the Old Order Amish or, like Ephraim and Jesse, have been excommunicated, but it is not enough currently to rock the stability of the group, which is growing in size. There is no impetus for the group as a whole to change. There are motives, though, for some individuals to risk and suffer exclusion. These motives must be powerful, because the emotional suffering involved (as the documentary demonstrated) is immense.

THE IMPETUS FOR CHANGE

The thrust of a rocket must reach extreme levels for it to escape the pull of earth's gravity. Similarly, an irrepressible force is required to shift a person outwards, out of their comfort zone from within the safety of their group. Illusions about the group are challenged at such times, but so too are illusions about oneself, in particular concerning one's innocence as a member of a group whose values and behaviour now seem tainted. Discovering similarities with people that we previously considered different and a threat, growing to appreciate what we had formerly considered worthless, necessitates a substantial reappraisal of one's attitudes.

Something intense has to happen to bring about such a change. Those involved are affected by nothing less than a spiritual force, the absolute force of truth, for example, of beauty, wisdom, wonder or love. It may be hard to describe, but the results are clear: 'something happens'.

What hit Ephraim and Jesse was a combination of Biblical insights and the knowledge that these had been corrupted and concealed by their elders. The effect was similar to that on the youth in the earlier parable when he experienced sunlight for the first time on the mountaintop. What he had been told by his tribal leaders was not lies but was, through their ignorance, incomplete. He knew in his soul that something vital was missing. The youth, like the Amish men, not just wanted but needed to seek and discover the whole truth. Partial or distorted versions no longer sufficed.

When we emerge from group membership and begin thinking independently, who we are, or who we think we are, is thrown into sharper focus. When something happens to shatter our innocence, there follows a widening of the distance and dissonance between the everyday ego and the spiritual self. We may be thrust into a higher trajectory than before, as well as being propelled forwards on the journey out of Stage 3 (see Figure 9.1).

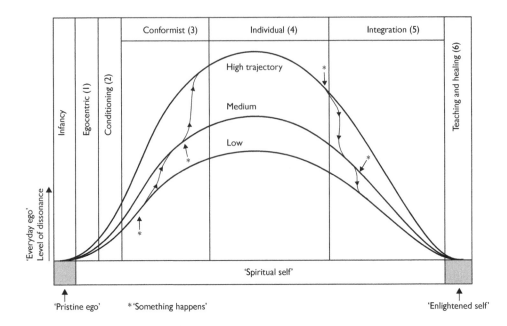

Figure 9.1: Trajectories of faith showing movement between trajectories when 'something happens'

By the time we reach Stage 4, we are seeking a new, individual identity. In some cases, this will be built largely out of what we knew before. In other cases, there will be a complete rejection of former beliefs and values, now associated negatively in our minds with the group we are committed to leaving behind. These are the circumstances for developing a kind of anti-identity.

For example, many people who leave religious groups turn their backs firmly on religion, and come to identify themselves as atheists. This gives them a renewed sense of meaning, purpose and belonging. Many people during Stage 4 similarly search out a new group to join, different from the old group, attempting to fulfil a continuing need to count and contribute somehow. Some try starting new groups. However, all groups, however liberal, invite exclusive behaviour and other aspects of Stage 3 mentality. The only exception is the much larger group to which everyone belongs: the entirety of humanity.

PARTIAL BREAKING AWAY

There may be Amish men and women who have broken away more completely than Ephraim and Jesse. However, at the time of the documentary, these two remained in transition, outside the original group but still physically close and substantially ideologically attached. Unlike the parable youth, they do not seem to be trying to change the entrenched culture of the remaining members and elders, but they are trying to live in a new style in some degree of compatibility with the old. They are in orbit, but have not yet broken fully free of the group's gravity to search elsewhere for spiritual sustenance and satisfaction.

SECOND GENERATION CHILDREN

Again, no criticism is intended by this observation. The situation remains unstable, however, particularly with regards to the children who are not growing up as members of the Amish parent group. Their future is less well mapped out, and they will necessarily have to think things through and make conclusions for themselves. We can only speculate on how their lives will unfold as they try to belong to two very different societies.

Problems associated with having no well-defined primary group

Many people find themselves growing up in the circumstances similar to this 'second generation', with no large and stable primary group with which to identify fully. Sometimes the children of migrants from one country to another, especially where different languages are spoken, have two distinct primary groups, and therefore two different identities to try to adopt according to a double set of conditioning.

In an ill-defined society, such as many find themselves inhabiting in the 21st century, 'non-conformism' has become one of the new ways of conforming. Traditional myths and values are spurned as irrelevant or worthless. Scientific rationality may have become overvalued. Polarization occurs easily, and personal identities are confused. The situation involves many people feeling at a loss, having no adequately defined and cohesive parent group with which to identify.

To use Erik Erikson's term, 'identity confusion' prevails. Caught up in it, people lack motivation, drive, meaning and purpose as well as a sense of belonging. Their self-esteem is at risk, and – lacking a robust sense of self-worth – they are at high risk of destructive behaviour. They also risk coming under destructive influences from other seemingly strong and goal-directed people, who may exploit them financially, sexually, criminally and in other ways. They are at great risk of dependency, including addiction behaviour involving alcohol, drugs, gambling, sex and other 'pleasures'. Careless for their own safety, they are attracted to dangerous activities and often also to violence. These individuals are also at greater risk of developing mental illnesses than the general population.

Often thwarting the education system, such hapless ones readily become a burden on many other social agencies, including the police, judiciary and prison services, hospital and health services, and social services. They respond less well to coercion (the usual strategy employed) than to being valued, heard and taken seriously as people with potential. Emotional healing and the capacity for social responsibility can only come when communication between their fragile egos and their spiritual selves will somehow be restored.

The group, clan, gang or underworld community to which some such lost souls conform during a distorted and destructive Stage 3 can give way to improvement; but 'something' has to happen. The process of spiritual growth needs to be kick-started into resumption. Stage 4 for them may be similar to that for 'second generation' people and others with no single, clear group with which to identify and conform during Stage 3. This includes many people excluded by mainstream society: the marginalized and stigmatized, forced prematurely into isolation.

Stage 4, for all of these people, becomes especially important. A way out is possible, a way forward towards Stages 5 and 6. A high profile example who made it is the current United States president, Barack Obama.

The spiritual development of a president
BACKGROUND

Barack Obama's early life had similarities to a 'second generation' child, although in his case, there were four rather than two sets of cultural influences: white American, black African, Asian (Indonesian) and black American.

Obama records in his autobiography,[4] written at the age of 33, that his mother, Ann, was a white American of European descent. His father, Barack Obama senior, from Kenya, was on a foreign student scholarship in Hawaii when the couple met in 1960. They were soon married, and the future president was born on 4 August 1961. His parents separated when he was two years old and divorced a year later. Barack senior returned to Kenya and saw his son only once more.

After her divorce, Barack's mother married an Indonesian student who was also attending college in Hawaii. After a military coup in his home country in 1967, all Indonesian students were recalled. The family had to move. From ages six to ten, Barack attended local schools in Jakarta, and was given additional tuition daily by his mother. A younger half-sister was born. In 1971, Obama returned to Hawaii to live with his white maternal

---

4   Obama, B. (2007) *Dreams from My Father: A Story of Race and Inheritance.* Edinburgh: Canongate Books.

grandparents and attend the respected Punahou School until high school graduation in 1979.

He went to college in Los Angeles in 1979, transferring to Columbia University in New York in 1981, graduating in 1983 before working for a year as a researcher at the Business International Corporation, and then at the New York Public Interest Research Group. He then moved to Chicago where he was a director of the Developing Communities Project on the city's far South Side. He worked as a community organizer there from June 1985 to May 1988 before going to Harvard Law School. Gaining his doctorate, he worked as a civil rights lawyer from 1991 until entering politics as an Illinois senator in 1997. He was elected to the US Senate in 2004, becoming the 44th US President in January 2009. Other facts about Barack Obama are a matter of public record.[5]

SPIRITUAL QUEST

His book, *Dreams from my Father*, first published in 1995, ends after a five-week visit to Kenya and his first meetings with many of his paternal relatives in 1988. In the Introduction, Obama notes that the book is 'a record of a personal, interior journey – a boy's search for his father, and through that search a workable meaning for his life as a black American'.[6] This announces and defines it as a spiritual quest. It is his search, both deep within himself and externally into his origins and roots, for an authentic and complete sense of identity.

We will see how he fails to settle into any one group identity and, feeling isolated, takes up the kind of search that typifies Faith Stage 4. Several experiences later usher him towards Stage 5, and he can be seen to grasp the wider universality of his true self. It is not only Barack Obama's story, therefore. In many respects, it mirrors everyone else's.

SOMETHING HAPPENS – AN UNEXPECTED LOSS

Obama's account of his odyssey begins in November 1982 when something unexpected happened. Unheralded, he received a telephone call from an aunt in Nairobi, informing him of his father's death in a car accident. As the news sank in, Obama began to reflect that he had grown up with more of a myth than a man as his father.

He realized that he had barely registered that his father looked nothing like the people around him in Hawaii, that he was 'black as pitch', while his mother was 'white as milk'. His own, albeit paler black skin, though, had

---

5   See, for example, http://en.wikipedia.org/wiki/Barack_Obama, accessed 29 May 2010.
6   Barack Obama (2007) *Dreams from My Father*. Edinburgh: Canongate Books, p.xvi.

become the focus of many doubts about his personal identity, and questions about his possible future and mission in life. His Asian experiences had complicated matters regarding his identity. Living in Jakarta from age six to ten presented different problems from living in America later. Skin colour was not such an issue; but he heard his mother, struggling herself with loneliness and a sense of isolation, making her attitude towards Indonesians plain: 'These are not my people.'[7] They were obviously not young Barack's people either, and he was left wondering who were.

In Hawaii later, Barack made up grandiose tales for his mainly white classmates about his father being a tribal prince. His ego, to avoid feelings of shame, created fiction as part of a false protective mask or 'persona'. Yet he admits that part of him 'knew that what I was telling them was a lie'.[8] Here his conscience is at work, demonstrating the split between personal ego and the all-knowing spiritual self.

In truth his father 'remained something unknown, something volatile and vaguely threatening'.[9] This image of his father was acting like his own dark Jungian shadow. They had been together only once, when Barack senior revisited Hawaii for about a month when his son was about 11 years old. Young Barack discovered then that he had five paternal half-brothers and a second half-sister living in Africa. He also listened to his father's stories of African tribes, 'That still required a young boy to kill a lion to prove his manhood',[10] and knew intuitively then that he had to get closer to this part of himself. But, like most adolescents, he tried out other, partial identities first.

ATTEMPT AT BELONGING LEADS TO ISOLATION

Barack made a conscious decision to become part of the world of basketball, practising for hours to make the high school team. He liked the idea that 'Respect came from what you did and not who your daddy was.'[11] Nevertheless, he later admitted that he was 'living out a caricature of black male adolescence, itself a caricature of swaggering American manhood'. Comparing himself with surfers, football players and would-be rock-and-roll guitarists, he describes the development of a persona to wear in public: 'Each of us chose a costume, armor against uncertainty.' At least on the basketball court, he said, he could find 'a community of sorts, with an inner life all its own'.[12]

---

7   *Ibid.*, p.47.
8   *Ibid.*, p.63.
9   *Ibid.*, p.63.
10 *Ibid.*, pp.69–70.
11 *Ibid.*, p.79.
12 Ibid., pp.79–80.

Obama recognized that he and his peers were confused and angry, and that this falsehood was how they dealt with their emotional pain. To join this social group was a typical Stage 3 response to the unhappy predicament he was in, but he was never sold on it. He was not just black skinned. He was, after all, living with white relatives, people he loved, so he understood that his situation was complicated and without a simple solution. After one particularly troubling incident, Obama experienced a powerful revelation. He knew for the first time, 'that I was utterly alone'.[13]

This is a characteristic insight of Stage 4, indicating the breaking out of one's former orbit around Stage 3 attachments. They no longer have the force to hold him back. Obama's search for a true identity continued at college in Los Angeles, where he spent time with other black students, many of whom 'chose to function like a tribe'; but he remained self-contained while doing so.

SOMETHING HAPPENS – A MOMENT OF INSPIRATION

Aged 19, Barack attended a rally in California supporting the African National Congress of South Africa, a country still in the grip of apartheid before the release of Nelson Mandela. Asked to make a brief speech, he found himself unexpectedly inspired.

Mounting the stage in a trance-like state, he reached the microphone and said:

> There is a struggle going on. It's happening an ocean away. But it's a struggle that touches each and every one of us... Whether we know it or not... Whether we want it or not... A struggle that demands we choose sides. Not between black and white. Not between rich and poor. No – it's a harder choice than that. It's a choice between dignity and servitude... Between fairness and injustice... Between commitment and indifference... A choice between right and wrong.[14]

With these words, he was demonstrating an intuitive grasp of the non-separateness of humanity. He was also accurately depicting his own crisis, and the choices he had still to make; yet with friends the same day, he tried to disown the speech. He was not ready yet to be a public figure. He remained assailed by:

> Constant, crippling fear that I didn't belong somehow, that unless I dodged and hid and pretended to be something I wasn't, I would

---

13   *Ibid.*, p.91.
14   *Ibid.*, p.106.

forever remain an outsider, with the rest of the world – black and white – always standing in judgement.[15]

Obama wanted to deny what seemed clear to others, that he had spoken from the heart, that he cared, and that he truly believed in something. The personal ego still governed him, but it was now more openly at odds with a powerful spiritual self that had momentarily broken through his defensive self-containment. There was to be struggle, but no turning back. This development was irreversible.

Obama remained in a confused frame of mind as he moved to New York: 'Two years from graduation, I had no idea what I was going to do with my life, or even where I would live.'[16] He wrote that he had come to understand himself as a black American, and was understood by others as such, but it was not enough. What he needed, he declared, was a community, and a place, where he could settle and test his commitment. He was ready for personal responsibility.

Obama applied himself fresh to his studies, and to thinking about his life. He started keeping a journal of daily reflections and poetry. He avoided going out drinking. His new-found discipline was deliberate and consciously protective for, in the city, he was surrounded by attractive possibilities:

> The beauty, the filth, the noise, and the excess, all of it dazzled my senses. There seemed no constraints on originality of lifestyles or the manufacture of desire – a more expensive restaurant, a finer suit of clothes, a more exclusive nightspot, a more beautiful woman, a more potent high. Uncertain of my ability to steer a course of moderation, fearful of falling into old habits, I took on the temperament if not the convictions of a street corner preacher, prepared to see temptation everywhere, ready to overrun a fragile will.[17]

In other words, he adopted a mature kind of wisdom that has much in common with monastic sensibilities. The breadth of his insight is breathtaking.

> Beneath the hum, the motion, I was seeing the steady fracturing of the world taking place. I had seen worse poverty in Indonesia and glimpsed the violent mood of inner-city kids in L.A.; I had grown accustomed everywhere to suspicion between the races... It was only now that I began to grasp the almost mathematical precision with which America's race and class problems joined:

---

15   *Ibid.*, p.111.
16   *Ibid.*, p.116.
17   *Ibid.*, p.120.

the depth, the ferocity, of resulting tribal wars... It was as if the middle ground had collapsed, utterly.[18]

Obama is describing what happens in a society where the dominant partisan, tribal, Stage 3 mentality leads to growing competition and pressure resulting in fragmentation. Self-interested, worldly values eclipse those of the spirit. Factions and rivalries emerge. The weak are marginalized and exploited or excluded. Mistrust and the threat of violence are everywhere.

Obama realized that he had to choose between either personal comfort or responsible engagement with social realities. Wisely, he took his time, writing later:

> Unwilling to make that choice, I spent a year walking from one end of Manhattan to the other. Like a tourist, I watched the range of human possibility on display, trying to trace out my future in the lives of the people I saw, looking for some opening through which I could re-enter.[19]

The balance of domination between the personal ego and the spiritual self is shifting during Stage 4, often very gradually. It may not be seen or felt, occurring invisibly like a seed growing into bud beneath the soil's surface. Once the process has begun, spiritual development of this nature is assured, responding according to kairos, God's time, however long it may take according to chronos, in terms of days, weeks and months.

Eventually, a year after the news of his father's death, Obama has a dream about his father saying to him, 'I always wanted to tell you how much I love you.' This provides the opening he seeks. Barack junior, aware that this dream-father is held in a prison cell to which he holds the key, awakens weeping. In finally facing this mythical shadow-figure, his black African father, he is no longer afraid. He is sad, but also energized to continue his search.

MOVING INTO STAGE 5

Ready to commit himself, Obama became a community organizer in 1983. The decision, he admitted, was impulsive and intuitive; but later he also understood that it formed 'part of that larger narrative, starting with my father and his father before him, my mother and her parents, my memories of Indonesia with its beggars and farmers...my move to New York; my father's death'. He comments, 'I can see that my choices were never truly mine alone.'[20]

These are the mature reflections of a man who no longer feels isolated. He has a new, much broader personal identity that allows him to feel a sense

18   *Ibid.*, pp.120–1.
19   *Ibid.*, p.122.
20   *Ibid.*, pp.133–4.

of belonging with many people, without distinction and discrimination on account of race, skin colour, place of origin or any other categorizing feature. This is the mentality of Faith Stage 5. The higher ideals Obama found himself ready to adopt included, 'To be right with yourself, to do right by others, to lend meaning to a community's suffering and take part in its healing'.[21]

His commitment and wisdom grow stronger as he attends neighbourhood meetings. Heartfelt reminiscences are shared here, and people remember with nostalgia how everyone used to help each other, reporting wistfully how this morality, based on sharing, seemed lost.

Obama describes the effect: 'The whole of what they recalled sounded vivid and true, the sound of shared loss,' he wrote. 'A feeling of witness, of frustration and hope, moved about the room from mouth to mouth, and when the last person had spoken, it hovered in the air, static and palpable.' To the astute reader, it is clear that this feeling also lodged in his breast. 'Then we all joined hands,' he concludes, 'and together we asked for the courage to turn things around.'[22] But he is not yet sure to who or what he is praying.

Listening repeatedly to what he calls 'sacred' stories of these humble Chicago people, sketchy biographies, stories full of terror and wonder, studded with events that still haunted or inspired them, he came to recognize that people carried within them some central explanation of themselves. He found this helpful. 'It was this realization, I think,' he wrote, 'that finally allowed me to share more of myself with the people I was working with, to break out of the larger isolation that I had carried with me to Chicago.'[23] He is grasping the universality of human experience, its spiritual dimension and, as a result, he is changing, unbending, letting go, growing.

It is clear that Obama soon became an effective community organizer. His account reveals a man of honesty and integrity, not boastful, and a man who is again inspired to speak up and persuade others when necessary. He is learning and growing through both failures and successes, through experiences that are decidedly personally challenging. One last experience described in his book confirms that his searching phase is coming to a conclusion. He is leaving Stage 4 behind.

CATHARSIS – 'SOMETHING HAPPENS' AGAIN

As the Developing Communities Project was a mainly church-based project, Barack necessarily met and worked alongside a number of Christian ministers. His mother's family had a Christian background, but were not churchgoers. Apart from a nominally Muslim father, Barack does not appear to have had

---

21   *Ibid.*, p.278.
22   *Ibid.*, p.178.
23   *Ibid.*, p.190.

any close personal connection with Islam. When once asked what church he belonged to, his answer was evasive. He said he was 'still searching'.[24] Someone said it might help his work as a community organizer if he became a church member somewhere. But, which church? 'It doesn't matter where really,' he was told.

Obama began to think about faith and where it came from. He decided he had faith in himself, but also concluded that this was never sufficient. The question lodged in his mind. At one church, Trinity, he met elderly professionals – engineers, doctors, accountants and corporate managers – who taught him something about trying to live without religion:

> They all told me of having reached a spiritual dead end; a feeling, at once inchoate and oppressive, that they'd been cut off from themselves. Intermittently, then more regularly, they had returned to the church… Many of their deepest spiritual needs were being met, in a way they had not been met while working in the big institutions.[25]

He added, honestly, that he remained 'a reluctant skeptic', doubtful of his own motives, wary of expedient conversion, and having too many quarrels with God to accept a salvation too easily won. But this is not his final position.

Shortly before leaving Chicago for Europe, Africa, and then his new position at Harvard Law School in 1988, Obama attended a service at Trinity Church. He was moved by the choir's joyful affirmation, singing 'I'm so glad, Jesus lifted me!' He was also deeply affected by a sermon on 'The Audacity of Hope', a meditation on a fallen world, based on the story of Hannah from Old Testament scripture.[26] While listening, he became aware of a conviction about this and similar tales from the Bible.

> Those stories – of survival, and freedom, and hope – became our story, became my story. The blood that had spilled was our blood, the tears our tears; until this black church, on this bright day, seemed once more a vessel carrying our story of a people into future generations and into a larger world.[27]

A boy leaned over and gave him a pocket tissue. Only then did the future president feel the tears running down his cheeks.

---

24 *Ibid.*, p.274.
25 *Ibid.*, p.285.
26 Hannah is a woman who knows bitter times, facing rejection and despair daily, but who longs for a son, prays to God, dares to hope and is finally rewarded. In gratitude, she offers her baby, the future prophet Samuel, to be a servant of God throughout his life. From 1 Samuel: Chapter 1 and 2. Obama later entitled his second book, *The Audacity of Hope.*
27 *Ibid.*, p.294.

This was an epiphany, another pivotal moment. Something highly significant had again happened in Barack Obama's life. The spiritual dimension had once more broken through into his conscious awareness, displacing the everyday ego, joining heart and mind. His tears indicate a powerful catharsis, a sorrowful cleansing heralding relief, healing and growth. Something shadowy, long held back and buried had been released within his mind. We will look again later at the emotional process involved.

A UNIQUE CASE?

Each person has their own story. That is why, as a separate and increasingly well-integrated person, it is necessary first to emerge from the comfort zone of the conformist stage, then to endure and grow through the isolation of the individual stage, in order to embark on the homecoming Stages 5 and 6. Is Barack Obama a unique case? The answer is surely both 'Yes' and 'No'. In terms of spiritual development, we are all unique, but there are also similarities. There is much that we share; hence the benefit of reading about other people's journeys. They offer guidance and hope.

That Barack Obama was born into such a complex and ill-defined cultural predicament was to his eventual advantage. It was also a blessing that he was gifted with intelligence, physical health and a number of other beneficial attributes. He was also fortunate in his education, and the self-discipline that came with it, including those valuable sessions with his mother early each morning in Indonesia.

Travel, his mixed background, his education and a questioning mind, allowed his spiritual self to retain a healthy influence over him, even during the troubled times of adolescence and young adulthood. Its inspiration came to him when he spoke at the rally, aged 19. Its moral guidance and discipline held him steady in the face of temptation and distraction in New York. Its sense of duty based on compassion, fellow-feeling for the poor and marginalized, led him to his work in Chicago, and a new, profound sense of belonging beyond boundaries of race or religion steered him gently to a tearful epiphany in Trinity Church.

Just as something happens to people early in the journey of spiritual development to increase the split between personal ego and spiritual self, to shift a person into a higher, more painful trajectory while also propelling them forward on the path, so too can something happen in the other direction, promoting ego-self harmony (see Figure 9.1). We will see in Part 3 how it is possible to increase the likelihood of these beneficial occurrences and experiences through spiritual practices and by developing spiritual skills.

Barack Obama's case is unique from one point of view, but it is also, more profoundly, universal. He is distinguished by being further forward on the spiritual path than 80 per cent or more of the rest of us. It seems fitting that, wherever in the world we are living, for as long as he remains true to his spirit, he is one of our leaders. Many people who elected him, obedient to deep intuitive impulses from their souls, will surely agree.

Summary points

1. *Aspects of Faith Stage 4*
Faith Stage 4 is about separating from your parent group and becoming an adult human being, and about thinking for yourself. It is also about the search for a setting in which to belong, and in which to find a genuine, rewarding and lasting sense of meaning and purpose.

2. *Moving on from Stage 3*
A shift out of the conformist comfort zone of Stage 3 begins when illusions about the parent group weaken. It can happen when the group starts to disintegrate as a result of external pressures.

3. *Potentially misleading elements*
Celebrity culture, while appearing to favour individuals, does not genuinely encourage people to think independently and to take responsibility for their actions and emotions. Caution is recommended when deferring to research evidence and expert advice, which may be incomplete or misrepresentative. Wisdom and truth involve more than simple factual knowledge.

4. *Spiritual skills*
Spiritual skills, wisdom and guidance help people achieve true individuality. Guidance may come through intuition, also from teachers and written resources. A key skill involves the acceptance of threat and loss with equanimity. Spiritual development involves letting go of numerous rigidly-held attachments.

5. *Partial separation – an example from the Amish*
As in the example of two men excommunicated from the Old Order Amish community, some people do not leave their parent group behind completely, but go into orbit around it, neither fully in nor out. The fate of the 'second generation' children is often compromised and uncertain.

6. *Lacking spiritual awareness*
Lacking spiritual awareness, caught up in 'identity confusion', many individuals lack motivation, drive, meaning and purpose or a sense of belonging, and readily become a burden on many social agencies, including

the police, judiciary and prison services, hospital and health services, and social services. A way out involving spiritual growth is nevertheless possible.

7. A presidential example of spiritual growth

US President, Barack Obama's early life is given to exemplify the spiritual quest for identity involved in Faith Stage 4. Reaching towards resolution of the difficult search, 'something happens' to him more than once. He also has to integrate many facets from his past and background. Eventually, recognizing the spiritual kinship of all who suffer and find hope, he can be said to have entered Faith Stage 5.

Exercises and questions for personal reflection and as a basis for group discussion:

1. Think about your origins and background. Describe your spiritual journey so far, either in writing or to someone else. Take your time. Make a start and add to it later. Think first whether your parent group was small or large, close-knit or poorly defined.

2. Now think about when you first became aware of yourself as a person, possibly when still a very young child. Think about whether and when you first started to become aware of yourself as significantly different (in appearance, thoughts, action, ideas or values) from others in your group or community.

3. Do you remember a period of isolation? Do you still feel somehow alienated from the mainstream of general society? How are you coping? Are you still trying to stay with or close to your parent group or original community? Have you been searching for a new, different community without the problems you wanted to leave behind? Have you encountered a new set of problems and a recurrence of the feeling, or fear (like that of Barack Obama in New York), that you do not belong anywhere?

4. Have you begun to recognize the truth of 'non-separateness', your kinship with everyone else, including the marginalized, weak, sick and poor? Discuss this with someone else.

Chapter 10

HOMECOMING

Returning towards home

Before I studied Zen, mountains were mountains and rivers were rivers. *While* I studied Zen with my master, mountains were no longer mountains and rivers were no longer rivers. *After* I studied Zen, abiding in the way of no-seeking, mountains have again become just mountains and rivers are again just rivers.

I remember this saying from the Zen Buddhist tradition, and it seems to be in agreement with what we have learned about the stages of faith development according to James Fowler.

The poetic statement compares with something more prosaic, based on the new psycho-spiritual paradigm, as follows: 'When I was in Stage 3, I knew what I believed and where I stood. There was no uncertainty. When I was in Stage 4, I no longer knew what I believed or where I stood. I was still seeking inner peace but beset by doubt. When I entered Stage 5, more accepting of the way of things, confusion gradually fell away and calm returned. Once again, I knew what I believed and where I stood.'

This is not simply travelling in a futile circle. Something is different. With maturity, we are different. Our comprehension of the world, ourselves and each other is expanded. Ego merges once again with Self. As T.S. Eliot puts it, in his poem 'Little Gidding', 'The end of all our exploring will be to arrive where we started, and know the place for the first time.'[1] The journey of spiritual development is taking us home.

---

1   Eliot, T. S. (2001) *Four Quartets*: quartet four, 'Little Gidding', verse five. London: Faber and Faber. Available at www.tristan.icom43.net/quartets/gidding.html, accessed 13 August 2010.

Numbers

Fowler's survey included 305 people over 13 years old, about 8 per cent of whom were recorded as having reached Faith Stages 5 or 6. Considerable benefit would be had from bringing this research up to date and extending the enquiry into adult spiritual development. In the meantime, by extrapolation from the 1981 figures, among the 50 million or so teenage or adult people in the UK, 4.25 million can be counted as spiritually mature. The comparable figure for the USA is approximately 16 million. Many unsung heroes are living quietly, doing good, in the midst of general society. Spiritual maturity should therefore not be considered either particularly rare or unattainable.

Letting go of attachments
CHANGING ATTITUDES

With the ripening of wisdom, a person's attitudes to many things change. They become more accepting of loss, softening particularly towards suffering and death. Earlier, we cast these as our enemies. We naturally seek to avoid them and minimize their effects, finding it hard to understand those who think to do otherwise. Apparently full of injustice, we consider loss, suffering and death to be feared. Only later may we come to accept them as inevitable, the great levellers of mankind. If we engage with the experiences of others, for example in the process of dying, death may become a vital and valuable teacher, preparing us to face its challenge in our turn.[2] Death may even appear to us, at last, as welcome, as a friend.

Mrs Cruikshank's story

A story about the final days of Mrs Eleanor Cruikshank serve to illustrate this point.[3] A proud lady in her eighties, I met her in 1977, when I was working in Australia, having taken over a friend's single-handed general practice while he returned to Britain for a long holiday. She had developed a cancer that had already become widespread when I first saw her, devastating her body; yet her mind remained alert. Making the predicament worse, she was also blind with dense cataracts. Nevertheless, she acted as if these were only minor indispositions, and caused her 60-year-old daughter, who was looking after her, much concern and frustration. Mrs Cruikshank did not appreciate the disruption she brought to her daughter's home, or the work she put her to.

---

2   See, for example, de Hennezel, M. (1998) *Intimate Death: How the Dying Teach Us How to Live.* Trans. C. B. Janeway. New York, NY: Vintage Books.
3   The following true story is adapted from Culliford, L. (2007) *Love, Healing and Happiness.* Winchester: O Books.

Never one to offer a word of either praise or gratitude, her nature was always critical and demanding.

After a heavy fall, in which her weakened, cancer-blighted right femur was fractured, and when her daughter could no longer cope with her, Mrs Cruikshank had to go into a private hospital where she would have a room to herself. (There was no question of operating on her leg. She was too frail.) Her first demand when I visited was to be allowed to go home. Astonished that she should even think it possible, I managed to persuade her to stay there for a few days and allow us to run some tests. The x-rays confirmed the very advanced state of the malignancy.

I thought Mrs Cruikshank would die soon, in less than a week, but she seemed to have other ideas. She lived on day after day, through one week into the next, and then the next. She began trying the patience of the nurses, asking daily when she could go home. Her daughter was in despair, completely unable to stand up to her domineering mother. Eventually, however, Mrs Cruikshank developed a chest infection and a fever. Her health deteriorating, she soon spent most of the time asleep, almost comatose; and so could not participate in the discussion about her treatment.

The ward sister, the patient's daughter and I then had a frank talk together. It was clear that the cancer was terminal, and that although the infection might respond to antibiotics, the eventual outcome was clear. She was close to death. The decision we reached was not to prolong life for the sake of it. All agreed that no antibiotic should be given. Mrs Cruikshank would be kept comfortable for her final days. But our predictions of her demise turned out again to be premature.

First, as a result of the fever and infection, she became delirious. Drowsy and disorientated, she became fearful. She thought the nurses were trying to poison her, and took to cursing them loudly in the most vivid language. She spat out all medication, and started refusing the food. One night she climbed out of bed, falling like a lumpy sack of turnips to the floor. After she climbed out a second time, cot sides were added to her bed. For a time, she had to be restrained as well as sedated.

It seemed impossible, but days passed and Mrs Cruikshank lived on. She was weaker. Her body was so thin. The irregular lumps of the cancerous tumours were visible everywhere. But live on she did. Then, one evening when I visited, many days after the fever began, she seemed more peaceful. She was sitting propped up on pillows in the bed. I took her hand and she turned towards me, just as if she could see. 'Is that you, Doctor?' she asked. I said it was, and she turned away briefly.

When she turned her head back, she suddenly seemed to fix me with a piercing gaze, despite those dull eyes being utterly sightless. 'You know, Doctor,' she said, 'I'm afraid.'

It was a big confession for her, and she seemed very relieved when, prompted by a kind of intuitive wisdom, I simply said I understood. I wanted somehow to validate her fear without being critical. 'Do you understand?' she replied. 'Do you really?' She almost visibly relaxed.

By the next morning Mrs Cruikshank's fever had subsided. She had beaten the infection. More than this, she retained her calm demeanour of the night before. She was compliant and grateful to the nurses, required very little pain relief, and resumed eating. When her daughter visited, she could not stop apologizing to her for being such a reproachful parent and such a heavy burden.

Something had clearly happened. The cancer and the fever of the infection had brought about a transformation, right at the end of Mrs Cruikshank's life. She continued to be alert, calm and a joy to be with for two or three more days before her long life came to its quiet, respectable and inevitable conclusion. She died peacefully in her sleep.

EMOTIONAL HEALING AND GROWTH

Mrs Cruikshank had been heavily conditioned early in life in the pioneer spirit tradition of not admitting to or showing any fear. It would have amounted to unacceptable weakness for her, so she always denied and banished it from consciousness. She found fear unacceptable in others too, especially in her daughter, and criticized it whenever she suspected it; but fear remained lodged within her soul, biding its time.

Weakened by illness, and unable to escape the reality of her own death, she had finally found the courage to face and admit to her fear. She confessed to me, her doctor, 'I'm afraid,' and felt relieved when I condoned it. Afterwards, the emotional conditioning of childhood overcome, no longer afraid of it or of what it might signify, she could simply experience the fear. It had lost its sting. All cause for dishonour was over.

Letting go of her shame allowed Mrs Cruikshank to experience the force of her fear, and then let go of that too. This was the final step she needed to achieve the contentment of emotional maturity. The split between ego and self had been healed.

IMPLICATIONS FOR THE DOCTOR

Mrs Cruikshank's final illness also affected me significantly. I knew intuitively that the transaction between doctor and patient over my acceptance of her confession of fear had made a difference. 'Something happened' to me also at the moment she gazed with sightless eyes into my face, as if she could see directly into my soul.

The experience stayed with me. Reflecting deeply about it later, I came to realize that there is a special kind of work to do in medicine, in addition to attempting simply physical cures: work involving the promotion of emotional healing and the fostering of personal growth.

Some years later, I wrote:

> This important episode was a turning-point, shaping and sealing my desire and ambition to continue studying the mind and its workings. I realized that I wanted, perhaps needed, to find out more about the mysterious process I had witnessed. From this moment, I was determined that further training would not for me be simply an academic exercise. It was to have the decided purpose of grounding me, if possible, in this very special, helpful and healing kind of knowledge and wisdom, enabling me to share it with others in need.[4]

I hope that the outcome and lasting effects of my spiritual encounter with Mrs Cruikshank will have benefited many of my patients and colleagues over the intervening years, and also the wider community to which I belong. The principle of reciprocity was at work, and (although I take no personal credit) I am confident that the consequences of such a deep and meaningful experience continue to spread out indefinitely, like ripples on the surface of an infinite lake. It was, for me, an epiphany. Over 30 years later, I still feel both humble and grateful.

A tough lesson

It is a tough lesson. But as our death becomes a reality for us, so begins our homecoming, a change in disposition from relative ignorance to wisdom, from grasping to contentment, from anxious and impatient industry to joyful serenity. In order to get there, we are required to give up attachments, to grieve.

A MEDIEVAL TALE FROM LITERATURE

There is a beautiful and instructive passage in Nobel prize-winning author Hermann Hesse's book *Narziss and Goldmund*.[5] It is a medieval tale, taking place in Europe at the time of the great plague, the Black Death. The character,

---

4   *Ibid.*, p.132.
5   Hesse, H. (1959) *Narziss and Goldmund*. Trans. G. Dunlop. London: Penguin.

Goldmund, is taken prisoner at one point, bound tightly, thrown into a dark cell and told he will be hanged at daylight for his crimes.

> He sat thus for a long while, miserably cramped, and striving with all his might to take this horror into himself, and know it; breathe it, let it fill him from top to toe... He must strive to learn that tomorrow he would have ceased to be. There he would dangle and be a thing, on which birds could perch... It was hard to make himself feel deeply, let it become part of his being... There were so many things from which he had never managed to free his heart, of which he had taken no farewell. The night hours were granted him for this.[6]

Here Hesse is listing his character Goldmund's as yet ungrieved attachments: to people, places and other things he has loved. Then he goes deeper.

> He must take leave of his hands, his eyes; of thirst and hunger, food and drink, of love and lute-playing, sleep and waking: of all... He seemed to taste the morning wind on moors, the sweet new wine, and young, firm walnuts, while into his fearful heart, like a memory, there crept the sudden realization of all the colour in the world, a dying pageant of farewells as the wild beauty of earth swept through his senses. He hunched himself up and broke into sobs, could feel the tears scald and trickle down his cheeks; moaning, he let this wave of grief sweep over him, crouched, and gave himself up to endless woe.[7]

Goldmund is reprieved at the last minute, but this account of the abrupt onset of a fit of grieving in the face of certain and an almost immediate death rings true. Vividly and movingly described, here is a natural catharsis of deep involuntary sorrow. The necessary emotional release of tears occurs as the most vital of attachments are relinquished. Farewell is made to life itself, and with it to the most basic of human faculties and experiences.

DETACHMENT ON THE PATH OF SPIRITUAL MATURITY

Happily, few people find themselves in such a dire predicament. Although we cannot necessarily count on it, we all usually have much longer than one night in which to number our blessings and take emotional leave of them. Relinquishing attachment is not, therefore, the same as giving up all association with the object of attachment. We may continue to benefit from and enjoy it for the time that remains to us, but less possessively and with less

---

6   Ibid., p.244.
7   Ibid., p.245

intense passion. A letting go, a freeing up, is all it means; a reduction in the amount of time, thought and emotional energy invested in the people, places, possessions and philosophies adhered to.

The reverse of attachment is 'detachment'. Being detached is quite unlike being indifferent. Rather than any kind of closing off, it involves uncoupling one's passion and desire, while remaining calmly alert and involved, moment by moment, with everyone and everything that takes one's attention. A spiritually mature person, no longer in thrall to distractions, can be thought of as a 'participant-observer'; at the same time both compassionate observer of life and wise participant in human affairs.

During the homecoming, Stages 5 and 6, major shifts in attitude tend to close the gap and reduce the dissonance between worldly ego and spiritual self. Intuitive epiphanies, like those of Barack Obama speaking at a rally and during the Sunday service in Trinity Church, do this. So too may encounters with suffering and loss of life.

Some people encounter death regularly in the course of their occupation, such as undertakers and health professionals.[8] On occasion also, 'something happens' to bring other people closer to the reality of death: encounters with, for example, fatal illnesses, suicides and attempted suicide, major accidents, man-made catastrophes, or natural disasters: avalanches, blizzards, earthquakes, famines, floods, forest fires, gales, hurricanes, tornados and tsunamis.

Being part of destructive events costing lives, even witnessing them remotely and repeatedly through the media, can change a person's attitudes and alter the trajectory of their spiritual journey. It can alter the path in either direction, depending on that person's preparedness. Some, finding their faith challenged and weakened by seeing and experiencing devastation, will feel helpless, bewildered, angry and afraid. Others, in contrast, will experience a spur to their resolve to live wisely, help others, and so accept and develop personal responsibility. This is spiritual maturity.

The example of plane crash survivors

There was much publicity when US Airways Flight 1549 crash-landed in New York's Hudson River on 15 January 2009. All the 155 passengers and crew survived. Some of those interviewed later gave reactions showing that the event had triggered a major review of their life's priorities and values. In several cases, this had prompted a significant change in their conduct.[9]

---

8   For example, see again Personal anecdote – encounter with death in Chapter 8.
9   Channel Four documentary *Miracle of the Hudson Plane Crash*, directors Christina Bavetta and Marc Tiley, producer Charlotte Surtees. Programme screened on 19 February 2009.

One regular aeroplane business commuter, a wife and mother, said, for example, that she had been questioning everything in her life, asking herself particularly whether she should continue with the same type of work. She could not help herself from wondering repeatedly what might happen next.

Picking up the theme, a male survivor reported his new attitude, saying that he knew there were other things that he felt he was supposed to do with his life. He also said that he thought all the 154 survivors now had something important that they were supposed to do with their lives. A grandfather contributed that his life had been touched by a miracle. His response was to say that he now felt compelled to give something back. He said that since the crash, he had been asking himself a big question. Thinking he might well have died, he was reflecting earnestly on whether he was the person he really wanted to be for the rest of his life.

Finally, another woman had already made plans for a major change of direction. She and her husband had signed up with an agency to adopt a baby, thinking of it as a second chance for a meaningful life.

Etty Hillesum

Great and prolonged adversity offers considerable opportunity for spiritual growth. Indeed, greater suffering could hardly be imagined than that of Jews and others as a result of Nazi persecution in the first half of the 20th century.

After the Nazi invasion of the Netherlands in May 1940, Etty Hillesum was given no second chance for life. She was murdered in Auschwitz concentration camp in 1943; but not before she attained and demonstrated remarkable spiritual maturity. Over a period of about 30 months, as her astonishingly revealing personal diaries and letters record, her life was completely transformed. These valuable documents were eventually published, although not until almost 40 years after her death.[10]

Etty was from a Dutch Jewish family living contentedly during her childhood alongside their non-Jewish neighbours. Her father taught classical languages and was headmaster of the school in a big town. Her mother came originally from Russia, having fled to Holland after violent, homicidal attacks on the Jews living there. Both parents and Etty's brothers, Jacob (Jaap) and Michael (Mischa), were alive as the diaries began in March 1941. An intelligent woman, with university degrees in law and Slavonic languages, Etty was at the time studying psychology and giving Russian lessons, living independently of her family in South Amsterdam.

10   *An Interrupted Life: The Diaries and Letters of Etty Hillesum 1941–1943.* Trans. A. J. Pomerans (1999) (rpt 2007). London: Persephone Books. See also Woodhouse, P. (2009) *Etty Hillesum: A Life Transformed.* London: Continuum.

INTENT UPON SELF-DEVELOPMENT

Born in January 1914, Etty had never been much of a conformist. As her diaries begin, at the age of 27, she was already independent-minded, preferring to think things through for herself; but she was only superficially confident. In her first diary entry she wrote, 'Deep down something like a tightly wound ball of twine binds me relentlessly, and at times I am nothing more or less than a miserable, frightened creature.'[11]

Intent on self-development, she is searching for love and wholeness, aware that she is growing as a person and eager to do so. This suggests that she was at Faith Stage 4 when her search for personal integrity led her to consult an unconventional Jungian analyst. She describes this man, Julius Spier, perceptively as 'a fifty-four year old in whom the struggle between the spirit and the flesh is still in full cry'.[12]

Burdened by inhibitions, a sense of shame and a tremendous fear of letting go, she wants him to 'bring order to my inner chaos, harness the forces now at loggerheads within me.'[13] He advises engaging in spiritual practices: reading philosophy, poetry and scripture, meditating, reflecting and praying. She reads the New Testament of the Bible as well as the Old, the words of Gustav Jung, and the wisdom of the poet Rilke, taking to heart his advice in particular, 'To go into yourself and test the deeps in which your life takes rise.'[14]

Within a short time, Etty reports progress, and her hope to become 'an adult, capable of helping other souls who are in trouble'.[15] 'The struggle itself,' she also says, 'is thrilling.'[16]

LOVE AND FRIENDSHIP

Etty is attracted to Spier, who has a fiancée living in wartime safety in London, and this is part of her inner conflict. Spier helps her see that love of mankind is greater than the love of one man, but Etty thinks she may also always be in search of a man of her own. The situation is complicated, because Spier is also attracted to Etty. Both are trying to be noble. Etty desires 'friendship', as she puts it, 'in its deepest and fullest sense'. She admits that part of her wants him to claim her as the only one, and to say he will love her for evermore; but at the same time she suspects, deeper down, that there is no such thing as eternal love. She feels possessive, but also writes that she neither wants Spier

---

11   *An Interrupted Life*, p.3.
12   *Ibid.*, p.4.
13   *Ibid.*, p.7.
14   Rainer, M. R (1954) *Letters to a Young Poet* (rev. edn). Trans. H. Norton. New York, NY: W.W. Norton, p.20.
15   *An Interrupted Life*, p.12.
16   *Ibid.*, p.22.

forever nor as the only one in her life. Her self-seeking ego and spiritual self are still in conflict. She is striving for non-attachment, and naturally finding it hard.

During the early part of Faith Stage 5, the personal ego, 'the flesh', with its possessive nature, its physical concerns and desires, is still in see-saw tension with 'the spirit', with the spiritual self, emerging from beneath the shadow. However gradually or jerkily, the pendulum swings definitively in favour of the latter throughout the integration stage. Etty seems aware of this; she has become an observer as well as participant in her own development, as she writes, 'Truly this spiritual contact [with Spier] gives me much greater satisfaction than the physical one.'[17]

Describing her personality as growing stronger, she later adds,

> There is a sort of lamentation and loving-kindness as well as a little wisdom somewhere inside me that cry to be let out. Sometimes several different dialogues run through me at the same time, images and figures, moods, a sudden flash of something that must be my very own truth.[18]

Truth, and the mature, selfless love she says she needs to fight for within herself, belong to the realm of the soul.

THE BIGGER PICTURE

Although described in an intimate way, Etty also connects her personal journey with the grim circumstances of life around her under Nazi occupation.

> You must remain your own witness, marking well everything that happens in this world, never shutting your eyes to reality. You must come to grips with these terrible times... I sometimes feel like a post standing in a raging sea, lashed on all sides by the waves. But I am firmly moored, and the years have helped to weather me.[19]

Etty's growing friendship with Spier is only one of several factors contributing to this firm mooring. Another is her love of nature, which she is able to appreciate with a deep, contemplative intensity. This reflective ability, applied to herself, is also very useful, but it is a skill she needs to develop. As she writes, 'There is a really deep well inside me. And in it dwells God. Sometimes I am there, too. But more often stones and grit block the well, and God is buried beneath. Then he must be dug out again.'[20]

---

17   *Ibid.*, p.61.
18   *Ibid.*, p.74.
19   *Ibid.*, pp.49–50.
20   *Ibid.*, p.53.

The excavation process proves very difficult at times. 'I am unhappy again,' Etty wrote in early September 1941. In response, following Spier and Rilke's advice to listen to her inner voice, she withdraws to a corner, head bowed: 'And sat there. Absolutely still, contemplating my navel so to speak, in the pious hope that new sources of inspiration would bubble up inside me.'[21] Etty describes her heart as 'frozen' and her brain 'squeezed in a large vice'. 'What I am waiting for,' she adds, 'whenever I sit huddled up like that, is for something to give, for something to start flowing inside me.'[22] Her faith is at work here, the source of courage and hope she needs to provide her with the strength and willingness to persist.

Eventually, this is rewarded. Heart and mind are unlocked. Etty's next report of a similar experience has a quite different quality.

> Now I sometimes actually drop to my knees beside my bed, even on a cold winter night. And I listen to myself, allow myself to be led, not by anything on the outside, but by what wells up from deep within. It's still no more than a beginning, I know. But it is no longer a shaky beginning, it has already taken root.[23]

'Something happened' to Etty within those few months. She has learned to meditate and literally to get on her knees and pray. She did not record a single moment of awakening or epiphany, but a gradually increasing awareness of divine influence, and her new consciousness was associated with profound gratitude and a natural and joyful sense of submission. One day she wrote, for example, 'The only certainties about what is right and wrong are those that spring from sources deep inside oneself. And I say it humbly and gratefully… "Oh God, I thank you for having created me as I am."'[24] Humility and gratitude, like faith, courage and hope, spring naturally and involuntarily like this from the soul, the spiritual self.

In December 1941, Etty was forced, 'almost automatically' to the ground in prayer by 'something stronger' than herself. She remembered Spier describing a similarly powerful experience that involved an encounter with a patient in therapy. He told her, 'At such moments you are completely at one with the creative and cosmic forces that are at work in every human being.' 'And these creative forces,' Etty added, 'are ultimately part of God.'[25]

---

21 Ibid., pp.53–4.
22 *Ibid.*, p.54.
23 *Ibid.*, p.96.
24 *Ibid.*, p.90.
25 *Ibid.*, p.90.

Faith Stage 6
EMOTIONAL MATURITY

Eventually, Etty Hillesum enters calmer reaches. Using the analogy from Chapter 1, by Faith Stage 6, the taught guitar string vibrates increasingly weakly, growing still and hushed. Similarly, as repeated hand-washing gradually wears away a bar of soap, so the barrier between personal ego and spiritual self is dissolved, allowing the two to merge, banishing the dissonance between them, resolving conscience by healing the split.

The emotional maturity resulting from this reunion involves no remaining confusion, no doubt, no anxiety and no compromise, only commitment. Anger, guilt and shame are quickly seen through as counter-productive, therefore redundant emotions. The sorrow felt is real, and often sharp, yet solely for the plight of others – including enemies and persecutors – rather than for yourself. Identification with suffering humanity has become your principal source of meaning and purpose, resulting in a near-total disregard for personal safety and well-being in the service of others. Self-sacrifice is experienced as resulting not in hardship but joy.

A WOMAN APART

The Nazi persecution that Etty Hillesum experienced, and the accompanying knowledge that her life was likely to be short, sets her apart from most of today's readers. She also reacted uniquely and stood apart from those around her at the time.

People less well advanced along the spiritual path often find the spiritually mature difficult to understand and accept. Those in the conformist stage may feel particularly threatened and react negatively, until perhaps won over by wisdom and kindness. The wise, with their selfless and compassionate perspective on things, are often unfairly deemed mad or bad, misrepresented and marginalized, even martyred.

Etty was included among other victims of extreme Nazi intolerance, and not singled out for separate treatment. This allowed her goodness to stand out. As she learned to pray, and to conquer her reticence to speak and write the name of God, the see-saw tension within, the doubts and shame, subsided. She discovered the strength and courage she needed to face both personal loss and the mounting challenges of Nazi persecution that were unfolding around her and drawing close. The timing was exquisitely fine. Calm and inner resolve protected and prepared her for increasing external destruction and chaos.

The situation for Amsterdam Jews worsened during 1941, and by the following year ordinary life had become impossible. The so-called Nuremberg

Laws[26] were introduced and enforced. Jews had to wear a yellow star. They were not allowed in certain shops and public places, or on public transport. Food was scarce and rationed. By late June 1942, Jews were not allowed to leave the city. Large-scale round-ups began and they were sent to camps, notably Westerbork, a camp over 100 miles from Amsterdam.

Etty knew the perils she was facing. At the end of June 1942 she wrote about her parents, 60 miles away:

> I am aware that there may come a time when I shan't know where they are, when they might be deported to perish miserably in some unknown place… The latest news is that all Jews will be transported out of Holland through Drenthe Province (the site of Westerbork) and then on to Poland… The English radio has reported that 700,000 Jews perished last year alone in Germany and the occupied territories.[27]

Commenting on this news, Etty demonstrates her strength of character, her willingness to face the facts, and her ability to retain hope:

> Even if we stay alive, we shall carry the wounds with us throughout our lives. And yet I don't think that life is meaningless… I know about everything and am no longer appalled by the latest reports. In one way or another, I know it all. And yet I find life beautiful and meaningful.[28]

Etty refused to consider attempting to flee the country or go into hiding. She wrote, 'Everyone who seeks to save himself must surely realise that if he does not go another must take his place… Ours is now a common destiny.'[29] She has taken on a universal identity, identifying not only with Jews, but with all who are poor, weak and oppressed. She expresses compassion for many of the Nazis too, victims also of powerful forces. She simply refuses to hate.

CHANGING CIRCUMSTANCES

Etty was employed by the Jewish Council, set up to maintain public order in 1941 after rising tension between the Dutch and the German occupying forces. In July 1942, she volunteered for work at the Westerbork camp, to help the internees there. Ill-health interrupted her plan and she returned to Amsterdam; but she returned to the camp again in July 1943.

---

26 The 'Laws for the Protection of German Blood and German Honour', passed 15 September 1935.
27 *An Interrupted Life*, p.184.
28 *Ibid.*, p.184.
29 *Ibid.*, p.211.

In the intervening period, she described her rare and remarkable state of mind in a series of diary entries. She speaks of 'hearkening to God' and of 'reposing' in herself, explaining that the part of herself, 'that deepest and richest part in which I repose, is what I call "God"…'[30] She also wrote, 'Those two months behind barbed wire have been the two richest and most intense months of my life, in which my highest values were so deeply confirmed. I have learnt to love Westerbork.'[31]

We might wonder if she has lost her reason, but she explains the value to her of experiencing 'life's innermost framework, stripped of all outer trappings'. Even now, she does not think of her life's work as being fully complete, not yet, as she describes it 'a rounded whole'.

A PERSONAL LOSS

On 15 September 1942, the very day the Gestapo came to take him away, Julius Spier died after a short illness. Etty wrote in her diary that night, as if speaking to her mentor, that he had become 'so much a part of the heaven that stretches above me that I had only to raise up my eyes to be by your side.'[32]

Her grief is tempered by this profound sense of ultimate universal unification in the spiritual realm. Earlier, in July, she had written:

> If I knew for certain that I should die next week, I should still be able to sit at my desk and study with perfect equanimity, for I know now that life and death make a meaningful whole… Death is a slipping away, even when gloom and abominations are its trappings.[33]

To know that life and death make a meaningful whole is a great blessing; the pinnacle of wisdom, one might say, from which all else follows.

LETTERS

On 6 June 1943, Etty returned to Westerbork camp for the last time. It was now just a transit place, in which people were rounded up, held for several weeks and then forwarded to extermination camps in the east. None of her diaries, if she wrote them, have survived from this time, but she did write numerous letters in which she comes across as compassionate, reverent, wise and often uniquely happy. Once she wrote to a friend, for example, 'I have a doctor who gets furious when I come into his office beaming. He says it's

---

30   *Ibid.*, p.249.
31   *Ibid.*, p.251.
32   *Ibid.*, p.244.
33   *Ibid.*, p.203.

unforgivable to smile at all in times like these. I think he's wrong: what do you say?'[34]

Her work at the camp involved helping inmates in extreme conditions of poverty and overcrowding. Over 10,000 people at a time were cramped into a few buildings. Etty did not complain, writing to a friend in June 1943: 'My soul is content, Maria. I was given four hospital barracks today, one large and three small; I have to check whether the people there need any food or luggage from the outside.'[35] Later, she was also given responsibility for the punishment barracks.

Etty continued to observe and enjoy nature and beauty, even in the face of stark horror. One day she wrote:

> The sky is full of birds, the purple lupins stand up so regally and peacefully, two little old women have sat down for a chat, the sun is shining on my face – and right before our eyes, mass murder...
> The whole thing is simply beyond comprehension.[36]

Her wry comment shows a mind fully open to the extremes of a simultaneously wonderful and terrible reality; and the self-awareness that to entertain both goes beyond rationality. That there is light in the darkness allows her to take an ironic tone, and this seems to express hope, not for deliverance from the ordeal she and those with her are facing, but from the risk of meaninglessness in their suffering, as her letters continue to imply.

A STRANGE STATE OF MOURNFUL CONTENTMENT

At the end of June 1943, Etty wrote encouragingly to friends in Amsterdam:

> The realms of the soul and the spirit are so spacious and unending that this little bit of physical discomfort doesn't matter all that much. I do not feel I have been robbed of my freedom; essentially no one can do me any harm at all. Yes, children, that's how it is, I am in a strange state of mournful contentment... Be of good cheer, my dear good friends.[37]

Another letter records:

> The misery here is quite terrible; and yet, late at night when the day has slunk away into the depths behind me, I often walk with a spring in my step along the barbed wire. And then time and again, it soars straight from my heart – I can't help it, that's just the way

---

34 *Ibid.*, p.317.
35 *Ibid.*, p.330.
36 *Ibid.*, p.332.
37 *Ibid.*, pp.347–8.

it is, like some elementary force – the feeling that life is glorious and magnificent, and that one day we shall be building a whole new world. Against every new outrage and every fresh horror, we shall put up one more piece of love and goodness, drawing strength from within ourselves. We may suffer, but we must not succumb.[38]

Etty Hillesum continues to feel responsible for others, at whatever personal cost. She is so busy in the camp, helping and comforting people. In addition, when she cannot alter history, she feels she has been chosen at least to record it – and her reaction to it – with unflinching honesty:

I have told you often enough that no words and images are adequate to describe nights like these (during which the weekly 'transport lists' of one thousand deportees' names are published). But still I must try to convey something of it to you.[39]

In the same long letter dated 24 August, she wrote:

If I were to say that I was in hell that night, what would I really be telling you? I caught myself saying it aloud to myself and quite soberly, 'So that's what hell is like'… 'God Almighty, what are you doing to us?' The words just escape me… We are being hunted to death all through Europe.[40]

Not so much a cry of despair, this is a chillingly accurate summary of the state of affairs for the Jewish people of the time, during which 83 trains carried over 90,000 people from Westerbork to the Nazi death camps of Sobibor and Auschwitz in Poland.[41]

Etty was still only 28 years old when these terrible things really happened. She is not blinded by the madness and cruelty of it, and remains always able to write something positive or wise about the situation. People in the camp die of a broken spirit, she says, 'because they can no longer find any meaning in life'.[42]

Like the better known concentration camp survivor, Viktor Frankl, in similar circumstances,[43] Etty understood that the primary cause of death was not the persecution, the malnutrition and ill-health, but the loss of meaning, a sickness of the soul.

---

38   *Ibid.*, p.355.
39   *Ibid.*, p.403.
40   *Ibid.*, pp.402–20. This was from the second of two of Etty's letters published illegally in Holland and circulated by the Resistance in 1943.
41   The other well-known Amsterdam diarist, the teenager Anne Frank, was also interned briefly at Westerbork, before being transported to Auschwitz and her death in September 1944.
42   *Ibid.*, p.356.
43   See Frankl, V. (2004) *Man's Search for Meaning.* London: Rider Books.

When she wrote to her friend, Maria, about love and about the balance between good and bad, her vision is completely holistic, another example of supreme wisdom. Expressing a clearly non-dualistic view, her words and ideas take on a truly mystical quality.

> Everywhere things are both very good and very bad at the same time. The two are in balance, everywhere and always. I never have the feeling that I have got to make the best of things; everything *is* fine just as it is. Every situation, however miserable, is complete in itself and contains the good as well as the bad.[44]

Etty mentions the tears she often sheds; but rather than tears of sorrow, they are tears of gratitude that run down her face. Like a prayer, she writes, 'You have made me so rich, O God… My life has become an uninterrupted dialogue with You, O God, one great dialogue.' She asks his help to: 'Please let me share out Your beauty with open hands!' In this same letter, dated just three weeks before she was taken from the camp to her death, Etty wrote, 'There are many miracles in a human life. My own is one long sequence of inner miracles.'[45]

Etty, no longer protected by the declining size and powers of the Jewish Council, was taken from Westerbork by the weekly transport on 7 September 1943. She threw a final postcard from the overcrowded train, addressed to a friend:

> Opening the Bible at random I find this: 'The Lord is my high tower.' I am sitting on my rucksack in the middle of a full freight car. Father, Mother, and Mischa are a few cars away. In the end, the departure came without warning… We left the camp singing… Thank you for all your kindness and care.[46]

FINAL WORDS ABOUT ETTY

On the same day, Etty's friend Jopie wrote to others in Amsterdam who knew her:

> It all happened so suddenly, so unexpectedly… And when the time came she, too, was ready and waiting. And, alas, she, too, has gone. She stepped onto the platform…talking gaily, smiling, a kind word for everyone she met on the way, full of sparkling humour, perhaps just a touch of sadness, but every inch the Etty you all know so well… With what grace she and her family left!

---

44 *An Interrupted Life*, p.391.
45 *Ibid.*, p.395.
46 *Ibid.*, p.426.

> After her departure I spoke to a little Russian woman and various other protégés of hers. And the way they felt about her leaving speaks volumes for the love and devotion she had given to them all.[47]

This letter powerfully and independently attests to Etty Hillesum's genuine faith and spiritual maturity. She died in Auschwitz on 30 November 1943.

Aspects of vocation

In city streets, in hospitals, nursing homes and hospices, material and emotional losses abound: loss associated with leaving the comfort and familiarity of home, with the changing nature of contact and communication between family and friends, with having few personal possessions to hand, with wearing allocated rather than personal clothing, with gradually or abruptly reducing faculties (including impairment of vision, hearing, mobility and memory), with the need for powerful medical, surgical and psychological treatments, with physical pain, and with imminent departure from life.

Health and social care professionals face and deal competently with all this on a daily basis. They are impressively committed, carrying out their emotionally challenging business with dignity, and often too with good humour. Arguably, what draws people towards this kind of work is compassion, a natural fellow-feeling for those who are suffering.

When conscious and deliberate, this is a characteristic of Faith Stage 5; but many are moved to help others less consciously at earlier levels of development. The child, Tam, described in Chapter 7, expressed a natural and spontaneous desire to help another child in difficulty. The desire may get submerged later, but compassion is rarely extinguished completely.

The Latin origins of the word 'compassion' mean 'to suffer with'. Compassionate thoughts and feelings are involuntary phenomena, arising from the purity of the spiritual self. Holding true to these higher instincts and values while establishing one's identity, forging one's way in the world in terms of education and employment, is to obey a sense of vocation – of being called into an occupation that benefits others. It usually also involves some degree of self-sacrifice.

In following a vocation, one also experiences significant rewards: a feeling of benefit, of being blessed, and therefore also gratitude. Putting oneself through training, engaging with the work, joining others as part of a professional body or team in the endeavour, witnessing results; all play a part in giving one's life a profound sense of meaning and purpose and a heart-warming sense of belonging.

---

47   *An Interrupted Life.* Letter from Jopie Vleeschhouwer, pp.426–30.

This is the situation when things are going well; but the drive to enact compassion needs tempering also with wisdom. We need to know our limitations and not strive excessively beyond them. We need to avoid putting results first, and to acquire the spiritual skills necessary to protect ourselves from exhaustion, from 'compassion fatigue' and 'burnout'. After all, as the medical students were encouraged to discover during the SSC (see Chapter 3), 'compassion hurts'. This is a lesson I too had to learn. (See Personal anecdote – compassion).

Personal anecdote – compassion

I became emotionally distressed, especially during the early part of my training in psychiatry, over the plight of several patients. I recall particularly one man whose intense depressive condition had failed to respond to years of treatment. He was very miserable, and tearful on a daily basis. I happened to speak of him to a Buddhist monk I encountered who asked me, perceptively, where the pain was. It took a while to realize that it was not 'out there' in the locked hospital ward. I was carrying it myself, in my heart.

Then the monk asked why I was suffering. I could not exactly say, so he told me it was because I cared about this man and my other patients. I immediately realized two things: that my compassion was involuntary, and that my emotional pain (which I had been thinking of as a problem) was a good thing.

Like many others, I had chosen to be a doctor and a psychiatrist from deep-seated motives over which I had no control. This was my vocation, my destiny. I was learning that compassion hurts, but that the pain is unavoidable. The monk advised that I should make such patients my teachers, rather than insist every time on being the one to give something to the other. I should allow the principle of reciprocity to work, and learn from those who suffer: learn my limitations, without being overwhelmed by anger, sadness, guilt, shame or any other painful emotion. On the contrary, because of the virtue of my intention to help people, even when it proved unsuccessful, I could feel at least a degree of contentment. These insights changed my working life. My enthusiasm for what I was doing was immediately renewed, and has remained robust.[48]

Losses associated with illness and ageing are normally considered and experienced as unwelcome. Being robbed by the Nazis of everything you possess, including ultimately your life, is the harshest of examples; but consider what happens as people are taken into day care, shelters, nursing

---

48 Adapted from Culliford, L. (2007) *Love, Healing and Happiness.* Winchester: O Books, pp.190–8.

homes, hostels, hospices, hospitals and the like. There are similarities. There is certainly the risk of a comparable loss of dignity.

Mrs Cruikshank's and Etty Hillesum's stories demonstrate that ill-health, persecution and all forms of material loss provide opportunities for spiritual gain for those prepared to acquiesce to natural or imposed attrition and decline in themselves and others. As we shall see in the next chapter, we benefit when we learn how to grieve.

Summary points

1. *Homecoming and recognition*
The journey towards spiritual maturity involves leaving a narrow certainty behind, passing through a period of confusion and doubt, before returning to confidence and recognition of a broader perspective. To paraphrase T.S. Eliot, the homecoming involves arriving where we started, and knowing the place for the first time.

2. *Many people are spiritually mature*
There are millions of spiritually mature people in the world, living quietly, doing good in general society. Spiritual maturity is neither rare nor unattainable.

3. *Changing attitudes*
With maturity, a person's attitudes change, softening particularly towards suffering and death.

4. *Lessons from a dying patient*
The author's patient, Mrs Cruikshank, survived cancer, a broken leg and a chest infection much longer than was expected. Something happened during the illness, allowing her to recognize and confess her fear and marking a turning point in terms of emotional healing. Her last few days were serene. The doctor, too, was beneficially affected, realizing that there is special work to do in medicine, as well as attempting simply physical cures.

5. *Lesson from literature*
Hesse's tale of Goldmund illustrates the importance of grieving in the face of inevitable death, and the emotional release of letting go of all mortal attachments.

6. *Detachment*

Detachment means a freeing up. It is not the same as giving up all association with the object of attachment, which people may continue to benefit from and enjoy, but less intensely and possessively.

7. *Lesson from plane crash survivors*

As survivors of a plane crash demonstrated, being part of life-threatening and destructive events can change a person's attitudes and alter the trajectory of their spiritual journey.

8. *Lessons from Etty Hillesum's story*

Dutchwoman Etty Hillesum's diaries and letters reveal a person growing to spiritual maturity while experiencing extremes of Nazi persecution that eventually led to her death in Auschwitz in 1943. She did not record a single moment of awakening, but a gradually increasing awareness of divine influence, profound gratitude and a joyful sense of both awareness and acquiescence towards whatever was happening, even in the face of stark horror.

9. *Characteristics of Faith Stage 6*

Etty's life showed how, by Faith Stage 6, the personal ego becomes thoroughly reunited with the spiritual self. No confusion, no doubt, no anxiety and no compromise remain, only commitment. Anger, guilt and shame are seen through as counter-productive emotions. Sorrow is felt as real, yet solely for the plight of others, including enemies and persecutors.

10. *Identification with others' suffering*

In Stage 6, meaning and purpose are derived entirely through identification with suffering humanity, resulting in a near-total disregard for personal safety and well-being in the service of others. Etty Hillesum was known for her compassion, love and devotion, right to the end.

11. *Human suffering brings out a compassionate response*

In city streets, in hospitals, nursing homes and hospices, material and emotional losses abound. Health and social care professionals are impressively committed, carrying out their difficult and emotionally challenging business competently, with dignity and often good humour.

12. *The basis of a vocation*

Compassionate thoughts and feelings are involuntary phenomena, arising from the purity of the spiritual self. Holding true to these higher instincts and values while establishing one's identity, forging one's way in the world, is to obey a sense of vocation, of being called into an occupation that benefits others but involves self-sacrifice. In following a vocation, one also experiences significant rewards: a profound sense of meaning and purpose and a heart-warming sense of belonging.

13. *Losses provide opportunities*
Losses associated with illness and ageing are normally considered and experienced as unwelcome, but these and other material losses can provide opportunities for spiritual gain.

Exercises and questions for personal reflection and as a basis for group discussion:

1. Think of any people you have encountered that seem spiritually mature to you. What makes you think that way about them? Is it a calm, cheerful disposition? Is it selfless, compassionate behaviour? Is it that they can be relied on for wise words and good advice? Can you think of anything else? Many people would count Mother Teresa and Nelson Mandela on their list. Do not only consider well-known examples. What about members of your family, your local community and your profession?

2. Have there been any occasions when an encounter with someone (because of something they said or did, or just because of who they were) made a real and significant difference to your life, causing you to pause and reflect, bringing about a change in your attitudes and behaviour? Was it a particularly influential school or university teacher? Was it a patient or someone else who came to you for assistance and ended up helping you too?

3. Have you been involved in any life-threatening or other potentially highly destructive events? What were the circumstances? How did the experience affect you at the time? How is the memory of it affecting you still? Please find and tell someone you can trust about these experiences.

4. What does death mean to you? Think about all that you have now and that you control. Think about the people you care about. Think about losing everything at the time of your death. Do you ever think about when it might happen?

5. Suppose you knew you were to die in four years' time; how does the idea make you react? What thoughts arise? What emotions? How would your values be affected? In the face of this knowledge, in what ways would you change your behaviour? Take your time over this.

6. Have you understood the distinction between 'detachment' and 'indifference'? Think about Etty Hillesum's story. Was she indifferent to the plight of Dutch Jews? Could it have been that an attitude of detachment enabled her to keep functioning, while being realistic about the limited effects of her efforts?

7. Do you have a sense of following a vocation? Are you aware of making any degree of self-sacrifice? What, for you, are the hoped-for rewards? Do you ever feel a deep sense of meaning and purpose, or a heart-warming sense of belonging and being useful? What would your life be like if you were not able to make a contribution to the welfare of others in some way?

PART 3

REMEDIES

'Sowing Live Seeds and Doing Good Deeds'

Chapter 11

SPIRITUAL SKILLS

Childhood and adolescence
EDUCATION
The process of spiritual development begins in childhood, hence the importance of education, which means sowing seeds; imparting information, values, codes of behaviour and so on. Education must also involve preparing the soil in which those seeds are to grow and flourish; and this means paying close attention to the true meaning of the word 'education', to make it a genuine 'leading out' of a person's innate wisdom and knowledge, to maximize their potential for the fine human qualities that attend spiritual maturity.

The point was made in Chapter 7 that schooling in contemporary Western culture is often deficient in terms of spiritual education. David Hay is emphatic about it, writing, 'Spirituality cannot be nurtured where education is purveyed as just another commodity distributed at arm's length. What is conveyed is a lack of spiritual awareness, sometimes paraded as a virtue.'[1]

In Hay's view, spiritual education 'is fundamental for the personal and political wellbeing of the community'.[2] He admits that there are difficulties due to 'the absence of a widely available, cross-curricular programme of spiritual education', and offers suggestions on what the schoolteacher can do to overcome the problem. These include 'helping children become aware of their (spiritual) awareness', and encouraging them 'to reflect on this experience in the light of the language and culture within which it emerges'.[3]

---

1   Hay, D. and Nye, R. (2006) *The Spirit of the Child* (rev. edn). London: Jessica Kingsley Publishers, p.148.
2   *Ibid.*, pp.133–4.
3   *Ibid.*, p.143.

A four-point plan for the teacher is recommended:[4]

1. helping children keep an open mind (gently encouraging or reawakening children's 'relational consciousness', their natural disposition to spiritual awareness)

2. exploring ways of seeing (such as exploring metaphors, ambiguity, paradoxes and exercises in empathy)

3. encouraging personal awareness (for example by sitting still with eyes closed and attending to the here-and-now, even for a minute or two, or experiencing as fully as possible the physical act of eating a piece of fruit)

4. becoming personally aware of the social and political dimensions of spirituality (recognizing that spirituality is concerned with self-transcendence, requiring people to go beyond egocentricity to take account of their relatedness to other people, the environment, the wider culture and the sacred wholeness of the universe).

Hay calls it important 'to offer a necessary scaffolding of language and cultural understanding that will enable children to come to grips with their spirituality – that is, their understanding of themselves in relation to the rest of reality'.[5] Many agree with him.

MEDITATION IN SCHOOLS

Other authors and researchers have begun exploring the same territory differently. Campion and Rocco, for example, report on a programme of meditation introduced into 31 Catholic schools in Australia in 2006, engaging over 10,000 students aged between 5 and 18 years.[6] Beneficial effects consistently reported included: increased relaxation and feelings of calm, reduced stress, reduced anger, improved concentration, and better interactions with others.

Some students described religious experiences during meditation. Others experienced altruistic thoughts and intentions, also a new appreciation of 'such things as food every day'. Negative effects reported include that meditation was 'boring', 'too long' and left students feeling 'sleepy' or 'tired'. Teachers and parents interviewed supported the students' reports of mainly beneficial effects. One teacher reported that his students 'were a lot calmer for

---

4   *Ibid.*, p.149.
5   *Ibid.*, p.157.
6   Campion, J. and Rocco, S. (2009) 'Minding the Mind: The effects and potential of a school-based meditation programme for mental health promotion.' *Advances in School Mental Health Promotion 2*, 1, 47–55.

the rest of the day', after a meditation session, and that they then 'deal better with each other' than at other times.

Fontana and Slack,[7] Erricker and Erricker,[8] among others, have also reported that teaching schoolchildren to meditate regularly, even for short periods daily (no longer than five minutes for younger children) improves their powers of concentration, helps them deal better with stress and reduces conflict between them. Some enthusiasts go further and suggest that meditation (sometimes called 'stilling') can contribute to improvement in schoolwork and grades, children's sporting abilities, their general levels of creativity, and their willingness to co-operate with each other. As a significant spin-off, it may also greatly improve teachers' working lives.

These investigations seem to show that meditation appreciably fosters physical and mental well-being among children. They hint too in the direction of spiritual benefits, such as increased gratitude for things previously taken for granted, and an increased consideration for the plight of those less well off.

Meditation as a spiritual skill
OPENING THE DOOR

Learning to be still and to meditate opens the door to many other possibilities. Meditation is the key, for example, to several other spiritual skills, the foremost of which is:

- being able to rest, relax and create a still, peaceful state of mind.

Although it is possible to achieve this without formally engaging in meditation practice, learning to meditate is a good way to improve one's capacity for restful calm. The resulting mental state has similarly quiescent characteristics, and will be more rapidly achieved and more stable. Meditation skills allow a person to remain still and relaxed for longer and in the face of greater distraction than before.

Other spiritual skills include:

- remaining focused in the present, staying alert, unhurried and attentive

- going deeper into the stillness and observing one's emerging thoughts and feelings with emotional stability, in a way that carries over into everyday life

- being honestly and sincerely self-reflective, taking responsibility for every thought, word and action

---

7   Fontana, D. and Slack, I. (2007) *Teaching Meditation to Children: The Practical Guide to the Use and Benefits of Meditation Techniques.* London: Watkins Publishing.
8   Erricker, C. and Erricker, J. (2001) *Meditation in Schools: A Practical Guide to Calmer Classrooms and Clearer Minds.* London: Continuum Publishing.

- using the capacity for deep reflection to connect with one's spiritual essence and values

- developing compassion and an extensive capacity for direct empathic communication with others

- emotional resilience: having the courage to witness and endure distress while sustaining an attitude of hope

- being able to give without feeling drained

- being able to grieve and let go.

These skills are interconnected and mutually reinforcing.

STILLING THE MIND

The essence of meditation involves reducing external stimulation: choosing a quiet place, becoming calm through stillness or repetitive, rhythmical activity while closing (or part closing) the eyes. This allows the mind to settle, so that internal stimulation is also gradually reduced. The mind now focuses naturally upon itself: upon the thoughts, emotions, sense perceptions and impulses that arise. Eventually, these too will subside, leaving the mind entirely clear.

This sounds easier than it usually proves to be in practice. At the beginning, the meditator is easily distracted. According to ancient Hindu scriptures, the Upanishads,[9] for example, meditation has been practised for thousands of years and in that period various techniques have been developed to help overcome the problem.

These techniques involve giving the mind a focus of concentration: the footsteps as one walks gently and rhythmically in a circle, for example, an actual or imagined visual image,[10] a sacred word, prayer or sound known as a 'mantra', the rise and fall of the chest and abdomen, or the passage of air through the nostrils during inward and outward breathing.

The aim is for 'mindfulness', and 'one-pointedness' of focus and concentration. Paradoxically, even when the mind seems empty of content, it remains full, filled with the single object of concentration. This mental state, devoid of ego, is expansive, seeming endless or bottomless, yet there is no partitioning, and no room within it for anything else.[11]

---

9   *The Upanishads*. Trans. J. Mascaro (2005) (New Impression edn) London: Penguin.

10   Such as a Buddhist mandala (a symbolic circular figure representing the universe) or Christian icon (a stylized image of a holy person. Icons are particularly associated with Byzantine or Orthodox forms of Christianity.).

11   This point is helpfully clarified by the Buddhist monk and teacher Thich Nhat Hanh in his book *The Miracle of Mindfulness: A Manual on Meditation* (2008 Classic edn) London: Rider Books.

The practice of these focusing techniques is not exactly the same as meditating. This is a more mysterious process, occurring spontaneously when the mind is engaged purely with itself; but proficiency in the techniques does allow the practitioner increasingly to let go of effort, allowing meditation simply to happen. Meditation techniques can be undertaken deliberately, but meditation itself cannot be forcibly guided or steered.

There are good biological and psychological explanations for meditation working its benefits and promoting spiritual growth.

THE BIOLOGY OF MEDITATION

The structure and function of the brain and nervous system are highly complex, and relatively difficult to study. Electroencephalography (EEG) and a variety of neuro imaging and scanning techniques have revealed a number of insights concerning meditation, as summarized and carefully explained in a recent publication.[12] There is much more still to discover.[13]

Although each meditation experience is personal and unique to the meditator, some generalizations are acceptable. In Chapter 1, we noted that the brain consists of a poetic right half-brain and a more practical left half-brain, both of which are important for spiritual awareness, and for full appreciation of and engagement with our environment.

Dr Nataraja writes that the stillness associated with meditation practice causes 'a lack of activity in the (brain's) *right* orientation association area (which) gives rise to the sense of unity and wholeness. At the same time a lack of activity in the *left* orientation association area results in the dissolving of the self/non-self boundary'.[14] This, and the closing down of the verbal-conceptual areas, she continues, leaves the meditator struggling to find a way of describing the experience to others.

Researcher Andrew Newberg and his colleagues have further shown that mystical experiences evoked by meditation appear to involve circuitry throughout the entire brain.[15] Brainwave (EEG) studies have also shown that meditation decreases compartmental activity in the brain and nervous system, so that it increasingly acts in a unified way, as a whole organ communicating with a whole body. A subtle degree of conscious awareness may be maintained.

---

12 Nataraja, S. (2008) *The Blissful Brain: Neuroscience and Proof of the Power of Meditation.* London: Gaia.

13 For a more detailed analysis of brain structure and activity during meditation, see Austin, J. (1998) *Zen and the Brain: Toward an Understanding of Meditation and Consciousness.* Cambridge, MA: MIT Press.

14 *The Blissful Brain,* p.89.

15 Newberg, A., d'Aquili, E. and Rause, V. (2001) *Brain Science and the Biology of Belief: Why God Won't Go Away.* New York, NY: Ballantine Books. Also, d'Aquili, E. and Newberg, A. (1999) *The Mystical Mind.* Minneapolis, MN: Augsburg Fortress Publishers.

As ever, spirituality concerns wholeness, and the unification of opposites. Left and right interact and work together seamlessly in concert. Both sides are necessary (as are light and dark, yin and yang) and it is unsurprising that the biology of meditation involves the unification of brain activity, together with seamless brain–body interaction.

A similar state to meditation is achieved during intense, purposeful activity. Athletes and artistic performers like musicians sometimes describe this as being 'in the zone'. Performance is enhanced to an optimal, near-perfect level. Concentration is intense and highly focused, coupled with the experience of the kind of automatism that is associated with quiescence of the personal ego.

At the start of meditation, experiences follow a chain of events that include activation of two key structures in the brain's 'limbic system'.[16] Reduced sensory input, contributing to reduced activity in the parietal lobe, results in the activation of the 'hippocampus', which in turn stimulates the 'amygdala'.

These two structures link emotional significance to our experiences. During meditation the process switches over, so that significance becomes attached to the *lack* of sensory input. In consequence, the activity of the autonomic nervous system is modified. First, a blissful, calm state arises (involving maximal activation of the parasympathetic nervous system). Then, a mentally clear state of alertness supervenes (through maximal activation of the sympathetic nervous system in tandem).

Meditation generates an ideal balance between these two interrelated systems, resulting in a 'relaxation response' characterized by calm, joyful alertness, accompanied by reduced breathing rate, oxygen consumption, blood pressure and heart rate, and increased skin resistance, blood flow to the internal organs and temperature of the extremities. In an experienced meditator, under the amygdala's influence, an optimal balance is regularly achieved and maintained.

THE PSYCHOLOGY OF MEDITATION

The limbic system, the seat of the emotions, takes the form of a circuit in each brain hemisphere with strong connections between the two sides. It forms a biological figure eight or infinity symbol.

The necessary research has not been conducted or reported, but the image serves well for the most basic and commonplace emotions of life with which

---

16   This account of nervous system changes during meditation is based on Nataraja, *ibid.*, pp.87–9.

we have become familiar throughout this book. We may presume them to be represented biologically in this double system of brain circuitry, extending through left and right hemispheres.

In one circuit are the painful emotions: of wanting and not-wanting (hunger and desire, distaste and aversion), of threat (bewilderment, doubt, anxiety and anger) and of loss (shame, guilt and sadness). In the other, conjoined circuit are their pain-free counterparts: contentment, clarity, certainty, calm, acceptance, self-worth, purity and joy (see Box 1.1, p.22). Where there are blocks and by-passes, some form of emotional suffering is implicated. When energy flows freely throughout the double system, all will be well.

The limbic system has close links to memory storage in the brain's parietal lobes, in a way that is also consistent with psychological effects arising during meditation, especially during the early stages of a meditator's practice. Meditation enables the 'letting go' of attachments.

DISTRACTIONS

At the first meditation session, a person is likely to be distracted by both external and internal stimuli, notably sounds and bodily discomfort. These are sense perceptions. The remedy is to re-focus on the image, mantra or breath each time, until the distraction fades.[17]

Eventually, it becomes easier to 'let things happen' (an ache or an itch, for example, the sound of voices, traffic noises or birdsong) rather than getting attached to and chasing after them with the mind. It is not necessary to try to shut out noise or other stimuli that arise, only to note them and avoid attachment to them, to avoid consciously following them.

Another level of distraction involves thoughts and impulses to act. An example is remembering while trying to meditate that you have left something undone (such as going shopping, or making a phone call) and remaining attached to the impulse to go off and do it right then. Eventually, using the same remedy, people become proficient at 'letting go', at detaching from such thoughts and impulses too.

The next level of distraction involves emotions, and these may be more difficult to manage. Some meditators become attached to the blissful and calm feelings they experience, and overindulge in the activity, neglecting other needs and responsibilities. It is a kind of addiction and indicates, like other addictions, that there may be painful emotions lying deeper needing release.

---

17 William James is reported to have once said, 'The faculty of voluntarily bringing back a wandering attention, over and over again, is the very root of judgement, character and will.' James, W. (1890, 2007) *The Principles of Psychology*. New York, NY: Cosimo Classics, Vol. 1, p.424. He added, 'An education which should improve this faculty would be the education *par excellence.*'

Meditation, the whole mind, emotional healing and spiritual growth

THE HEALING POWER OF MEDITATION

As already described in earlier chapters, desire leads immediately to the threats both of not having what is desired and of losing what has been gained. Suffering, associated with both threat and actual loss, is inevitable. Painful emotions arise in this way, and emotional healing only takes place subsequently when the whole scale or spectrum of emotions has been present or somehow represented in the conscious experience of the sufferer.

Crying is nature's way of bringing healing to our emotional system, to our hearts and minds. This kind of emotional release is known by the Greek word for cleansing, 'catharsis'. Energy that has been invested in some form of attachment is liberated: the attachment itself is loosened or even relinquished completely. (The Greek word for this uncoupling is 'lysis'.)

Crying is very important, just as bleeding from a wound begins the physical process of healing. It may be helpful to moderate it, but it is not helpful to stifle it altogether. It is necessary to bleed, and to allow clot formation so the body's natural repair system can get to work. It is equally necessary to release tears, to cry, to sob, to wail over loss; in other words, to grieve. In many instances, emotional readjustment and the restoration of equanimity cannot take place otherwise.

Sometimes, when the loss is relatively slight or when we have been able to prepare ourselves for it, relief may be experienced as well as, or even instead of, sorrow. It may be of such a degree that we laugh, rather than cry. Laughter is another form of catharsis, of emotional release, that brings healing and growth.

Similarly, the experience of intense embarrassment, shame, makes people blush; and blushing is another involuntary form of readjustment and release. When we blush, we are forced (at least momentarily) to acknowledge some part of the ego's shadow that has been causing us shame.

When all the emotions have been present, and the sequence completed, the painful aspects simply flow away, leaving contentment in the place both of desire and distaste. Anxiety, for example, becomes transmuted into calm; bewilderment into clarity; anger into acceptance; and sadness into joy.

Furthermore, this healing process is accompanied by permanent gain in the form of personal growth. After weathering a significant loss, people are left able to experience a wider range of emotions – painful and pain-free – and in greater intensities than before. We develop increasing emotional resilience, rebounding more quickly to calm equanimity after each setback. Generally less fearful, we tend to live with greater joy, spontaneity and freedom than before.

This is why, after an episode of emotional trauma, for example brought on by severe illness, someone might say they would not want to go through it again, but were somehow glad that it happened. This affirms that there can be purpose in suffering.

Fear of something terrible that *might* happen had blighted the life of such a person beforehand. With the arrival of what seemed at first like a personal disaster, they began to discover both unsuspected inner wisdom and strength and outward assistance from others. This enabled them to survive the unpleasant experience and the associated losses involved, experiencing the whole spectrum of first painful and then pain-free emotions in the process.

MEDITATION AND THE WHOLE MIND

Meditation fosters these emotional processes of healing and growth. In experienced meditators, by reducing external stimulation and streamlining the passage of energy through the limbic circuits, it raises emotions into consciousness all at once, as if in a bundle.

Just as, when all the colours of the spectrum are bundled together, brilliant white light is experienced, so, when all the emotions of the bi-modal set are bundled together, blissful calm is experienced. Emotional healing occurs naturally and spontaneously in this way, without cathartic upheaval, and without therefore resulting in undue distress.

Some kind of prism is necessary to separate the colours of the spectrum. For the emotions, that prism takes the form of the personal ego, the source and seat of desires and aversions.

The true, spiritual self is free of desire. Meditation, therefore, little by little, releasing desire, aversion and resulting attachments from the ego, allows it to be restored gradually to its purer state. The power of the everyday ego is diminished by regular meditation, as a lit candle is shortened and a bar of soap is gradually worn away. The true self is revealed in its place.

Meditation enables this by improving the practitioner's ability to 'stay in the moment', to remain consciously focused in the here and now, untroubled by distracting or painful memories and imaginings. In promoting calm and clarity in place of anxiety and bewilderment, it does so also through fostering the kind of clear thinking that gives spontaneous access to wisdom.

Thinking that is no longer self-serving or partisan, arising in the clear, calm contentment of the meditator's mind, locked on to the spiritual realm, the Absolute, the Divine, however one might choose to express the supreme and seamless totality of existence, has certain additional beneficial attributes.

This kind of thinking is super-rational. It is holistic, intuitive, creative, empathic, compassionate and wise. Indeed, when the mind is not focused separately and energetically on sense perceptions, thoughts, emotions or impulses, but is allowed to become still, the higher functions (intuition, creativity and empathy among them) will tend to emerge.

Intuitive, holistic thinking is 'both/and', rather than 'either/or' thinking. It is characterized by the kind of universality that allows us, when it operates, to see things from different perspectives at the same time. It therefore precludes partisan, 'us and them', 'right or wrong' attitudes and encourages sympathetic understanding of the circumstances and opinions of other people. Hence it not only fosters compassion but also understands the deep-seated wisdom behind it.

The emergence of holistic thinking, intuition, wisdom and compassion through meditation practice may seem mysterious, because the meditator cannot account for how he or she knows how it appears spontaneously in the mind with no ego-driven effort of will. Nevertheless, associated with the absence of doubt (along with the absence of bewilderment, anxiety and so on), what arises in meditation is accompanied by feelings of certainty. This contributes to its mystical quality. The resulting insights appear incontrovertible, completely argument-proof.

This is one of the hallmarks of wisdom. 'I know this to be true. I know this course of action to be correct... But I cannot easily say how I know.' Often such ideas also appear counter-intuitive, suggesting that true wisdom (a sacred form of knowledge) lies deeper than everyday instincts and hunches.

Many who have benefited from its insights would also declare a spiritual, rather than personal, origin to such thoughts by saying, for example, 'Heaven has answered my prayer,' or, 'It was a kind of revelation,' or even, 'It was like hearing the voice of God.' Others will simply say, or think, 'Something happened... Something remarkable happened.' The accompanying feeling might well be one of relief. It might equally be one of awe (see Personal anecdote – a convincing communication.)

Personal anecdote 5 – a convincing communication

On returning from Australia to England in the early 1980s, I took a long break from psychiatry. I considered several other options, without being able to decide. One day, as I was emerging from meditation, I 'heard' in my head (but as if from outside it) a clear message: 'You have trained as a psychiatrist. Go and do that!' It was as if God or the Universe had spoken. Shortly thereafter I answered an advertisement in a medical journal for the position in a prestigious Medical School Department of Psychiatry that led to the resumption of my career.

The confidence I derived from the certainty that this was meant to happen undoubtedly helped me convince others at very competitive interviews for this and subsequent posts. The resulting rock-solid sense of purpose also protected and energized me through a number of stressful challenges in psychiatric settings over the following years.

MEDITATION RELIEVING EMOTIONAL SCARS AND INJURIES

In less experienced meditators, when the everyday ego is bound strongly to its attachments, the experience of whole-mindedness (also referred to as 'mindfulness') is less common. Painful feelings resulting from earlier psychological trauma, scars and injuries, previously somehow buried in memory, sometimes emerge and surface into consciousness during meditation, when they are easier to experience without being overwhelmed. Another personal anecdote illustrates the point.

Personal anecdote 6 – healing through meditation

About 30 years ago, when I began meditating regularly, I had been seated in meditation for about 15 minutes when I experienced the image in my mind's eye of a cat. At the same moment, I experienced a strong pang of sadness, bringing tears momentarily to my eyes. Remembering this afterwards, I recalled for the first time in many years the family cat, which had died while I was away at school at the age of about ten. I had not shed tears when informed of the loss, and it was as if I was now (albeit briefly) grieving for the first time. My emotional attachment to the cat, already attenuated by the passage of time, was finally relinquished.

It seems remarkable that simply sitting quietly allowed this lost memory and unfinished emotional business to emerge and be dealt with relatively painlessly. Even more remarkable was that not only did I feel better after the episode, but a fairly severe allergy I had developed to cats instantly improved. Both biological and psychological benefits had clearly resulted from meditation in this case.

Not every catharsis is as abrupt and complete as mine involving memories of the family cat. A very gentle and gradual process is also common, leaving people gradually less encumbered by attachments (to people, places, activities, objects, success, wealth, celebrity, ideas, ideologies, beliefs and so on) while remaining fully engaged with their lives.

Either way, accommodating losses is made easier. Tears of sorrow and other forms of emotional release may well up in the mind of the meditator, often briefly and intensely, before being allowed to evaporate, the energy flowing naturally out of them. Each person's experience, although similar in some ways, will be unique.

TEMPERAMENT

Everyone's temperamental profile involves preferences for some emotions over others. We feel attachment to some and aversion to others, and do not necessarily simply like the pain-free feelings and dislike those that are painful. Sometimes one emotion arises and, on fading again, reveals another that it has been masking. If attached to anger, for example, perhaps because it generates feelings of power and a sense of being in the right, we may discover in meditation that it has been shielding us from other emotions.

Temperamentally irritable and angry people can also be people for whom fear, shame, guilt and sadness are seen as unacceptable indications of weakness. As we saw (in Chapter 10), Mrs Cruickshank was such a person for most of her life, intolerant of weakness in others, until she was able to face and admit her fear, overcoming her shame to do so.

In meditation, such a person might experience anger, fear, shame, guilt and sadness, whether blurred together, one after the other, or repeatedly, together and separately, over a number of sessions, before becoming finally free of them. Remnants of the past, no longer fuelled by real events, they need simply to be experienced and endured until they mutate towards sadness and finally fade away. Anger is usually associated with resistance to loss. Sadness arises only when the inevitability of the loss is acknowledged and acceptance begins. This emotion, sorrow, enables catharsis and starts the healing process, whereas anger tends mainly to inhibit it.

The situation can involve an additional layer of complication, such as when someone is fearful of anger (even their own), then immediately feeling ashamed of it and guilty whenever they experience and express it. Such people have strong tendencies to suppress their anger. For healing and growth to occur, they must first experience it, allowing it to pass. Then they can begin grieving their losses and lost opportunities, feel the underlying sadness and begin to heal. Regular meditation practice makes this much easier to do.

The work of the meditation eventually begins to carry over between sessions. Corrective emotional experiences can then occur spontaneously in everyday life, triggered by real events, memories and dreams.

MEDITATION AND THERAPY

Meditation has long been reported as a useful adjunct to some forms of psychotherapy.[18] Mindfulness meditation is also central to the successful programme of the Stress Reduction Clinic at the University of Massachusetts Medical Center, where many people with a wide range of medical disorders, notably chronic pain, often unresponsive to other forms of treatment, have benefited.[19]

A more recent development has been the successful use of mindfulness meditation with cognitive behaviour therapy in the treatment of depression.[20] Although insufficient research has been conducted, in either general medicine or psychiatry, on the illness-prevention capabilities of regular meditation practice, such reports as are available suggest significant benefits.[21]

Meditation and Faith Stage development
MOVING FROM STAGE 3 TO STAGE 4

It follows from the discussion about emotional healing and growth that experience in meditation practice will promote Faith Stage development. According to Fowler's research, moving from Stage 3 to Stage 4 is the most common transition facing adults. As we saw in Chapters 8 and 9, for those on a high trajectory pathway of spiritual development, this is likely to be difficult, involving letting go of multiple, steadfastly held attachments, particularly to the group of origin, its culture and values, people (including family) and places.

Other spiritual practices enable a similar type of shift in spiritual development, as we shall see in the final chapter. Like some of these other practices, meditation allows a person experience of a new, individual perspective, liberated from the attachments formed by years of conditioning through childhood and adolescence. It fosters the capacity for thinking independently of the group, and for seeing matters from a more neutral

---

18 See, for example, Kutz, I., Borysenko, J. Z. and Benson, H. (1985) 'Meditation and psychotherapy: A rationale for the integration of dynamic psychotherapy, the relaxation response, and mindfulness meditation.' *American Journal of Psychiatry 142*, 1, 1–8. Craven, J. L. (1989) 'Meditation and psychotherapy.' *Canadian Journal of Psychiatry 34*, 7, 648–53. Bogart, G. (1991) 'The use of meditation in psychotherapy: A review of the literature.' *American Journal of Psychotherapy 45*, 3, 383–412. Germer, C. K., Siegel, R. D. and Fulton, P. R. (2005) (eds) *Mindfulness and Psychotherapy.* New York, NY: Guilford Press. Epstein, M. (2008) *Psychotherapy Without the Self: A Buddhist Perspective.* Yale, CT: Yale University Press.

19 Kabat-Zinn, J. (1990) *Full Catastrophe Living: Using the Wisdom of Your Body and Mind to Face Stress, Pain and Illness.* New York, NY: Delta Books.

20 Williams, M., Teasdale, J., Segal, Z. and Kabat-Zinn, J. (2007) *The Mindful Way through Depression: Freeing Yourself from Chronic Unhappiness.* New York, NY: Guilford Press.

21 See, for example, West, M. (1987) (ed.) *The Psychology of Meditation.* New York, NY: Clarendon Press/Oxford University Press.

and less tribal position, taking full and unbiased account of the people and perspectives of those once thought of as different, even as enemies.

Travel in foreign places may have this effect, for example. Seeing changes of attitude and behaviour as a necessary part of the pathway to personal growth makes us less keen to resist and more likely to embrace them. It makes change easier first to accept and then to accomplish.

MOVING FROM STAGE 4 TO STAGE 5

Meditation and other spiritual practices also help in completing the transition between Stages 4 and 5. A phrase sums it up: 'I want to be free more than I want what I want.' Liberation from earlier attachments not only becomes a paramount aim, but also allows us to see how others are powerfully bound up, still gripped by their passions, desires and aversions.

We come to realize our limitations, and that the only thoughts, feelings, words and actions we can truly hope to influence and control are our own. In this, we become free of the wish to change directly the thoughts and ways of others, especially those from our original group. We may continue to hope to influence them through our words and example, but we also steadfastly honour their capacity for independence from us, even when they do not appear to appreciate it. In this, we model the ideal, in the hope that some at least will follow.

Moving from Stage 4 to Stage 5 involves recognition of our 'non-separateness', of 'interbeing' – the seamless interconnectedness of all things – and the principle of 'reciprocity' at work. The regular practice of meditation helps develop these key insights. Another personal anecdote, comparing a river trip with meditation experiences, illustrates both this point and other aspects of this form of spiritual practice (see personal anecdote – lessons from a canoe trip).

> *Personal anecdote 7 – lessons from a canoe trip*
> With friends one summer in the 1990s, taking camping equipment, food and supplies for several days, I took a canoe trip down 100 miles of the Spanish River in Ontario, Canada, which (except at our starting and end points) was inaccessible by road. There were no man-made landings or supply stores in this beautiful wilderness area.
>
> I was new to canoeing, but my Canadian friends were experienced. They provided good canoes, maps, enough food and proper equipment. The weather was fair. With guidance, I was soon able to master sufficiently the necessary skills and techniques.
>
> Setting off from Toronto for the 200-mile drive, vehicles heavily laden, we failed to arrive at our launch site until dusk. By the time we

had unloaded the vehicles and prepared the canoes, it was dark and there was nowhere nearby to make camp. We had to embark on the river. As the only newcomer to canoeing among eight people, I was feeling anxious.

By torchlight, we soon found an adequate landing and campsite. Getting there and setting up proved to be a pretty hectic and fraught business. We were also hungry, and had somehow to prepare food. It was tricky. Nevertheless, in the morning we had all slept and were ready to paddle downstream.

We worked hard during the next four days, sometimes paddling for ten hours. We had repeatedly to empty water from the canoes, occasionally running aground or capsizing. We would shoot the safer rapids. This was exhilarating. We also had laboriously to carry canoes, tents, equipment and supplies around the more hazardous falls. At the aptly named 'Graveyard Rapids', a place worryingly littered with the wreckage of many boats and canoes, one friend was pulled in and under the water trying to let the force of the flow clean out an empty food bag. As it was dark and no one had seen it happen, he might easily have drowned. The river disgorged him, though, leaving us all later to reflect on the proximity of death. Also, I was warned, there were bears.

The morning of our fourth day dawned brightly, and there was a change of mood. We were feeling especially happy. By midday we reached the final section of our trip, designated on the map as a 'Royal Ride', where the water runs swift and smooth through a long, straight, rock-sided channel. Here, we effortlessly doubled our previous average speed and covered the final 20 miles in just two hours to reach our destination. [22]

As I learned canoeing skills, so do many people learn meditation: in the company of others. These people often swiftly become spiritual friends and companions in a deep and rewarding, generous kind of friendship, tending to get you at least pointed in the right direction…downstream. It is possible to make progress alone, but it may be slow or more limited without proper instruction, comparable to heading against the current and expecting too much too soon. It is best to find good meditation teachers, to help avoid mistakes and discouragement.

For many people, as it was for me on the Spanish River trip, you start barely prepared and more or less in the dark. There are obstacles and difficulties at the beginning, interspersed with exhilarating high points and breakthroughs. Later, as your technique and skills improve, what seemed against you now turns in your favour. There is no need to resist or struggle.

---

22 Adapted from Culliford, L. (2007) *Love, Healing and Happiness.* Winchester: O Books, pp.136–40.

The flow eventually becomes smooth and you find yourself on a royal ride. Perseverance is recommended. Often good progress is being made, even when things seem to be going badly. There is no easy way of judging. It is important to accept that sometimes the flow dwindles or backs up, just like water in a river. There may on occasion be barriers to negotiate; emotional barriers, the need to grieve and let go of something. Meditation enables nature to take its healing course. It is necessary simply to maintain practice; to keep moving, return to the water, head downstream and stay afloat.

The allegorical comparison between the canoe trip and meditation can be extended. The water in the Spanish River has fallen as rain on some of the oldest rocks of the earth's crust: beautiful, glacier-sculptured pink granite. It flows in streams through dense spruce and pine forests alive with moose, bears, wolves, eagles, chipmunks and butterflies, before joining beaver and trout on the banks and in the river.

Several timescales are represented here: those of the rocks, of the trees, of the animals, of me and my friends (the canoeists), of me now (the writer) bringing together into the present, using my mind and imagination, these different aspects of the past. Now the reader (at a different time) can do the same, build up a picture of that place and the events described. This kind of seamless and interdependent continuity reflects a powerful truth about existence. It is not fragmented. It is whole.

The Spanish River flows on still. It flows beyond where my friends and I left it into a sequence of lakes and eventually through a dam, from which it provides power and electricity for the far-off city of Toronto. The water then continues into Lake Huron, over Niagara Falls and into Lake Ontario, then to the St Lawrence River, and so to the Atlantic Ocean from where it evaporates, falling as rain again: an endless cycle.

This is the kind of vision that grows to be a part of everyday experience during Faith Stage 5 for those who meditate regularly. The influence of the personal ego subsides, giving over dominance to the spiritual self. Mindfulness is no longer confined to separate and deliberate meditation sessions. It increasingly becomes the natural and autonomous mental state, one of alert, focused, calm, contented and joyful equanimity. As it does so, you move inexorably towards Stage 6 and the goal of spiritual development.

Other spiritual skills
MEDITATION AS THE BASIS OF OTHER SKILLS
Meditation practice, however, is not for everybody. Some people experience it as unproductive or boring, or are dissuaded from practice by doubting its potential efficacy. Others find themselves too restless or distracted to be

still and concentrate. Such people often benefit through engaging in other spiritual practices, such as those discussed in the following chapter.

For many people, on the other hand, regular meditation practice enhances their capacity for the spiritual skills listed at the beginning of the chapter:

- being able to rest, relax and create a still, peaceful state of mind

- remaining focused in the present, staying alert, unhurried and attentive.

With time, a strong mental stability supervenes during the sessions. This firm equilibrium allows the individual to experience thoughts, impulses and emotions without immediately reacting, by becoming an observer as well as the main participant in the process. It is akin to depressing the clutch briefly, while the mind's motor is still running. There is then a brief instant in which to deliberate about whether to respond or not, and how to do so.

In meditation, the aim is to continue observing, watching how the mind's contents come and go, as if on a shifting cinema screen. This is instructive, giving you valuable insights into the patterns of thought, feelings and behaviour that have been governing your life so far; patterns that have been learned, conditioned and ingrained by earlier experiences. You can often see how destructive they have been. Also you can see ways in which change might improve your life and the lives of those with whom you come into contact.

This is how meditation can continue to affect personal life outside the sessions. When the degree of stability attained is sufficient, it will continue for a time. Then you have a secure, calm base to which to return – 'within the space of a single breath' – whenever you recognize that you have become even slightly distracted or emotionally upset.

The effect of 'putting in the clutch' allows us to modify our words and actions as the impulses arise, giving greater freedom to speak or stay silent, to act or refrain from acting. It allows us to reflect and choose more often to deliver words and actions based on affection, calm, clarity and joy, for example, than on disaffection, envy, anger or fear. These refer to the following skills:

- going deeper into the stillness and observing one's emerging thoughts and feelings with emotional stability, in a way that carries over into everyday life

- being honestly and sincerely self-reflective, taking responsibility for every thought, word and action.

As meditation becomes deeper, the ego subsides and the mind, focusing on itself, seems to disappear into mindful emptiness. Now intuitive, even mystical experiences become more likely, during which 'something happens' and the spiritual realm is briefly experienced in full harmony with the temporal world.

With the mind naturally attuned to the spiritual dimension at such times, the spiritual essence or 'soul' of the individual can be thought of as in direct communication with the great, pervading spirit or life-force of the universe. Another spiritual skill is thereby enabled:

- using the capacity for deep reflection to connect with one's spiritual essence and values.

The values mentioned are those of universality, of 'interbeing', of knowing oneself to be an indivisible part of the entirety of humanity, bound to others by a principle of reciprocity. They are values associated with the harmonious combination of compassion and wisdom that is love.

The next skill involves empathic communication. Empathy and sympathy are related but not quite the same. In the context of therapy, empathy involves the direct experience of another person's emotional state. The person has to be in the room with you, and the feeling is a direct perception.[23]

To be skilled empathically involves being able to empty one's mind of self-regard and avoid being distracted by one's own emotional state, which must therefore be completely quiescent. Meditation practice helps this, and also improves the degree of concentration you can give to the often subtle sensations that result from direct empathic communication received (like a kind of 'gut feeling') from someone else.

Putting emotions into words is also a valuable therapeutic skill. The purest form of empathy concerns emotional states; so a therapist might be able to say, confidently, on the basis of empathic skills, 'You seem angry', 'You seem sad' for example. The therapist is sometimes aware of this before the patient, and is often also able to articulate it more clearly.

These matters are pertinent to the next spiritual skill:

- developing compassion and an extensive capacity for direct empathic communication with others.

The remaining skills on the list concern the well-being of people who, either through the demands of their profession or in the general course of their lives, engage with those who are suffering:

- emotional resilience: having the courage to witness and endure distress while sustaining an attitude of hope

---

23 Sympathy, on the other hand, is a supportive fellow-feeling, based largely upon a combination of supposition, understanding and some knowledge (or assumptions) about the other person. It may be expressed in a kindly way as follows, 'I have heard about your predicament and imagine how unpleasant/difficult it must feel.'

- being able to give without feeling drained
- being able to grieve and let go.

It is very important to remember that one's ability to help others involves giving adequate priority to one's own welfare. Meditation practice enhances all three skills by providing access to the spiritual source of emotional equanimity and hope, vital energy, and the wisdom to acknowledge the inevitability of loss.

Summary points

1. *Education*

Spiritual development begins in childhood, hence the importance of education. A four-point plan for teachers is recommended.

2. *Meditation helps schoolchildren*

In school meditation studies, beneficial effects consistently reported include increased feelings of calm, reduced stress, reduced anger, improved concentration and better interactions with others.

3. *The key to spiritual skills*

Meditation is the key to several spiritual skills (nine are listed), the foremost of which is being able to relax and create a still, peaceful state of mind.

4. *Focusing techniques help reduce distractions*

Meditation involves reducing external stimulation, allowing the mind to settle. Several techniques involve giving the mind a focus for concentration. Internal stimulation is thereby also gradually reduced.

5. *The whole brain working seamlessly with the body*

Meditation decreases compartmental activity in the brain and nervous system, so that it increasingly acts as a whole organ communicating with a whole body. Biological effects, which involve the limbic system, are described.

6. *The psychology of meditation*

Forms of emotional release, including cathartic crying, laughter and blushing, enable the liberation of emotional energy invested in attachments, promoting healing and personal growth.

7. *Meditation enhances spiritual development*

The true, spiritual self is free of desire. Meditation, therefore, little by little releasing desire, aversion and resulting attachments from the ego, allows it to be restored gradually to its purer state, easing transition through the stages of faith.

Exercises and questions for personal reflection and as a basis for group discussion:

1. Think about your schooling. Do you recall any teachers who were good at helping you keep an open mind and at exploring ways of seeing? Were there any lessons or activities that seemed to encourage spiritual awareness and development? Do you feel that you were actively discouraged from developing spiritual awareness, and from having and talking about spiritual experiences?

2. Have you tried learning to meditate? If so, try writing down your experiences and/or sharing them with someone else. Do you still meditate? What have been the effects of meditation practice on your thoughts, emotions and behaviour?

3. If you are not familiar with meditation, think about your attitude to it. Are you generally in favour, against or neutral? Do you use any other methods allowing you to rest, relax and create a still, peaceful state of mind?

4. Use an internet search to look on-line and inform yourself about the range of meditation retreats and classes in your area. Try to identify different methods and traditions available, including Buddhist, Christian, Transcendental and other types of meditation. See if you can discover what they have in common.

5. Gather a few raisins. Alternatively, prepare a segment of tangerine or a thin slice of apple. Sit quietly for a few minutes with these to hand. Adopt an upright posture, letting your hands fall into your lap or resting on your thighs. Close, or part close, your eyes. Take a breath and release it, allowing your breathing to settle into a natural rhythm. Pay attention to the breath, to each in and out breath, to the air passing back and forth at the nostrils, or the rise and fall of chest and abdomen. Note any distractions that arise, then bring your mind back to focus on the breaths. Repeat this as often as necessary. Remain still and calm for a few minutes then, without opening your eyes any wider, and without unnecessary movement, pick up a raisin or piece of fruit. Feel the shape and texture before lifting it gently to your nose. Take a breath and smell the fruit, focus on appreciating the aroma to the full, even if it is faint. After a few more breaths, put the fruit onto your tongue and gently close your mouth. Spend some time (the space of several more breaths)

appreciating the taste before swallowing. Stay with your eyes shut for a little longer. Ask yourself, 'How was that?'

6. Think about how quickly, and with what limited attention, you normally eat your food in comparison with the fruit in the previous exercise. Do you ever consider where your food comes from, who cultivates, harvests, transports, sells, buys and prepares it? How many people do you think you might be connected to by a single piece of fruit? Think also about your connections through this fruit to nature, to sun, soil and rain. Do these observations seem simply commonplace to you, or do they give you a sense of wonder?

7. Do you remember any occasion when, perhaps to your surprise, you found yourself in tears? (Remember Barack Obama's experiences in Trinity Church in Chicago as he reacted to the music of the choir and a sermon about hope.) As you reflect on the experience, does it seem as if it brought the healing release of painful emotions? Can you think what hurt, what emotional wounds or scars, were being touched on? Was this any kind of turning point for you, even in a small way? Did it mark the start of a period of personal (spiritual) growth? If so, try describing your experience in writing (perhaps in a journal, to which you can return and make further entries) or in words with someone you trust and respect.

Chapter 12

SPIRITUAL PRACTICES

What is spiritual practice?
DEVOTION

According to spiritual principles, faith development (in its broadest sense) is the only essential work and purpose of a lifetime. Any commitment or regular activity that promotes spiritual development can be considered a spiritual practice. It is always timely, therefore, to engage intentionally in such practices, which can usefully be distinguished into 'religious' and 'non-religious', although there is no rigid boundary between the two.

Many people engage in spiritual practices without identifying them as such, and an aim of this chapter is to help readers clarify such practices. People often make pledges and do things that contribute to their lives in a spiritual way, giving them meaning and adding to a sense of purpose, a feeling of belonging, of working towards being whole, living wholesome lives and being their true selves.

Spiritual practices
MAINLY RELIGIOUS

- belonging to a faith tradition
- ritual practices and other forms of worship
- meditation and prayer
- reading scripture
- listening to, singing and playing sacred music

- pilgrimages and retreats.

MAINLY NON-RELIGIOUS (SECULAR)

- contemplation

- yoga, t'ai chi and similar *disciplined* practices

- maintaining physical health

- contemplative reading of literature, poetry, philosophy, etc.

- engaging with and enjoying nature

- appreciation of the arts and engaging in creative activities, including artistic pursuits

- joining clubs and societies

- co-operative group or team activities, sporting, recreational or other, involving a special quality of fellowship

- maintaining stable family relationships and friendships

- acts of compassion.

Spiritual practices (saying prayers, for example, or shopping for a disabled elderly neighbour) often form an important part of someone's daily or weekly routine. Impulses of devotion and duty arise from within, from one's spiritual essence, often accompanied by a willing sense of personal dedication, of deliberately making space and time to honour them. This is one way for us to recognize aspects of our true self. Worthy impulses feel agreeably life-affirming when we honour them. Try to ignore them, and they tend to persist or recur.

With increasing spiritual maturity, devotion and duty come to feel less like burdensome servitude, more like joyful liberation; but these rewards are not always felt. Routine activities sometimes seem less meaningful and more of a chore than a delight. The temptation naturally grows to abandon them; and this is especially so at the beginning.

Regular meditation, for example, starts as a practice, as simply an exercise, before becoming a skill. Patience and perseverance are required, and both come more easily when a person finds faith in the process. Another aim of this and the preceding chapter is, therefore, to be reassuring. Readers can be confident that spiritual practices do work and eventually bear fruit.

A gentle warning must be sounded in addition though; that those who look too early and too eagerly for the rewards have their minds focused incorrectly, and will frequently be disappointed. It is important to remain focused on the present moment and on the activity in hand during spiritual practice; to attain one-pointed concentration, as during mindful meditation; then the process will flow. The rewards will come; slowly and gradually at first, later in cascades of small epiphanies, and sometimes in quantum leaps of magnificent and mystical proportions.

Mainly religious practices

These general comments lead us into examining some of the principal types of spiritual practice, beginning with those of a mainly religious nature.

BELONGING TO A FAITH TRADITION

Researchers have found that belonging to a faith group or tradition, and participating in associated community-based activities, has significant health benefits.[1] Associated with this kind of commitment, involving a measure of faith, a range of illnesses are prevented or moderated in frequency and severity. Recovery is quicker and more complete. Lasting distress and disability are endured more easily. This occurs, even when the people studied were not actual worshippers to any significant degree. To belong to the group and participate socially were sufficient.

RITUAL AND SYMBOLIC PRACTICES, AND OTHER FORMS OF WORSHIP

The word 'worship' is a contraction of 'worth-ship', and implies an activity honouring God, a Supreme Being or deity, with thanks and praise. Repetition, ritual and symbolization are common aspects of church services and other forms of religious worship, often accompanied by prayer and music (see below). Acts of worship can be satisfying in a number of ways, and frequently enable the mind of the worshipper an opportunity to expand communication with the spiritual dimension in a deeply personal way.

When two, three or more people are gathered together in worship and prayer, a deep, satisfying and often enduring sense of fellowship and mutual support can develop between them. This kind of spiritual camaraderie has also been linked to physical and psychological health benefits.

MEDITATION AND PRAYER

As a bar of soap is worn away by repeated use, so meditation causes the dissolution, little by little, of the false ego. It is a spiritual practice that has

---

1   See, for example, Koenig, H., McCullough, M. and Larson, D. (2001) *Handbook of Religion and Health*. Oxford: Oxford University Press.

been associated for many centuries with Buddhism, Christianity, Hinduism, Jainism, Sufism and other religions. Involving mindful communication with the divine, meditation is closely akin to silent prayer, an important aspect of which is listening, being receptive to the promptings of the inner soul in intimate communication with the life-force, the great pervasive spirit of the universe.

Other forms of prayer (which include giving thanks and praise, asking forgiveness, and making requests) depend first on developing this level of communion with the Absolute, with the Almighty. It is normal for actively religious people to pray regularly, morning and evening, and often more frequently. Some elderly Buddhists in Ladakh, India, for example, have been encountered uttering a prayer or 'mantra'[2] almost all the day long while continuously turning their mechanical prayer wheels.

There are many instances of prayer being helpful for those suffering physical or mental illness. Brenda was such a person (see Vignette in Chapter 4). Prayer was vital to helping her cope with the symptoms of schizophrenia.

READING SCRIPTURE

Holy scriptures from different religions comprise a rich treasure house containing abundant folk histories, illuminating human stories and much timeless wisdom.

It is hard to imagine anyone reading parts of the Old and New Testaments of the Bible, the Hindu Upanishads and Bhagavad Gita, the Holy Koran, the Dhammapada of the Buddha, Lao Tsu's *Tao Te Ching* or Chuang Tsu's *Inner Chapters*, without gaining some new and valuable insights into life and how to live, into worthwhile values, and into the spiritual dimension of existence. To maximize the experience requires that scripture be read mindfully, paying it devoted attention, without hurry in an open and expansive way, attuned to the sacred purpose of the author.[3]

SACRED MUSIC (LISTENING TO, SINGING AND PLAYING) SONGS, HYMNS, PSALMS AND DEVOTIONAL CHANTS

Music opens us up and is capable of transporting us in mind and imagination to sacred realms, both hellish and sublime. It may help develop in us the

---

2   Etymologically, the word 'mantra' means 'to protect the mind'. The Tibetan mantra, *Om Mani Padme Hum*, translates as, 'sacred jewel at the heart of the lotus'. The phrase is said to express in a condensed, symbolic way the essential qualities of a deity, in this case the Tibetan Buddhist deity Avalokiteshvara, the personification of the Buddha's compassion. See Batchelor, S. (1987) (ed.) *The Jewel in the Lotus: A Guide to the Buddhist Traditions of Tibet*. London: Wisdom Publications. Prayer wheels contain written prayers that are 'prayed' over and over by turning the wheel.

3   In Christian monastic circles, this contemplative method of reading is known as Lectio Divina.

capacity to view pain, cruelty and destruction without flinching and turning away, with a degree of calm detachment. This allows us to respond appropriately, when we are called on to do so, without being incapacitated by disgust or despair. In this way, also by transporting us on occasion towards bliss, engagement with devotional music can aid spiritual growth.

As a powerful and moving focus, music can aid our powers of concentration while liberating our emotional reactivity from the stiff bonds of temperament. Fostering cathartic release, music can enable us to release attachments of which we may have been unaware, and which we cannot describe, promoting maturity through improved emotional spontaneity and freedom.

PILGRIMAGES AND RETREATS

A pilgrimage is a journey in search of meaning, understanding, beauty and blessing, to (and back from) a place that is both sacred and significant to the pilgrim. It is frequently undertaken in the company of others with whom one often establishes a deep sense of fellowship. Other people are met and befriended similarly, in passing, on the way.

Phil Cousineau writes that pilgrims are people seeking completion and clarity, 'a goal to which only the spirit's compass points the way'.[4] He describes the journey evocatively as a sequence of stages or components, all of which are important for the transformative process: The Longing, The Call, Departure, The Pilgrim's Way, The Labyrinth, Arrival and Bringing back the Boon. Preparation is a key aspect of the journey, and Cousineau's section on 'the labyrinth' reveals that matters seldom proceed smoothly. The pilgrim faces outer difficulties and inner challenges involving loss, the threat of further loss and the need to let go.

There are similarities to pilgrimage when a person goes on a planned retreat. The main opportunity is for a period of silence and solitude. Leadership and guidance may also be available, and the company of others.[5] Many retreats involve periods of meditation practice. There is usually a tranquil setting with food and accommodation provided, allowing the retreatant to settle and focus with a clear mind both on the surroundings and their inner, mental landscape.

---

4   Cousineau, P. (1998) *The Art of Pilgrimage: A Seeker's Guide to Making Travel Sacred.* Newburyport, MA: Conari Press, p.14. Another excellent book about pilgrimage is Forest, J. (2007) *The Road to Emmaus: Pilgrimage as a Way of Life.* Maryknoll, NY: Orbis Books.
5   See www.thegoodretreatguide.com, accessed 29 May 2010.

Mainly secular practices
CONTEMPLATION (DEEP REFLECTION)

Contemplation involves thinking continuously about something, studying and musing over it, usually something worthwhile and important, pertaining to life and meaning. When this kind of reflective activity goes very deep, when a person becomes still and highly focused as they ponder, the ego dissolves temporarily and contemplation becomes increasingly like meditation.

Contemplation, however, may be less of a deliberate and regularly performed activity. It may just happen; when we are taking a long bath, for example, or going for a walk. Sometimes it is triggered by an event, something someone says or something we read, by a dream or a memory. Contemplation is a common activity, and supports the idea that everyone – whether religious or not – engages with the spiritual dimension from time to time.

The kind of thinking involved in contemplation may begin with rational, linear, cause-and-effect, 'either/or', exclusive, 'right-or-wrong' thinking. When this approach is reapplied to the same problem or situation from several angles in a short space of time, though, thinking becomes more holistic, intuitive, super-rational, 'both/and' type and inclusive.

During contemplation, we tend to take more account of our emotional experiences and reactions to whatever is the focus of our contemplative attention. Our emotions may themselves become that focus, until troubling feelings soften and equanimity is restored; then we may, with a clear mind, return our attention to the original train of thought (see Vignette – Peter).

Vignette – Peter

Peter's family had been aware for several months that he was unhappy. His mood was often irritable. It seemed to improve during the weekends, and deteriorate during the week. One Sunday evening he erupted in anger over a relatively trivial matter, shouting at his wife and frightening his two young children. The following morning, driving to work, he became angry and impatient as the traffic built up. He yelled at a driver whose vehicle was moving slowly, and undertook a sudden, dangerous manoeuvre to get past it. Having done so, he was furious when the traffic light in front of him suddenly changed to red, forcing him to brake hard.

It was 60 seconds before the light turned green. During that brief period, aware of the slower driver coming up behind him, Peter began to feel guilty and ashamed of his actions. He also remembered his wife saying, the night before, that he was behaving uncharacteristically and asking what was wrong. He had denied any problems, but now began to think about the situation more objectively.

Peter began to consider his present anger and his general unhappy mood, asking himself what could have been going awry. After the lights changed, he pulled off the road to contemplate, to consider the matter for a while.

Peter's boss had been promoted and replaced a few months earlier. The new manager was very efficient, seemed fair to most of his colleagues and even likeable. Thinking about it, though, Peter realized that the change of personnel had upset him. The new boss reminded him of his authoritarian father, who had always seemed to demand more effort and seldom gave any praise. Peter realized he had been dreading the managerial meetings held every Monday morning. Despite improving results each month, he felt increasingly exposed, imposed upon and frustrated.

Peter, who had taken up karate the previous year, sat in his car until he felt calm and in control again. Armed with the new insight into what had been troubling him, he formulated a plan. The first part involved telephoning his wife to apologize for his recent moodiness, arranging a dinner date with her the following Friday, and a special treat day out with the children on Saturday. He was going to make it up to them too. Peter was determined that family life would regain priority over his work, even if it might eventually mean switching jobs.

The second part of the plan was to use the morning meeting to say something, calmly and privately, to his new manager about how he had been feeling overstretched and undervalued. This began a new and happier phase between them, as his boss admitted that he was in awe of Peter's record and had been thinking of him as a rival rather than as a colleague. In the days after their discussion, the manager took Peter into his confidence and asked for his advice more frequently. They were able to work much better together as a team, and soon set about ensuring that others among Peter's colleagues felt fully appreciated for their work contributions and no longer taken for granted. The productivity level of their department quickly improved to superior levels, to everyone's satisfaction.

YOGA, T'AI CHI AND SIMILAR DISCIPLINED PRACTICES

As mentioned in Chapter 2, many authorities refer to four types of yoga, each representing a major path of spiritual development.[6] In Western society, hatha yoga, t'ai chi,[7] and martial arts like judo, karate and taekwondo are increasingly popular. These martial skills combine exercise and the sport of combat techniques with a philosophy emphasizing meditation and self-

---

6   See footnote 17, p.52.
7   A Chinese system of slow-movement callisthenics developed centuries ago by a Taoist monk.

defence. These practices are therefore both disciplined and devotional. Karate, in particular, is a deeply philosophical practice that teaches profoundly ethical principles, with strong spiritual significance for its adherents.

MAINTAINING PHYSICAL HEALTH

For those who do not engage regularly in yoga or similar physical disciplines, maintaining physical health through other methods can be considered good spiritual practice: through exercise and diet, by avoiding toxins and intoxicants, and through seeking appropriate health checks, advice and treatment when necessary. This honours the principle of non-separateness between body, mind and spirit.

CONTEMPLATIVE READING

The secular equivalent of reading scripture involves a similarly contemplative and devotional attitude to reading great literature, biography, drama, poetry and philosophy. Reading about science may be included too. Reading and applying oneself to the contents of some of the more enlightened self-help literature may equally prove beneficial.

ENGAGING WITH AND ENJOYING NATURE

It seems fairly obvious to include engaging with nature in this list of spiritual practices and pursuits, but city-dwellers in particular may need reminding of the benefits of regular and frequent contact with diverse, beautiful, awe-inspiring landscapes, growing plants, animals, waterfalls, sunsets, snowstorms and similarly evocative objects, suitable for direct experience and contemplation. Flowering plants, shrubs and trees inviting cultivation offer the added opportunity for beautifying the home and managing a personal garden, however small and modest or grand and spacious. The garden offers meaningful activity, a perpetual source of wonder, reasons for both joy and gratitude, and is such a place of solace that it becomes for many their true temple of wisdom and worship.

APPRECIATION OF THE ARTS AND ENGAGING IN CREATIVE ACTIVITIES, INCLUDING ARTISTIC PURSUITS

Other creative activities echo the benefits and blessings of gardening, whether pursued professionally or as a regular hobby. Listening to and making music that does not necessarily have religious or devotional intent can have similar benefits, as can painting, sculpture, craftwork, even activities like crochet, needlework and knitting. Critically, these creative processes require one-pointed concentration. There may also be something soothing and rhythmical about the activity, which allows the mind to settle into a kind of meditative state, fostering imaginative and intuitive processes as the insistent ego gradually grows quiescent.

Direct contact with great art, as with sacred music, offers the opportunity to engage meaningfully with what may appear hellish and infernal, at one extreme, or beautiful and sublime at the other. Exposure to both can help us grow.

JOINING CLUBS AND SOCIETIES

Joining a club or society compares with belonging to a faith tradition. There is a degree of commitment and a social aspect to the kind of sports, hobbies and other activities already listed as secular spiritual practices. Friendships and a special quality of human fellowship often exist within such groups, clubs and societies. As with religious groups, there are dangers of partisanship, of 'us and them' thinking, of destructive exclusiveness, to be wary of and avoided. In the main, however, joining and experiencing a sense of belonging is helpful.

CO-OPERATIVE GROUP OR TEAM ACTIVITIES, SPORTING, RECREATIONAL OR OTHER

The same dynamic arises involving a higher level of commitment, cohesion and quality of fellowship when people come together to form a group or team with a specific purpose; to produce a play, for example, or play competitive sports. The personal ego of each member is necessarily subordinated to the group for the success of the enterprise, providing a learning experience that often carries over into everyday life. People are not separate and self-sufficient. We are intimately interconnected. We do well to realize this – to 'make it real' for ourselves – and recognize that we need each other.

MAINTAINING STABLE FAMILY RELATIONSHIPS AND FRIENDSHIPS

We can relinquish group, team or club membership whenever circumstances change and the time feels right. However, family relationships, marriages and some special friendships, especially those involving high levels of trust and intimacy, are ideally and potentially lifelong. They require working at if they are to be maintained and stay rewarding. Keeping in touch; being available, ready to listen and console during periods of hardship; being there similarly to share in celebrating joys and successes: these are among the privileges and duties of such relationships. They are devoted relationships, and they hold and require a spiritual quality to be sustained and successful.

ACTS OF COMPASSION

If commitment to helping a relative or close friend is considered a spiritual practice, even more so will be any similar commitment to helping one or more strangers. Such activities require self-centred, ego-driven impulses to take second place to those of the naturally compassionate spiritual self.

This kind of 'devotion to others' approach can be applied to any kind of employment. It is a noble attitude, where 'service' to others has nothing to do with demeaning forms of 'servitude'.

When your work involves caring for others and includes an element of compassion, it may be a truly uplifting calling or 'vocation'. Health and social care employment exemplifies this. It involves looking after designated patients and clients. It also involves colleagues sharing both burdens and successes, and looking after each other. This kind of teamwork gives an extra dimension to this advanced form of spiritual practice, requiring as it does the regular deployment of spiritual skills.

Doing good
TEN WAYS OF GIVING

To examine one's life and list the spiritual practices to which you regularly commit time and effort is a valuable form of honest self-appraisal. Building, maintaining and re-examining a profile from time to time (based, for example, on the list above) can itself be considered a form of spiritual practice.

We could also check to what extent we make use of the 'ten ways of giving' listed in the following section. They are based on scientific enquiry.

Ten ways of giving

The way of celebration: gratitude

The way of generativity: helping others grow

The way of forgiveness: set yourself free

The way of courage: speak up, speak out

The way of humour: connect with joy

The way of respect: look deeper and find value

The way of compassion: feel for others

The way of loyalty: love across time

The way of listening: offer deep presence

The way of creativity: invent and innovate[8]

---

8   From Post, S. and Neimark, J. (2007) *Why Good Things Happen to Good People: How to Live a Longer, Healthier, Happier Life by the Simple Act of Giving.* New York, NY: Broadway Books.

Author of *Why Good Things Happen to Good People* Stephen Post, is a professor of bioethics and family medicine at Case Western Reserve University in Cleveland, Ohio. He is also President of the Institute for Research on Unlimited Love, founded in 2001. In this capacity, he has funded over 50 social science and health outcome studies in numerous universities. Stephen Post reports that strong evidence now supports the idea that benevolent emotions, attitudes, and actions centred on the good of others, contribute to the giver's happiness, health and length of life.[9]

In the Preface to *Why Good Things Happen to Good People*, Otis Moss tells of meeting a religious woman, Sister McNair, in hospital soon after she has had her diseased legs amputated. She remained positive, despite the inevitable prospect of future disability. 'I have been here in my bed thinking about all the wonderful things I'm going to do with my hands when I go home,' she told him, adding, 'I think I will bake you a cake'.[10] Despite her great loss, she still felt whole, and retained a sense of humour.

Demonstrating a high degree of spiritual maturity, wisdom, courage and humour, a vital sense of purpose emerged when Sister McNair contemplated and accepted with equanimity the reality of the loss of her limbs. From her wheelchair, we are told, she went on living fully thereafter. Moss says there are many people like her everywhere, and implies that they are both receivers and givers of gifts. He calls it the power of love: love heals both givers and receivers. Stephen Post tells that this doctrine is scientifically sound.

He writes that giving is good medicine because it switches off the 'fight or flight' response to challenge, and reduces the intensity of painful emotions contributing to stress-related physical and psychological illnesses. This is consistent with the link between spirituality and emotions emphasized by the psycho-spiritual paradigm presented throughout this book; that painful emotions subside following catharsis, when losses are anticipated and accepted, and that emotional healing leads directly to personal growth.

The research with which Post is associated looks at the ten ways of giving,[11] divided into four areas or 'domains' of life: family, friends, community and humanity.[12] Much of the research is based on a 200-point 'Love and Longevity Scale' developed by psychologists at the University of Miami, with 20 questions for each way of giving.[13] Readers can generate a score under

---

9   Post's co-author, Jill Neimark, is a widely published science writer and former features editor of *Psychology Today*.
10 *Ibid.*, p.xiii.
11 *Ibid.*, pp.21–3.
12 *Ibid.*, pp.18–20.
13 The 20 questions each allow for answers from 'strongly agree' to 'strongly disagree' on a six-point scale, allowing a maximum score of 120. They are printed for readers' use at the end of each of the ten relevant chapters in *Why Good Things Happen to Good People*.

each heading, and the book provides sensible suggestions on how to improve your score and your life.

These ten ways relate closely to spiritual values, notably honesty, generosity, tolerance, patience, perseverance, courage, compassion, wisdom, beauty and hope. They are also necessarily associated with the development of spiritual skills. They have much in common with spiritual practices, and similarly overlap and reinforce one another. There follows a brief summary of each.

THE WAY OF CELEBRATION: TURNING GRATITUDE INTO ACTION

Celebration involves the expression and sharing of joy. According to Post, celebration wells up from a state of gratitude, creates a circle of love among those we interact with, moves us from fear to faith, and 'shifts us from tired to inspired'.[14]

Post gives the example of a doctor's words: 'A spirit of transforming love came to life in our burns unit. The burn victims began to experience gratitude for life once again. They began to celebrate themselves.' Many health professionals have similar stories to tell. Celebration takes many forms, from a simple 'thank you' and a smile to a big awards ceremony and extended party. Post and Neimark encourage us to think about what we, and those around us, have to celebrate.

THE WAY OF GENERATIVITY: HELPING OTHERS TO GROW

People who nurture others are also likely to nurture themselves. Generativity, helping others to discover and make use of their own gifts and strengths, has been studied extensively. It is linked to leadership qualities and high levels of self-esteem.

According to a lifetime study started in California in the 1920s, covering almost 200 people, generativity in high school predicted good physical and mental health in late adulthood, over 50 years later.[15] This is in part due to better health habits. Generativity was also found to be linked to spirituality, worldly success, good family relations and social competence. At the biological level, nurturing behaviour has been found to result in increased levels of dopamine in the brain. Dopamine is a neurotransmitter associated with pleasure and reward experiences.

---

14 *Ibid.*, pp.27–9.
15 See Wink, P. and Dillon, M. (2002) 'Spiritual development across the adult life course: Findings from a longitudinal study.' *Journal of Adult Development 9*, 1, 79–94; and Dillon, M. and Wink, P. (2007) *In the Course of a Lifetime: Tracing Religious Belief, Practice and Change.* Berkeley, CA: University of California Press.

Generativity might involve, for example, being a mentor or teacher, inspiring and encouraging others, especially the young. These and other kinds of altruism are thought to benefit givers by resulting in a more active lifestyle, a greater sense of meaning in life and an improved feeling of competence. The feeling of being socially integrated is also enhanced, and people usually cope more successfully with their own problems when remaining alert to and engaged with the difficulties of others.

THE WAY OF FORGIVENESS: SETTING YOURSELF FREE

Bearing a grudge means holding on to emotional pain after being hurt by someone. When we suffer some kind of threat or actual loss at the hands of another, it is natural to experience the spectrum of emotions from anxiety through to anger and sadness. The more severe the harm, the more difficult it is to forgive. By holding on, however, we prevent the healing process from reaching resolution. The way of forgiveness is undeniably hard. It requires courage and maturity to feel the pain, accept the loss and move on. Doing this, letting go of resentment, is however the way to peace.

There is now abundant research supporting this point of view.[16] Chronic anger has well-documented harmful effects on the immune and cardiovascular systems. Forgiveness has been found to lower stress hormones, boost mood and reduce anger. It has also been shown to improve health and alleviate depression. People who score highly on forgiveness as a personality trait are less likely to be depressed, anxious, hostile or exploitative, and are also less likely to become dependent on drugs or cigarettes.

According to Post and Neimark, forgiveness is sometimes misunderstood. They emphasize that it is not about forgetting, condoning or excusing what has happened. It does not involve forgoing justice, relinquishing claim to any legal or financial reparation that is due, and it does not mean reconciliation with a perpetrator of harm in any way that may endanger the victim's health or safety.[17]

The concept of forgiveness has a central role in many religious traditions, which provide norms, role models and psychological resources that help people learn to forgive. This has obvious social benefits, reducing the general level of discord and conflict between people.

Forgiveness requires deep, honest reflection, and may take a long time. Combat veterans with post traumatic stress syndrome have been found to suffer fewer symptoms, and are less depressed, when they are able to

---

16 See, for example, McCullough, M., Bono, G. and Root, L. (2005) 'Religion and Forgiveness.' In R. Paloutzian and C. Park (eds) *The Handbook of the Psychology of Religion and Spirituality*. New York, NY: Guilford Press. For more detail see McCullough, M., Pargament, K. and Thoresen, C. (2000) *Forgiveness: Theory, Research and Practice*. New York, NY: Guilford Press.

17 *Why Good Things Happen to Good People*, p.81.

forgive *themselves* as well as others. Forgiving oneself, an important aspect of forgiveness, is often the harder thing to do. Many people find it helpful to seek the assistance of a higher power, for example through the spiritual practices of confession and prayer, and seek to make amends for their harmful attitudes, words and actions in some meaningful way. The rewards are often found to match or exceed the effort. As those who achieve it attest, inner peace is a goal worthy to aim at, an inestimable prize.

THE WAY OF COURAGE: SPEAKING UP AND SPEAKING OUT

Post and Neimark describe different types of courage: physical, moral and psychological. Physical courage involves what they call 'activism', the attempt to change things. Moral courage involves 'being assertive' (without being aggressive), standing up for yourself, speaking out for what you need in relationships and setting boundaries. Psychological courage requires 'perseverance', steeling oneself to face each day despite hardship and the additional difficult practical, economic and emotional problems it may bring.

Bravery of any type requires emotional resilience. It needs optimism, so as to be able to face tough situations and emerge from them both stronger and wiser. Sometimes it is necessary for people to reach a crisis or turning point. Mrs Cruikshank, for example, reached a crisis of courage when, during her final illness, she faced a fear that she had been carrying most of her long life; the fear of appearing weak, of not measuring up to the high expectations of others (see Chapter 10). Honesty triumphed eventually, and she was finally relieved of a great psychological burden.

Writer, William Faulkner, wrote often of 'the human heart in conflict with itself'.[18] His short story 'Barn Burning' describes the crisis of a young boy, forced by conscience to find the courage to stand up to his father.[19] 'Something happens', and he not only refuses to help his father commit a crime in retaliation against his employer, but also reports the wrong-doing, so that the father and his older brother are both shot while burning down a barn.

At first the boy is torn between fear, family loyalty and self-interest, and the higher motives of fair play, justice and the protection of others. He is

---

18 The phrase comes from his Nobel Prize acceptance speech delivered in Stockholm on 10 December 1950, published as a preface in Faulkner, W. (1955) *Faulkner's County*. London: Chatto and Windus.

19 Included in the collection *Faulkner's County*, pp.309–26. It is also available in Faulkner, W. (1993) *Selected Short Stories of William Faulkner*. New York, NY: Modern Library. I have written in more detail about this gem of a story in Culliford, L. (2007) *Love, Healing and Happiness*, pp.93–7.

ambivalent, uncertain.[20] Almost too late, compelled from within to go forward, he gives the warning. Soon afterwards, he hears the shots. Knowing intuitively that his father has been killed, the moment of spiritual crisis is upon him. Instead of 'sticking to their own blood', as the family tradition and the bullying ways of the father tried to insist, he has courageously, and at great cost, chosen honour and honesty. Now he must live with the consequences.

Faulkner makes clear that this is a genuinely transformative experience. Exhausted, as night falls, the youth sleeps. Meanwhile, nothing prevents movement within the cosmos, as Faulkner writes, 'The slow constellations wheel on.' In the morning, the boy's breathing is easier. He decides to get up and move forward; and, Faulkner tells us, 'He does not look back.'

We can seldom know beforehand the full results of any act, including any act of courage. In facing down risk, we must therefore have faith in the outcome. Faith, the spiritual dimension, is at the heart of courage. Its motives lie very deep. To risk health, happiness, financial security, reputation, peace of mind or life itself on behalf of another involves an act of great generosity, an act of love.

Research has shown that bravery is rewarding. Contemporary moral leaders and social activists interviewed in a study at Stanford University, for example, were described as leading lives, 'of striking joy, great certainty, and unremitting faith'.[21] In another study, 90 per cent of whistle-blowers standing up against injustice in the work place said they would do it again, despite the threat of harsh consequences. People who witness bravery report themselves feeling inspired to act bravely themselves. Acts of courage contribute to everyone's welfare.

THE WAY OF HUMOUR: CONNECTING WITH JOY

Folklore has long had it that 'laughter is the best medicine'. This approach was adopted by physician Hunter 'Patch' Adams in the USA in 1971. Trained as a clown as well as a doctor, he founded the Gesundheit! Institute in West Virginia where they continue to organize events that bring hope and joy to orphans, patients and many other people.[22] For many years, Dr Adams has successfully been running a medical community employing and promoting a holistic healthcare model. Relying on humour and play, he teaches students to develop compassionate connections with all their patients.

---

20 Faulkner brilliantly captures this mood with a phrase. On the way to give the alarm, we read of 'the terrific slowness under his running feet'. The boy wants to run faster, but is delayed by a mysterious kind of reluctance, a longing to postpone what must happen.

21 See Colby, A. and Damon, W. (1992) *Some Do Care: Contemporary Lives of Moral Commitment.* New York, NY: Free Press.

22 See www.patchadams.org, accessed 29 May 2010.

The medical profession began taking serious notice of the advantages of humour in the late 1970s when an article appeared in the New England Journal of Medicine describing the benefit of watching Marx Brothers and other humorous films as a way of coping with severe and enduring back pain.[23]

In 1996, psychologist Robert Holden developed his original 'laughter clinic' and, with colleagues, set up the Happiness Project in the UK.[24] Top psychologists, life coaches, business leaders, spiritual ministers, leading physicians, great musicians, actors and poets, all of whom are 'fired with a passion to serve and inspire', have come together in the project with the aim of promoting 'laughter medicine'.[25] This is one example of multiple initiatives worldwide.

Laughter has been found to relax the whole body, lower stress hormones, boost the immune system, protect the heart, release endorphins and decrease pain. As predicted by the psycho-spiritual paradigm, the emotional catharsis involved relieves painful emotions like anxiety and shame, relieves stress, promotes resilience and enhances feelings of joy and zest for life.

The established social benefits of humour and laughter include the defusing of conflict and strengthening of relationships, the promotion of harmony, bonding and teamworking. Healthy laughter sounds warm and inviting. It will be at nobody's expense and does not embarrass or ridicule. It is important to be aware, though, that humour can be destructive. When it sounds hollow and is directed against someone, in a sneering or jeering manner, it is usually linked to low self-esteem and poor social functioning on the part of the would-be comedian. This is the reverse of being courageous, and no one is ultimately served by it.

Laughter is very common, but research suggests that only about 15 per cent of laughter follows a joke. Laughing is contagious, occuring much more frequently in social settings than when people are alone. Good humour is not all about laughter, radiating naturally from people who are relaxed and at peace with themselves; from those, in other words, who are spiritually mature.

THE WAY OF RESPECT: LOOKING DEEPER AND FINDING VALUE

At Faith Stage 3, we feel safer within a group to which we conform in terms of beliefs, behaviour, traditions and values. We think in 'either/or' terms,

---

23 The author was Norman Cousins, who went on to write *Anatomy of an Illness as Perceived by the Patient* (1979) New York, NY: W. W. Norton.

24 See www.happiness.co.uk, accessed 29 May 2010.

25 Also in 1996, Mumbai physician Dr Madan Kataria started a 'laughter club' and is now Founder-President of the Laughter Club International, with 70 branches in Mumbai, more than 400 nationwide in India and offshoots in major cities throughout the world.

of right or wrong, of 'Us' and 'Them'. The way of respect goes beyond all this. Diversity is welcomed. Differences are not denied but celebrated. Accordingly, people develop tolerance and friendly feelings towards those who seem different culturally and in other challenging ways. They do so by travelling, learning about other cultures, by seeking out rather than avoiding differences. As Mark Twain said, 'Travel is fatal to prejudice, bigotry and narrow-mindedness.'[26] It is also possible to develop increasing tolerance within your neighbourhood without going far, for example by joining in a project with people from a different background, especially a project that involves teamwork and helping people.

Post and Niemark make similar points, and also suggest that hierarchies are inevitable in the human, as in the animal, world and that rank and social status are especially significant during difficult times. The antidote to stress resulting from the social pecking order, they say, is routinely to respect other people.[27]

Courtesy, civility, tolerance, etiquette, simple good manners – saying 'please' and 'thank-you', stepping aside to let another pass, waiting your turn, offering your seat in a crowded public vehicle – all of these help to make people feel comfortable. Being considerate, putting people at their ease will also make you feel good.

In health and social care settings, it is always best to respect and get alongside the person you are trying to help. It is important first to discover and then honour their wishes. Seeking to understand why they want what they want is usually important. An elderly woman refusing laser treatment for her eyes had exaggeratedly false notions of the risks involved, for example. She thought her brain could somehow be fried; and swiftly changed her mind when properly informed that this simply couldn't happen.

Respect for people is important for our well-being, and so too is respect and reverence for nature. Feelings of reverence help us recognize what is truly sacred.

Haidt and Keltner describe two core features of awe as 'vastness' and 'accommodation'. The former refers to anything we experience as far larger than ourselves. (Similar experiences can also be had in connection with things that are minuscule.) The latter means that, in feeling somehow absorbed into this immensity (or infinitesimal smallness), we make a psychological shift to accept and accommodate it.[28] This is at the heart of spiritual experience, a kind of mystical feeling.

26 Twain, M. (2003) *The Innocent Abroad.* London: Penguin Classics, p.498.
27 Post, S. and Neimark, J. (2007) *Why Good Things Happen to Good People: How to Live a Longer, Healthier, Happier Life by the Simple Act of Giving.* New York, NY: Broadway Books, pp.154–7.
28 See Haidt, J. and Keltner, D. (2003) *Approaching Awe: A Moral, Spiritual and Aesthetic Emotion.* In Russell, J. (ed.) *Pleasure.* Hove: Psychology Press, pp.297–314.

THE WAY OF COMPASSION: FEELING FOR OTHERS

Much has already been said about compassion in these pages. Post and Neimark remind us that the Latin origin of the word means 'suffering with', and add that it involves an immediate impulse to act whenever we encounter another's pain, especially when it is right in front of us.

Compassion has been described as a 'classical human strength', one that may promote health by a variety of mechanisms. It is a powerful force for good parenting, for example, from the instant a child is born, and possibly earlier, in the womb, for mothers. It has been linked to the release within the brain of a hormone, oxytocin, which floods the nervous system and is reliably associated with pair-bonding, devotion and nurturing attachment.

Oxytocin studies have also been found to suggest a link between compassion and other powerful 'feel good' experiences like connectedness and spirituality. Brain imaging studies quoted by Post have revealed that acts of compassion light up certain areas of the brain associated with nerve cells that 'mirror' the experience of another person, as if we are having the same experience at the same time.[29] This seems to be the biological basis of empathy, a key element in compassion. The conclusion is remarkable. Compassion involves the ability to sense and empathize with another person's pain yet, despite this, it triggers positive emotions.

In addition to the research reported by Shanida Nataraja (see p.203), recent studies in long-term meditators support this idea. A group of Buddhist monks, expert meditation practitioners for between 15 and 40 years, were found to have permanently heightened activity in an association area for the positive or pain-free emotions, with a corresponding reduction in an area linked with painful emotions.[30] Spiritual skills can therefore have important biological consequences. More research will undoubtedly confirm and clarify this.

THE WAY OF LOYALTY: LOVING ACROSS TIME

Loyalty is a form of steadfast and selfless identification with another person, group or organization. A manifestation of 'non-separateness', it is a form of love.

The best studied form of loyalty concerns marriage. According to research on 456 inner-city men over a long period conducted by Harvard psychiatry

---

29 Post and Neimark, *ibid.*, p.180.
30 Brofezynski-Lewis, J.A., Lutz, A., Schaefer, H.S., Levinson, D.B. and Davidson, R.J. (2007) 'Neural correlates of attentional expertise in long-term meditation practitioners.' *Proceedings of the National Academy of Sciences 104*, 27, 11483–8.

professor, George Vaillant,[31] marriage is one of the most supremely balancing and healthful commitments people can make. Other studies have found that good marriages, where initial passion has transformed into deep, trusting love, contribute to the well-being of both men and women.[32] Findings are consistent that people are physically and mentally healthier, and live longer, if married. They experience less anxiety, depression, hostility and loneliness, and are more likely to say they are happy.

In another study involving 147 couples, the key to marital success was commitment: people sticking to their vows were able to weather and grow through the difficulties.[33] Good marriages also provide good parenting environments, with highly significant beneficial consequences on the physical and psychological health and development of children.

Camaraderie (forged, for example, among troops in combat conditions) and having a 'best friend', palling-up, 'mateship' are examples of enduring friendships that also turn out to have measurable health benefits, protecting against depression and boosting self-esteem. These are usually social relationships between people of similar values, personal characteristics and backgrounds, confirming the idea that, 'I like you', often follows from 'I am like you'. Friendships turn out to be more important for emotional well-being than family relations. Post and Neimark comment that loyalty is what distinguishes deep from casual relationships. They add that betrayal breaks up friendships, while forgiveness is what heals and saves them.

During Faith Stage 3, the temptation to exclusivity, to put 'us' before 'them', operates once again in a way that is often destructive through corrupting the spiritual purity of loyalty. Patriotism, for example, in a world the parts and nations of which are now so obviously globally interconnected, can no longer be considered an absolute virtue. When conflict is invited or undertaken through a claim of 'patriotism', it arguably exemplifies false loyalty to one's country, because aggression brings pain and loss to the perpetrator as well as the victim. This follows the spiritual principle of reciprocity, which prevails whether or not there are either immediate direct retaliatory consequences or longer-term grudge-bearing and enmity. What goes round will surely somehow come around in such a case.

---

31 See Vaillant, G. (1977) *Adaptation to Life*. Boston, MA: Little, Brown. (Reprinted with a new preface in 1995 by Harvard University Press: Boston, MA.) Vaillant has been Director of the Study of Adult Development at Harvard University Health Service for over 30 years. He is also the author of *Spiritual Evolution: A Scientific Defense of Faith* (2008) New York, NY: Broadway Books.

32 See Waite, L. J. and Gallagher, M. (2001) *The Case for Marriage: Why Married People Are Happier, Healthier and Better Off Financially*. New York, NY: Broadway Books.

33 Fenell, D. and Weinhold, B. (2005) *Review of Counselling Families: An Introduction to Marriage and Family Therapy* 3rd edn. Denver, CO: Love Publishing.

A similar warning is appropriate against ill-considered institutional, political and religious loyalties. Implying the same lack of respect and reverence for differences between people and organizations, they can be as destructive – to both perpetrator and victim – as can military aggression. There is no place in a spiritually attuned world for the aggressive use of knowledge, advantage and power. There is no place either for greed.

THE WAY OF LISTENING: OFFERING DEEP PRESENCE

Students at Brighton and Sussex Medical School were instructed to 'take a spiritual history' from one or more patients of their own choice.[34] They were asked simply to 'have a conversation' with them, armed only with two types of question:

- Do you think of yourself as religious or spiritual in any way?

- What helps you most when things go badly wrong (such as when you are ill)? What sustains you?

Students were encouraged to discover where their patient turned for strength, hope and support. They were looking for sources of inner strength and of external help, both practical and emotional. The success of the venture depended much on the students' ability to listen attentively and empathically.[35]

The process involves watching people too, on the alert for visual clues from their body language and facial expressions. The emotional tone of information is of special importance. As students discovered, in terms echoed by a public information leaflet published by the Royal College of Psychiatrists, 'A gentle and unhurried approach works best... As well as gathering information, the process can have important therapeutic value.'[36]

It helps to take a loving and caring, compassionate interest, to acknowledge, accept and thereby validate people's accounts of themselves and their often troubled predicaments. Post and Neiman emphasize that this is also a form of generosity, honouring the person's deepest being as they reveal aspects of their true self.

The release of oxytocin has again been found beneficially enhanced by this positive form of social interaction. Scanning studies also show that listening activates the so-called 'mirror neurons' in parts of the brain apparently hard-wired for empathy.

---

34 See Chapter 3.
35 See Appendix 1: Taking a Spiritual History.
36 See *Spirituality and Mental Health* from the 'Help is at Hand' series, published by the Royal College of Psychiatrists, London. Also available as a free download at www.rcpsych.ac.uk/mentalhealthinformation/therapies/spiritualityandmentalhealth.aspx, accessed 29 May 2010.

According to Greg Ficchione, of the Institute for Research on Unlimited Love,[37] when a doctor (or any professional) listens empathically, both the physical and emotional components of pain that the patient is carrying are being processed by the same part of the brain of the listener: the anterior cingulate gyrus, associated with positive, pain-free emotions.

This suggests an explanation for the greater effectiveness of some professional interventions over others that is worthy of further research. For example, listening to others in distress has been found to quieten their stress responses. Does this depend on a kind of reciprocal empathy, the patient feeling directly the warmth and positivity emanating from the physician? In support of the idea are reports that patients' complaints about their medical attendants tend to centre more on their frustration at not feeling listened to, than on doubts regarding their professional knowledge and expertise.

It is interesting that the word 'psychiatrist' (from the Greek words 'psyche', meaning mind or soul, and 'iatros', meaning doctor) was once used of physicians using their own minds, empathically attuned, to heal the distress and disability associated with their patients' diseases. There are still 'spiritual healers' employing similar principles today.[38]

According to Post and Neimark, people are less likely to let their health deteriorate if they feel valued and heard. It particularly helps when their feelings are accurately reflected back to them; for example, 'You seem to be feeling sad (or angry, or anxious) today.' This often encourages the person to open up more.

Empathic listening not only helps the sufferer. It can benefit the listener too. Schwartz and Sendor studied 132 patients with multiple sclerosis (MS).[39] Five of these MS patients were given additional help, and trained for a two-year period to give telephone support by making monthly calls to half of the remaining cohort. (Patients from the other half were taught coping skills for comparison.) The surprise finding involved the psychological health of the five MS patients who were also supporters. They improved most of all, reporting dramatic changes in how they viewed themselves and their lives. They were significantly less depressed, with much improved self-esteem and self-confidence. Report author Carolyn Schwartz is reported by Post and Neimark[40] as saying, 'This group of five people were very good at listening compassionately to others.' She added that, by the end of the study, they had undergone 'a spiritual transformation'. The implications for health and

---

37   As reported by Post and Neimark, *ibid.*, pp.236–8.
38   See www.thehealingtrust.org.uk (accessed 29 May 2010), the website of the National Federation of Spiritual Healers Charitable Trust Ltd.
39   Schwartz, C. and Sendor, M. (1999) 'Helping others helps oneself: Response shift effects in peer support.' *Social Science and Medicine 48*, 11, 1563–75.
40   Post and Neimark, *ibid.*, p.243.

social care professionals are clear, and reflect the genuine potential benefits of engaging in this kind of admittedly challenging work.

THE WAY OF CREATIVITY: INVENTING AND INNOVATING

Howard Gardner has described creative people as falling into five main types.[41] They are:

- problem-solvers: setting questions and working out answers

- builders of theory: shedding new light on reality

- creators of works: including writers, painters, composers, architects and so on

- ritual performance builders: dramatists, theatre directors and choreographers, for example

- high-stake public performers and change activists: creators in the social realm; leaders and figureheads.

Many people favour one style, but this is not always so. Leonardo da Vinci, for example, became famous for being a painter, an inventor, theory builder and a problem-solver. It turns out to be important for personal satisfaction, and therefore psychological health, to discover one's talents, finding some worthy way to give something back to the world.

Creativity is strongly associated with divergent thinking, which is linked in turn with personal development and maturity, with what Carl Rogers called 'self-actualization'.[42] Post and Neimark quote Shelley Carson, who researches creativity, as saying, 'The more creative an individual can be, the richer their life. We're going to appreciate beauty more, we're going to think in analogies more, we're going to work out novel experiences more.'[43] Other authors have discovered a circular link between creativity and joy: the two reinforce one another.

Creativity requires a willingness to break away from convention, from conformist thought and behaviour. It may take courage and a spirit of adventure to discover and implement one's creative abilities, but this is a necessary aspect of emerging from conformist Faith Stage 3 towards Stage 4 and beyond.

---

41 Howard Gardner is the Hobbs Professor of Cognition and Education at the Harvard Graduate School of Education. See, for example, his book *Five Minds for the Future* (2007) Harvard, MA: Harvard Business Press.

42 Carl Rogers (1902–1987) was a celebrated founder of the humanistic approach to psychology and 'person-centred' therapeutic methods.

43 Post and Neimark, *ibid.*, pp.267–8.

The advice from Post and Neimark includes studying the creativity of others, reading about well-known thinkers, creators, artists, explorers, inventors and social activists, visiting museums, art exhibitions, novel buildings, and performances of new and newly interpreted drama, ballet and opera. They recommend that we take up or deepen our interest in a creative personal hobby; share what we create with others; teach creative skills if we can; join a peaceful walk or demonstration for a moral cause; and perhaps get involved in (rather than just donate funds to) a worthwhile charity. These are all ways of receiving while we are giving, protecting us from spiritual stagnation, lack of fulfilment and the risk of despair.

These observations hold good for all ten ways of giving. Everyone we know will benefit. If the holistic principles of non-separateness and reciprocity hold true, everyone – including those we don't know – will benefit too. This vital subject is worthy of deep personal reflection. The spirituality theme park repays every moment of exploration.

Conclusions

These ten ways of giving are bound up closely with spiritual values, spiritual skills and spiritual practices, this holistic bundle forming the firmest and most reliable basis for good physical, psychological, social and spiritual health.

The heart (representing the emotions) and head (representing awareness, the physical senses and thinking) interact harmoniously as 'soul'. Soul, in turn, works through the hands – hands of friendship – ensuring that thoughts, words and actions are driven by both wisdom and compassion, by the most mature and selfless form of universal love.

With maturity, passing through the six stages of faith, aspects of the false self, the everyday ego, gradually diminish to reveal and release from domination the true spiritual self, the soul, seamlessly linked and attuned to the divine. Hearts, heads and hands, free of the encumbrances of attachment and aversion, are no longer inhibited or in conflict. The caring and cared-for need and depend on each other. This is a goal to envision: a poetic vision of human togetherness with self, others, nature and the totality of existence.

Looking at the world today, faced with frequent natural catastrophes and threats like those associated with global warming; listening to the daily news of widespread conflict, from warfare to street and domestic violence, often fuelled by alcohol and drug misuse, and of pervasive crime associated with these destructive human addictions, it is not hard to conclude that more spiritually minded and mature people are urgently needed within our communities. We would do well to rediscover and reinvent the 'sabbath mind', the monastic way and the 'Bodhisattva ideal'.

Greater proportions of the population will be required, one by one, to leave the fragile, fearful and ultimately false comfort zone of Stage 3, passing on to take more responsibility for themselves through Stage 4, to reach a more reliable, joyful, truthful and contented Stage 5. We are all in this predicament together. Can we change? Can we each do what has to be done? The recent words of an elected world leader ring true. His proud, confident and emphatic response to these questions: 'Yes we can.'[44]

Spirituality is a deeply personal matter. Although each individual must find their own unique pathway of growth, a routine practice involving three elements can be recommended as helpful. The first involves devoting quiet time each day to prayer, meditation or deep reflection. The second element is regularly to read and study appropriate spiritually inspired literature, including scripture, poetry and philosophy. The third involves cultivating supportive family bonds and friendships with people sharing similar spiritual values, aims and aspirations.

Yes, we can change. Evolutionary momentum seems to insist that we must. Let me conclude, therefore, with the hope that this account of the new, holistic, psycho-spiritual paradigm be accepted as a useful contribution to the educative effort required. It is an introduction that I hope will stimulate further enquiry into the psychology of human spirituality. Let it not be the last word.

Summary points

1. *Devotional living*

Spiritual development, in its broadest sense, is the only essential work and purpose of a lifetime. Any commitment or regular activity serving the quest for spiritual maturity can be considered a spiritual practice.

2. *Religious and non-religious practices*

It is never too late to engage intentionally in such practices, which (despite overlaps) can usefully be distinguished into 'religious' and 'non-religious'. Six examples of the former and ten of the latter are described. Rewards are assured; arriving slowly and gradually at first, later in cascades of small epiphanies, and sometimes in awesome quantum leaps.

---

44 Senator Barack Obama's remarks in his speech after he won the Democratic presidential primary in South Carolina on 26 January 2008: 'Don't tell me we can't change. Yes, we can. Yes, we can. Yes, we can.' Available online at www.guardian.co.uk/commentisfree/2008/jan/27/yeswecan, accessed 11 June 2010.

3. *Ten ways of giving*

There is strong evidence that benevolent emotions, attitudes and actions contribute to the giver's happiness, health and length of life. Ten ways of giving are described that relate closely to spiritual values. They are also associated with the development of spiritual skills, have much in common with spiritual practices, and similarly overlap and reinforce one another.

4. *Conclusions*

Final comments about the world today lead to the conclusion that more spiritually minded and mature people are urgently needed within our communities. A routine practice – involving regular quiet time, appropriate reading and study, and the formation of spiritual bonds and friendships – is recommended. We are all in this together; we can change, and we must.

Exercises and questions for personal reflection and as a basis for group discussion:

1. Make an inventory of your spiritual practices, based on the lists of religious and non-religious commitments and activities at the beginning of the chapter. Reflect quietly for a while on the ways they sustain and help you.

2. Make a similar appraisal of the 'ways of giving' you use, based on the ten methods listed. Do you feel devoted to the welfare of other people? Does this refer mainly to your family, friends and others like yourself, or does it also include strangers, people with whom you have less in common, the poor, disadvantaged and sick? Does it include wrong-doers, particularly people who threaten or harm you? Are there, or should there be, limits to compassion? Discuss these questions – and your answers – with somebody else.

3. What does maturity mean to you? Have you grasped how it may be achieved through regular spiritual practices? Do you understand the concepts of a false, personal ego gradually weakening, revealing the true, spiritual self it has been masking all along? Try taking a fresh bar of soap, setting it aside and using it just once a day to wash your hands. (Don't let anyone else use it.) Make yourself aware of how the soap diminishes, eventually wearing completely away. (You can substitute speedier exercises if you feel impatient. Either light a small candle and watch it burning down to nothing, or put a boiled sweet or some candy in your mouth and pay attention to how it gradually dissolves away as you suck on it gently.)

4. Plan a pilgrimage for yourself. Where would you like to visit? It can be somewhere within walking distance or much further off. You decide. Can you think, for example, of somewhere associated with one or more of the hobbies or interests to which you feel devoted? Check the internet or look up books for suggestions, if you like (see Appendix 2: Further reading). What special significance does the place have for you? Imagine making preparations, setting off, the challenges of the journey, arrival…and returning home. Think about what might be holding you back.

5. Go back to the first page, read through this book and re-explore the spirituality theme park once again. If you were to teach a course based on this book to young people (teenagers or college students) pick six topics or chapters to focus a one-hour session on. Which seem the most helpful or the most important to you? Why?

6. Finally, choose and read (mindfully) at least one of the books listed in Appendix 2: Further reading.

The ultimate aim of the quest must be neither release nor ecstasy for oneself, but the wisdom and power to serve others.

Joseph Campbell
From *Myths To Live By*
(1995, London: Souvenir Press)

Appendix I

Taking a Spiritual History[1]

Taking a spiritual history is easy. Anyone can do it.

To put it colloquially, you are simply trying to find out what makes someone tick, what motivates them and keeps them going. It is best thought of as a clinical skill to acquire and hone, rather than an activity to be performed by recipe or rote.

Taking a spiritual history involves engaging with the other person as an equal and listening empathically. You are listening for what might not be being said as well as what is. You are watching as well as listening, picking up non-verbal clues from facial expressions and body language. You are trying to identify the emotions being experienced by the other.

You are encouraging the person to speak about deeply personal matters: what makes sense to them and what puzzles them, what motivates them and what holds them back. It often encourages them to know that you know how they are feeling, so it can be important to say they seem anxious, angry, sad and so on, at the appropriate moment.

Taking a spiritual history requires patience. It works best in a comfortable, quiet and confidential setting. A gentle, unhurried approach is recommended. More than one conversation may be necessary. It pays to let people say what they want to, but also to be thorough. This means maintaining a reasonably systematic approach, for example by taking a chronological approach, or by having a list of topics in mind that need covering.

A good way in is to start by asking whether the person is religious or spiritual in any way, and asking them to give details if they answer yes. They may just need an occasional prompt, like 'Please go on', or 'Could you please tell me more about that?'

At some point, whether religious, spiritual or not, it is often useful to ask, 'What helps you most when things get really bad?' You are looking for sources of inner strength, courage and hope as well as external emotional and practical supports from family, friends and organizations (including religious groups and communities).

---

1   Based on Culliford, L. (2007) 'How to take a spiritual history.' *Advances in Psychiatric Treatment 13*, 3, 212–19, and the leaflet *Spirituality and Mental Health* published by the Royal College of Psychiatrists, London. Also available as a free download at www.rcpsych.ac.uk/mentalhealthinformation/therapies/spiritualityandmentalhealth.aspx, accessed 29 May 2010.

Taking a chronological approach, the following series of questions[2] may be helpful:

SETTING THE SCENE
What is your life all about? Is there anything that gives you a particular sense of meaning or purpose?

THE PAST
Emotional stress usually involves some kind of loss, or the threat of loss. Have you experienced any major losses or bereavements? How have they affected you? How have you managed to cope?

THE PRESENT
Do you feel that you belong and that you are valued? Do you feel safe, respected and with a sense of dignity? Can you communicate freely with other people? Does there seem to be a spiritual aspect to the current problem? What particularly needs to be appreciated about your religious background? Would it help to involve a minister of your faith, or someone from your faith community?

THE FUTURE
What does the immediate future seem to hold? What about the longer term? Are you worried about death and dying; or about the possibility of an afterlife? What are your main fears regarding the future? Do you feel the need for forgiveness about anything? What, if anything, gives you hope?

REMEDIES
What would you find helpful? How might you find such help?

A number of lists are available as prompts for taking a systematic approach.[3] The most recently published is the mnemonic FAITH, designed for medical students and doctors.[4] The letters stand for:

F – Faith, spiritual beliefs (and practices)
Do you have any particular faith, religious or spiritual beliefs (or practices)? What gives your life meaning? What helps you cope in times of stress or illness?

A – Application
How do you apply your faith in everyday life? Do you belong to a church (synagogue, mosque, temple, gurdwara) or faith community? Is prayer or meditation important to you?

---

2   From the Royal College of Psychiatrists leaflet *Spirituality and Mental Health*.
3   Other mnemonics include 'HOPE' and 'SPIRIT'. See Culliford, L. 'How to take a spiritual history,' *ibid.* for more details.
4   Neely, D. and Minford, E. (2009) 'FAITH: Spiritual history-taking made easy.' *The Clinical Teacher 6*, 3, 181–5.

I – Influence, Importance (during illness)

How do your faith and spiritual beliefs influence your life? How do they affect you during this illness? Have they altered your attitudes and behaviour? Has this illness influenced your faith? What would be helpful for your doctors and health workers to know about how your beliefs might affect healthcare decisions?

T – Talk, Terminal events planning

Is there someone you trust to talk to about spiritual or religious issues? Do you have any specific requests if you were to become terminally ill, such as terminal care options, making a living will or end of life requests?

H – Help

Is there any way people like me in the healthcare team can help with religious or spiritual concerns? Do you require assistance or help with prayer? Would you like to speak to a chaplain (from your faith background)? Would you like to discuss spiritual issues with your doctor?

David Neely and Eunice Minford say that FAITH provides a flexible and comprehensive tool to aid spiritual history-taking which is applicable in a wide variety of medical settings including general practice, hospital and hospice. It could easily be adapted also for use in social care settings, in the office and in people's homes.

In addition to the chronological and systematic approaches described, readers of this book could assess people on the basis of the spiritual practices – religious and non-religious – with which they are regularly engaged (see Chapter 12). Some thought to the spiritual values they adopt, and the spiritual skills they have acquired, may also be given.

Quantitative methods, and more complex qualitative methods of assessing people's spirituality have been devised,[5] but these are well beyond the scope of this book.

After taking a spiritual history from an elderly woman on a hospital medical ward, a female student in her twenties told her classmates, 'That is the first time in three years studying medicine that I have definitely felt that I have actually helped a patient.'[6] This comment exemplifies two things: the therapeutic potential of spiritual history-taking, and the positive effect on the enquirer.

Taking a spiritual history is relevant and beneficial to all concerned, in all medical, psychiatric and social care settings. For good reasons, the holistic, 'bio-psycho-socio-spiritual' model of health and social care is being adopted increasingly widely. The psycho-spiritual paradigm outlined throughout this book, building on rather than displacing what has gone before, is definitely gaining ground.

---

5   See Culliford, L. and Eagger, S. (2009) 'Assessing Spiritual Needs.' In C. Cook, A. Powell and A. Sims (eds) *Spirituality and Psychiatry*. London: RCPsych Publications.

6   See Culliford, L. (2009) 'Teaching spirituality and health care to third-year medical students.' *The Clinical Teacher* 6, 1, 22–7.

Appendix 2

Further Reading

BIOGRAPHY

Jim Forest (1991, revised 2008) *Living with Wisdom: A Life of Thomas Merton*. Maryknoll, NY: Orbis Books.

Barack Obama (2007) *Dreams from My Father: A Story of Race and Inheritance*. Edinburgh: Canongate Books.

Patrick Woodhouse (2009) *Etty Hillesum: A Life Transformed*. London: Continuum.

MEDITATION, MINDFULNESS

Shanida Nataraja (2008) *The Blissful Brain: Neuroscience and Proof of the Power of Meditation*. London: Gaia.

Thich Nhat Hanh (2008) *The Miracle of Mindfulness: A Manual on Meditation*. London: Rider Books.

PHYSICS

John Gribben (1984) *In Search of Schrödinger's Cat: Quantum Physics and Reality*. London: Corgi Books.

Gary Zukav (1984) *The Dancing Wu Li Masters: An Overview of the New Physics*. London: Flamingo.

PILGRIMAGE

Phil Cousineau (1998) *The Art of Pilgrimage: A Seeker's Guide to Making Travel Sacred*. Newburyport, MA: Conari Press.

Jim Forest (2007) *The Road to Emmaus: Pilgrimage as a Way of Life*. Maryknoll, NY: Orbis Books.

PILGRIMAGE PLACES

Dan Cruickshank (2005) *Around the World in 80 Treasures*. London: Weidenfeld and Nicolson.
James Harpur (1994) *The Atlas of Sacred Places: Meeting Points of Heaven and Earth*. London:
Cassell.

SPIRITUALITY: GENERAL

Larry Culliford (2007) *Love, Healing and Happiness*. Winchester: O Books.
Thomas Merton (1993) *Thoughts in Solitude*. Boston, MA: Shambhala Pocket Classics.
Mother Teresa (1995) *A Simple Path*. (Compiled by Lucinda Vardey) London: Rider Books.
Evelyn Underhill (1993) *The Spiritual Life: Great Spiritual Truths for Everyday Life*. Oxford:
Oneworld Publications.

SPIRITUALITY AND DEATH

Marie de Hennezel (1998) *Intimate Death: How the Dying Teach Us How to Live*. (Translated by
Carol Brown Janeway) New York, NY: Vintage Books.

SPIRITUALITY AND PATIENT CARE

Jon Kabat-Zinn, (1990) *Full Catastrophe Living*. New York, NY: Delta Books.
Harold Koenig (2002) *Spirituality in Patient Care: Why, How, When and What*. Philadelphia, PA
and London: Templeton Foundation Press.

SPIRITUALITY AND PSYCHOLOGY

David Fontana (2003) *Psychology, Religion and Spirituality*. Oxford: BPS Blackwell.
M. Scott Peck (1978) *The Road Less Travelled: A New Psychology of Love, Traditional Values and
Spiritual Growth*. London: Arrow Books.
M. Scott Peck (1988) *The People of the Lie: The Hope for Healing Human Evil*. London: Arrow
Books.
Victor L. Schermer (2003) *Spirit and Psyche: A New Paradigm for Psychology, Psychoanalysis and
Psychotherapy*. New York and London: Jessica Kingsley Publishers.

SPIRITUALITY: SELF-HELP

Patrick Whiteside (2001) *Happiness: The 30 Day Guide*. London: Rider Books.

SPIRITUALITY AND TIME

Jacob Needleman (2003) *Time and the Soul*. San Francisco, CA: Berrett-Koehler Publishers.

RELIGIOUS TEXTS

Buddhist

Thomas Byrom (1976), translator *The Dhammapada: The Sayings of the Buddha*. London: Rider
Books.

Christian

The Holy Bible – Old and New Testaments (including, especially for newcomers to Christian
texts, The Gospel of Mark; Acts of the Apostles)

Hindu

Juan Mascaro (1965), translator *The Upanishads*. Harmondsworth: Penguin.
Swami Prabhavananda and Christopher Isherwood (1944), translators *Bhagavad Gita: The Song of God*. Hollywood, CA: Vedanta Press.

Islam

The Koran

Judaism

The Torah; The Old Testament of the Bible

Taoism

Chuang Tsu (1974) *Inner Chapters*, translated by Gia-Fu Feng and Jane English. London: Wildwood House.
Lao-Tzu (1989) *Tao Te Ching*, translated by Stephen Mitchell. London: Kyle Cathie.

REFERENCE BOOKS

Harold Koenig, Michael McCullough and David Larson (2001) *Handbook of Religion and Health*. Oxford: Oxford University Press.
Raymond Paloutzian and Crystal Park (2005) (eds) *The Handbook of the Psychology of Religion and Spirituality*. New York, NY: Guilford Press.
Thomas Plante and Carl Thoresen (2007) (eds) *Spirit, Science and Health: How the Spiritual Mind Fuels Physical Wellness*. Westport, CT: Praeger.

Index

Lightning Source UK Ltd.
Milton Keynes UK
UKOW06f2319121015

260410UK00001B/116/P